The
CASE of the
BAFFLED
RADICAL

The CASE of the BAFFLED RADICAL

HAROLD ROSENBERG

The University of Chicago Press
Chicago and London

For many years Harold Rosenberg was art critic for *The New Yorker* and professor in the Committee on Social Thought and in the Department of Art at the University of Chicago. His imaginative grasp of the contemporary artist's aesthetic and cultural situation influenced not only the field of art criticism but also the practice of art and the process of selection that proclaimed the importance of such major postwar figures as Barnett Newman, Arshile Gorky, Jackson Pollock, Franz Kline, Mark Rothko, and Willem de Kooning. Other titles by Harold Rosenberg available from the University of Chicago Press are *The Tradition of the New, Discovering the Present, The Anxious Object, Artworks and Packages, Act and the Actor, The De-definition of Art, Art on the Edge,* and *Art and Other Serious Matters.*

The University of Chicago Press, Chicago 60637
The University of Chicago Press, Ltd., London

94 93 92 91 90 89 88 87 86 85   5 4 3 2 1

Library of Congress Cataloging in Publication Data

Rosenberg, Harold.
   Case of the baffled radical.

   Includes index.
      1. Art—Addresses, essays, lectures.   2. Art, Modern—
20th century—Addresses, essays, lectures.   3. Artists—
Interviews.   I. Title.
N7445.2.R67   1985   709'.04   84-27996
ISBN 0-226-72692-4

Contents

Publisher's Note

This volume is a selection of previously uncollected essays and interviews which were being compiled by the author for two separate volumes at the time of his death in 1978. The publisher has combined the pieces into a single volume arranged chronologically under the headings *Unfinished Works and Fugitive Essays* and *All about Everything*. These pieces comprise the last uncollected writings and ideas of the critic.

Unfinished Works
and Fugitive Essays

1

The Case of the Baffled Radical

A new literature seems to have made its appearance—the literature of conscience of the ex-Communist.

Primarily a movement among journalists, the literary abnegation of "The Party" has already produced some outstanding novels, notably Ignazio Silone's *Bread and Wine* and Arthur Koestler's *Darkness At Noon*.

This literature of the Communist backslider has little in common with the epics of Party conversion known as "proletarian" writing a decade ago. The dramas of Bolshevik piety drew their main thinking, naturally, from the organization into which the initiate was delivering himself. In contrast, the work of the deconverted Red belongs to the main stream of modern writing; it is part of the tradition of doubt and negation which has occupied first place in literature for the past 100 years. Upon the Communist precepts and practices Koestler lets loose the disintegrating machinery of skepticism, ambivalence and psychiatry—weapons of the type used by Joyce in assaulting Catholic education, by Mann against the ethics of middle-class duty, or by Gide against the accepted morality of personal relations.

Reprinted from *Partisan Review*, vol. 11, no. 1, Winter 1944.

Measured by the accomplishment of the masters of the past generation, both the art and the skepticism of Koestler are quite thin. But as one of the best chroniclers of the moral Flight From Moscow, he brings to the novel something new or long-neglected—political sophistication and a serious sense of the human drama of public events. Koestler understands how modern man is defeated in the conference rooms and the daily press, on the battlefields and in the dungeons of Europe. He is aware of viciousness and weakness not only, as the older writers knew it, as something inherent—he knows it also as something *made,* even *made* "according to plan." . . . Perhaps the task of the artist today is rendered more difficult by the increased brutality of our culture; he is forced to deal with new problems and areas of data from which his art, as such, will gain nothing—just as the soldier at the front finds it harder to keep alive though the quality of his life is not raised by these difficulties.

Koestler's *Arrival and Departure* is the story of the education of Peter Slavek, fugitive ex-Communist, in the dubious sources of his own revolutionary heroism. Upon his arrival in "Neutralia" (there ought to be a law against such place-names), with which the book begins, Peter has already given up his connection with The Party, after many months in a Nazi concentration camp. Why? Because the very intensity of the sufferings he had borne without cracking had helped to convince this 22-year old son of the middle class that his resistance was due to some other source than loyalty to the Party. The rank-and-file Party members had succumbed to the tortures of the Gestapo and had betrayed their oath, and they admired this faithful Peter as a hero. But isn't there something suspicious, Peter asked himself, in being a hero?

Yet when he jumps ship at Neutralia, Peter is still a carrier of banners, determined to get back into the battle through offering himself as a volunteer to the British. While waiting, however, for the slow processes of the Consulate to lift him out of neutrality, he falls in love with a French refugee, Odette, a girl whose moral philosophy is neatly summed up by Koestler in the phrase, "After all—why not?"

The love affair, which Koestler handles rather spottily, ends abruptly when Odette leaves without warning for America. The sudden abandonment proves too much for Peter; he is smitten with a psychic paralysis of the right leg, on which the Nazi torturers have left fatal stigmata of cigar burns. The most exciting sequence in the novel is the unexpected physical collapse of Peter as the scar of the burn in the bend of his knee becomes a hole through which "the strength had run out of his leg like water out of the bath of Sonia," the female psychoanalyst in whose apartment he is staying.

The core of the book is the psychic analysis itself, during which the half-allegorical figure of Dr. Sonia Bolgar rocks in her chair by the bedside of the fallen warrior, drawing from him the tale of his deeds and his dreams. The surface layers of Peter's mental tissue contain the horrors of his actual experiences in Nazi Europe—his capture, the black-clad torturers, the "mixed transports" in which captured girls, gypsies and Jews are dragged across the continent to nightmarish fates. But when these memory fabrics are torn up by the analysis, they bring with them, like an uprooted sod, growths belonging to still deeper fears and defeats: childhood crimes, expiations and vows to which all his adult life has chained itself through symbolic transferences and confusions of identity. When the bottom is reached, and the original sin disinterred—the "accidental" putting out of his brother's eye at the age of five, which he knew subconsciously was not an accident at all—Peter is cured, "cured of his illusions, both about objective aims and subjective motives."

The new Peter decides to cast aside all political totems— "What real good had come of those quixotic crusades?" But a certain uneasiness springs up in connection with this plan too.

However disillusioned he may have become, Peter is dedicated to political action, "he is not the type to back out and cultivate a garden." Below the values uprooted by psychoanalysis, judgments continue to form themselves, perhaps simply out of the need to act, characteristic of Peter and his generation.

The final episodes of *Arrival and Departure* indicate clearly the poles of Koestler's thinking—they are the same as those that appear in the works of Thomas Mann and a good deal of other modern literature. On the one hand, the road of a relaxed yielding to events, cessation of struggle, and personal self-indulgence (identified with love): "After all—why not?" On the other, a leap in the direction of "duty," duty *felt*, not arrived at by reason and even opposed to reason: "Here we go" is the phrase Koestler uses as a key.

"Don't you think," the shot-up British flier asks Peter, "that it's rather a boring game trying to find out one's reasons for doing something?"

Thus, as Castorp in *The Magic Mountain* is last seen advancing across No Man's Land, the baffled Peter reaches action and even consciousness of possessing moral values when he leaps out over enemy country in a parachute. At the last moment, he had quitted the ship that was to take him to America and the immoral Odette—since duty is better than giving way. And he had made the final discovery that reasons are a thing of the past, for we live at the end of the age of science and "a new god is about to be born." "Here we go," trusting ourselves happily to the void in the cradle of a parachute; perhaps out of this act of self-abandonment the future deity will take shape.

Because of the intelligence, and particularly the *relevance*, of his novels, it is easier to praise Koestler than to indicate the correct proportion of his lack. His thinking tackles boldly some of the most real dramatic situations of our time. And it never forgets the personal sufferings of those who are caught in them. At the same time there is a pervading glibness in Koestler, the journalist satisfying himself with devices aimed at the reader's opinions. This glibness is not altogether a vice, since it permits the author to put down quickly and cleanly events whose meanings a more painstaking investigation might not reveal for a long time or might even find to be out of reach entirely. Haste is especially important for the chronicler of political conscience, since the background of the drama changes so rapidly today that details of doubt recorded about, say, Spain in 1935 no longer have the same point if described in 1943.

But for the readiness of his formulas, Koestler pays a high price. For instance, his handling of the psychoanalytical process is extremely well planned, but the quality of the symbols is uneven; some are subtly selected personal images, others are text-book clichés. The writing, too, is marred by easily acquired phrases and ideas: phrases like "another symbolic toy which he had hung on the Christmas tree of his guilt"; ideas like the theatrical notion of Peter that he has the duty to save mankind and that at the time of the Flood "there should have been at least one who ran back into the rain, to perish with those who had no planks under their feet."

Also, for all its philosophical fashionableness, the conclusion of *Arrival and Departure*, with its assertion of the *necessary* failure of the modern mind in the face of historical problems and its call for a new deity, is intellectually gross. For the book has not even raised the problem of socialism versus fascism which it pretends to exhaust. It does not criticise the particular political philosophy of Peter—he might as well have been a heroic Protestant minister. It merely argues that heroism is always the result of infantile guilt feelings, that the political always violates the personal, and that any reasoned political action involving sacrifices is therefore always wholly neurotic.

The notion that psychoanalysis gives plausibility to these conclusions is extremely superficial. The analysis is shown to have destroyed Peter's ability to make a judgment of fascism, whereas, actually, by removing his dream interpretation of the enemy, analysis should have deepened his consciousness of what fascism means. Koestler has all but left himself in the position of trying to demonstrate the contradiction that without neurotic compulsions man cannot behave intelligently.

Koestler approaches politics with a fixed philosophical dualism that distorts his understanding of the tragedy of the left intellectual of the past decade. In *Darkness at Noon,* also a novel of atonement, he did not attack the jailers of Rubashov for specific violations of socialist values, but placed the responsibility on Rubashov himself as representing with them a metaphysical absolute—"the logic of history"—opposed to the individual by the nature of things. The effect of this mechanical dichotomy (which also appears in Koestler's essays) was to cause Rubashov, introduced as one of the revolutionary founders of the USSR, to conceive his political life as nothing more than a series of crimes against the individual—it was the guilt he incurred in "representing history" that he expiated in confessing at the trial. Such a criticism of The Trials is a metaphysical not a political or historical criticism, and in effect it accepts the political and historical claims of the Communists while rejecting their moral ones.

But without concrete politics, no concrete political characters. Unlike Silone, whose fascists are living types, Koestler's novels of guilt talk about characters more often than they reveal them dramatically. The scene between Peter and Radich, Chief of the Political Department, is a marvellous dramatic opportunity—utterly missed. The same is true of Koestler's Communists; they remain invisible behind their "ideas."

No doubt the ex-Communists are baffled in the face of the present world situation. Koestler's prophecy that "a new god is about to be born" has no other content than this bafflement. The new god is a religious or mythological device which fills his hero with serene enthusiasm by ending his need to understand what is taking place. In this shape, confusion is positive and homeopathic. The trouble is that it makes "Here we go" identical with "After all—why not?" and political action into a sexual experience.

2

Evidences

One will be struck directly by the resemblance of these photos to reproductions of advanced contemporary paintings. Aaron Siskind's collection is like the catalogue of a show of "best Americans" that may take place next month in a leading New York art gallery. Here are the dual picture planes, the calligraphy, the post-Cubist balances, the free strokes and aerial perspectives, the accidental landscapes, galaxies hinted in stains, of half a dozen vanguard styles. Illuminated by these, the camera's eye has plucked from fences, beaches, rocks, strips of material, images of possible canvases as if someone had had the ingenuity to paint them. Perhaps someone will paint them. Certainly, they contain an intelligence of painting from which many painters can profit.

Siskind's photos are inseparable from painting. Yet they have nothing to do with that movement in photography, abetted by professional vanity, that seeks to establish the photograph as "fine art" to be hung alongside the canvas on the walls of museums and galleries. These magnificent black and whites dis-

First published as the Introduction to *Aaron Siskind Photographs* (New York: Horizon Press, 1959), © 1959 by Aaron Siskind.

dain "interpretation" and the devices—blurring, angle shots, foreshortening, double exposure—by which "creative" photography attempts to simulate the effects of modern modes in painting. No fake Seurats, Renoirs, Mondrians, rediscovered in the streets and fields with the aid of the dark room. Siskind has retained as fully as in a news shot the classical function of photography as a reporter, "a direct communications medium," as Steichen calls it. Like the best of his painter contemporaries he has simplified his means in order to concentrate on the act of choice.

Instead of scenes that seem like paintings, Siskind's pictures *are* paintings as they appear on the printed page—which is where people today see most of the paintings that they see. They are reproductions, though reproductions that have no originals. Or, if you prefer, they are reproductions of "works" which came into being through the collaboration of anonymous men and nature when neither they nor it were engaged in their more typical creations.

These indifferent compositions, often animated by the chemistries of decay, which were on display anywhere, have here been made part of our art culture by a man who combines in himself the faculties of the artist and the connoisseur. He has gathered them as evidences of the response of the physical world to the freshest assertions of art, as one might have shown the new influence of Rubens on the female form had it been possible to take photos in the early years of the seventeenth century.

Siskind has used the camera to make a book on modern art. It is a book that *teaches* in the same degree as a book on Picasso or on post-Impressionism. Our sensual pleasure in its shapes and textures—it is in his wonderful grasp of surfaces by the modulations of his greys that Siskind almost makes us forget that these are not paintings—will be one with our intellectual pleasure in recognizing them as extensions of our esthetic tradition. In turn, they reveal possibilities in that tradition that have often gone unperceived by painters. Siskind's photos comment on art today, not in terms of particular artists or schools, but as a general development of experience and knowledge.

As pictures to be *perused,* these photographs have the grand advantage over other book art that their qualities are all here, on the page. A reproduction of a painting is at best a substitute, and a poor one. It is art living under reduced circumstances; it cannot engage our interest without raising questions, concerning the scale, color, texture, etc. of the original, which it cannot answer. In looking at an art reproduction the mind is divided between the present image and the one that is absent. In a Siskind photo we may forget its source. Neither our delight nor our learning would be in any sense augmented if we were told that this blackness was a night sky or a piece of tar paper. Though "ready-mades" and "found" art are today accepted as authentic works, no one could be so naif as to imagine that the actual object from which Siskind drew his image could match the beauties he has brought to the print. Whatever was there before he clicked his shutter would not look like this until his impeccable choosing determined in what light, from what distance, in what quantity, it was to be seen. In each of these photos it is the separate and unique making, as well as the inspired selecting, that we experience; were the pictured boards or stretches of sand to be physically delivered to us, nothing in them could make up for the loss of Siskind's eye and mind.

As reproductions of works of art made by nobody and recorded by genius, these photos bring to photography an order of thought generally lacking in it. Unlike a painting, which we get into deeper the more we look at it—finding the artist himself in the hue, line, rhythm of paint strokes—the photograph, within whose areas of light and darkness the hand does not intervene, can catch and hold us only through its overall effect, that is, its idea. Yet cameramen take it for granted that a "good" photo speaks for itself, a meaning being somehow guaranteed by the reality of the thing in the picture. This assumption of intrinsic significance is a fallacy that photography shares with its twins, the newspaper and naturalistic literature. The fact is that most photographs, however charged with the mood or story reference of the "frozen instant," simply stare back at you with the dumb stare of physical fact.

The inanity of duplicated "life" was less noticeable when photos were met with mainly in the family album—what and who Aunt Sadie in her graduation dress was, or why anyone should want to look at her likeness, could be settled by memory and sentiment. Today, however, with the picture weeklies, tabloids and armies of amateurs in every land intent on packing all that exists into the one-eyed black valise, the illusionary realm of photography has taken on an independent life. Out of the capacity of the machine to produce resemblances has risen a world of aimless artifice that stands between both nature and art. In it reality is rectangular and instantaneous; translated into these dimensions the bearded Cuban revolutionist, the inside of a mushroom, a Paris merry-go-round, a pitcher's wind up, the skull of a war victim, become equivalents. The natives of Africa seem to have been justified in their fear of being kidnaped into the cubic void where, converted into tastefully composed moments, creatures lose their solidity and flicker in an infinity of "scenes." The black and white universe has become the agency of an immense stupefaction, which its refraction into false hues threatens to make still more acute.

Against the break-up of experience into bits of scattered appearance, Siskind uses the camera to establish the continuity of contemporary visual understanding as well as of his own personality—"the start," he says, "is from a previous picture." This is another way of saying that Siskind makes a *moral* use of the camera. Through this eye trained to look by modern art (which is something more than being trained to look at modern art), the seen world recovers its human unity in the unity of plastic norms freed of local associations. Each of his studies penetrates the idea of its subject and joins it to the objective system of the art of this century. In this context, the smear, the bubble, the odd bit of lettering, seems less random than the Eiffel Tower or a president addressing a crowd.

People who believe that paintings ought to be like photographs believe that photographs can be like paintings. Siskind has not fooled himself into trying to make of his pictures the vocabulary of an artistic identity. His work is as removed from the obsessive patterning of the "abstract" photographer as from the symbolism of the film impressario of blasted trees and ghostly monuments. With the instinct of a master for the philosophic basis of his medium, he has comprehended the camera as an instrument turned outward to variety rather than as a tool for inscribing a signature. As a group and separately, his images evoke a commonly accessible world—though one which, unlike that of "boy and his dog," has as its strict entrance requirement an educated sensibility. What this is, Siskind here demonstrates in practice, page by page.

3

Gorky and History
An Exchange

Paul Goodman's review of my book on Arshile Gorky (*PR*, Summer 1962) is actually a counter-statement on the relation of the artist to history, except that Goodman did not understand my side of the discussion and his presentation of it consisted of some half-gnawed quotations left over from gobbling up my book into his thesis. But anything that Goodman does not understand is worth further examination.

Not that my account of Gorky's development was so complicated; there was really no need for Goodman to discover in it the operation of a "double dialectic." Both the complexity and the dialectic arise rather from Goodman's attitude toward history. This attitude is indeed amazing. Goodman conceives the history of our time as unreal, or as real only negatively; and then he finds that there is another history, the real one, which he doesn't describe but which has to do, I suspect, with noble events chosen by him out of the entire past. Rosenberg, he complains, "takes the crazy details of current history too seriously as real history." To understand this criticism you do need a double dialectic: one for what actually happens and one for

Reprinted from *Partisan Review*, vol. 29, no. 4, Fall 1962.

what is real. You might even find a third dialectic handy, to choose what is serious in the "crazy details" and what is comical in the real history.

For Goodman's next statement is even more startling than his theory of the two histories. The crazy details, though not serious, may have consequences fatal to mankind: "they are," writes Goodman, "real enough in that they may do us in, but they do not much recommend themselves for humane discourse." Current history may kill us but it can't interest us. Nor can it influence the artist. Fate and action are in one bin, intellect and art in another. Goodman demonstrates at City Hall as a war resister, but real history is whatever he chooses to talk about, as in the "historical" confabulations of *The Empire City*. I wonder if Goodman realizes that in this split between fact and discourse his classicism has come very close to mere academic idealism.

But if it was a mistake to think that the history of the twenties through the thirties influenced Gorky, how about *real* history? Did that influence him? Goodman doesn't say. Gorky was not in the range of his humane discourse—and, in fact, doesn't seem to interest him very much.

Through his gift of the "double dialectic"—i.e., my dealing with Gorky as responsive to history and dealing with him as an artist—Goodman generously tries to share with me his view of the double reality and while so doing to clarify me a bit, as they used to say on the Left. Besides my mistake about current history, I take current art too seriously as the art of our time, but when, says Goodman, I discuss Gorky's best work I "really treat all this as mythology" and present Gorky as "quite outside of *that* history and very much like the artist of any age." (Goodman's italics) Thus, according to Goodman, I am contradicting myself—either art or history ought to be kept out. But my contradictions are true and wise, because in bringing in this mess of contemporary history and contemporary art by which I am taken in, I am describing, all unawares, "the paradox of being trapped and therefore representative and indeed existing at all, and of escaping and becoming one's self and realizing some value." In other words, the history of the twentieth century is the mask of an eternal psychological drama, and while I failed to see through the mask and thus dealt with it as the real thing, I did touch on the drama, which was the same for Gorky as for Giotto.

Well, that's telling me what I think but it is not telling the reader what I said. In my book, there was only one history, *that* one, and no artist "quite outside of that history." Real or unreal, seriously or seriously in quotes, dialectically and comically, the history was the history of our time, in whatever degree that history absorbs, repeats, fulfills or negates past history. Gorky and his contemporaries were stuck with it and the artist at any point of his creative effort was stuck with its art; neither Gorky nor his paintings ever got out of either.

I wrote of Gorky as a man stuck with the history and the art of our time and *conscious of being stuck.* There are two ways of giving effect to this consciousness. The first way is to attempt to figure out history's next move—this was the spirit of the thirties in its political ideology and in its rationalized approaches to art. The second way is to discard the ideology of the next move and to trust to action or to the unhindered gesture to evoke the new out of the unknown—this was the spirit of the War period, with its abandonment of "ultimate objectives," which has survived the Cold War years. Gorky tried both ways, first one then the other, each in "the right time" (that is—since Goodman questions what "right time" means— going along with the rationalizing effort and shifting at the moment when that way had been collectively exhausted). Thus Gorky's history was "exemplary." But the important thing is that *in both phases,* Gorky was responding to historical actuality with historical consciousness and intention.

Goodman makes much of my inability to "unite the two strands" of history and art in Gorky's career. One may gather from the above that no such uniting was necessary, since there was no separation—again, the problem is Goodman's, not mine. Gorky's career was linked simultaneously to political and social history and to esthetic experiment by the problem of *location*. The drama of this refugee from war and from famine is entirely a drama, almost a saga, of self-placement; in this drama all of his intellectual and emotional powers came into play.

The consciousness of being stuck with, or in, history is simply outside of Goodman's comprehension. For him, as we have seen, the actual historical moment is unreal or unserious, and to feel hedged in by this unreality of triviality is to be the victim of an illusion that needs to be translated into a more basic symbolism of traps, *e.g.,* the womb.

But how can one who denies or displaces Gorky's anxious consciousness grasp the tension of his thought? Even if Goodman were right about history, his impatience with determinism would make him wrong about Gorky. Not that it is necessary to agree with the artist in his feeling about history. But it is necessary to respect that feeling as a fact and not brutally to substitute for it one's own ideas of what the "real fact" is. After all, the critic has not, like the head doctor, been called in to straighten anyone out to that extent.

Nor does the problem of self-location exist for Goodman. It did exist, but Goodman long ago solved it to his own satisfaction. It is his great creative feat, in fact, and the mark of his own pioneering intelligence, that back in the thirties he consciously situated himself in a Manhattan set within a combination of semi-real Nature and a fiction of Athens, and that within this symbolically transformed environment he established, discovered, or pretended to discover a "community" of friends and disciples, the "humane discourse" about whom overlay the "crazy details" of current history in *The Empire City*. But what Goodman has done he cannot understand other people failing to do. Gorky, with far fewer social, intellectual, symbolic and psychological resources, had to keep searching for a spot, on the map and in the human world—it was to this end that he sought to decipher the history of painting as if it were the code in *The Gold Bug*. Gorky had come to New York, but for an artist in those days New York was the wrong spot; the real spot was Paris.[1] The struggle for location, which was the connection between Gorky and history, thus provided the meaning for him of the fall of Paris and the arrival in New York of the exiled surrealists: by being and working there, they authenticated New York for Gorky—in commenting on this dramatic relationship, it is presumptuous of Goodman to introduce his opinions of Breton and Matta as "international hipsters"; no one claimed that they influenced *Goodman*.

Goodman lacks the dramatic imagination required to visualize the outlines of another's life, as formed by his limitations and the dilemmas that arise out of those limitations, and to apprehend the particular genius by which he surmounts them (when he does surmount them) and the anguish in which he sinks under their weight. Goodman is a sage with answers; he is weak on problems. Thus he reduces the concrete drama of Gorky's struggle with place, time and human environment, the conditions of his creative leap, to the mush of "the artist's mature liberation in terms of his temporarily good marriage, getting a decent income [Gorky never got a decent income] and a little public acceptance [Gorky had just as much public acceptance in the thirties but by different people, and it was the difference that counted for him] also his rage of jealousy and fear of oncoming death [by the time of Gorky's cancer operation his new style had been in full development for five or six years] for

1. Since this was true for American artists generally, the wrong spot was the right spot in terms of the change that was to take place in American painting.

these are the things that free us from obsessional self-consciousness and give the real self a chance to breathe."

In sum, Goodman demands that we discard as "fancy psy-
chologizing" the exploration of Gorky's thought and experience, his development through conflict with the strangeness of
his time and place and with the hard issues of influence and
originality, and accept instead some abstractions of therapeutic
psychology. History and the artist are to be kept firmly apart.
As flippantly as he dismisses from serious "discourse" the facts
that may do us in, he announces that he is "profoundly unim-
pressed" by the human and cultural crisis (the War and the
conquest of France by Hitler) through which the personal-his-
torical complex of Gorky and other artists underwent transformation and ushered in a new period in American painting.

For Goodman the only choice in regard to current history is
either to paralyze oneself by "role playing" in it or to ignore it.
Once Gorky shook off the error of asking "What next?" he
had, according to Goodman, no longer anything to do with
history and became "an artist of any age." The fact is, however, that Gorky's later paintings were both far more expressive
of their time than the earlier ones and far richer in historical
content—this content was described in detail in my analysis of
his painting, *The Diary of a Seducer,* but Goodman, overlooking "the crazy details," read this analysis as a demonstration of
"classical art theory." Being mesmerized by the idea of solving
the historical riddle had actually kept Gorky "out of history,"
as it did to a large extent the American Marxists. Once he re-
nounced this effort, he was able to recognize that he already
was in history and to act as one who belonged there. André
Breton communicated this sense of proprietorship of history
very powerfully, and its effect on Gorky's confidence was incalculable. By ceasing to push for the next step, Gorky arrived at
it, the irony being that had he not pushed so hard the door
would not have opened when he stepped back.

Goodman is, of course, aware of these processes, but only when they take place in his own laboratory. It horrifies him to think of history sitting on someone's back and frustrating his solutions. It offends him almost as much to think of history shoving someone *toward* solutions. It is not only that Goodman is opposed to willed roles, he wishes to deny also imposed roles, the world of tragic struggle and irony. He wishes to deny as unreal any power not emanating from within the individual and which cannot be controlled by inner movements—you relax and things relax. This assumption of total freedom is not only Utopian, it leads a daring soul to primitive magic. Inside yourself (on good days, that is) "solutions" occur that way. And "humane discourse" ought to have a good dose in it of the consoling belief that things so happen too in the world.

But Utopianism and magic won't do as a means for understanding the lives of others. *They* live in situations made up of details, including the nutty ones. *They*—dammit—live in determinism; *they* have to fight it out with imposed limitations; for *them* the Chinese Emperor's Easy Way is not a sure formula. *They* are in history; if not their whole ("real") selves, then their actions, including the actions of painting pictures or composing book reviews. For all his classical wishes, Goodman's own good work is not achieved outside *"that"* history.

4

Insurrection

Though the British literary quarterly *Scrutiny* ceased publication ten years ago, it and Dr. F. R. Leavis, its "editorial protagonist," as he calls himself, are still hot issues on both sides of the Atlantic. In England, it is recalled that *Scrutiny* caused a civil war in literary criticism, and it is always difficult to know when and if any such war has ended. As for Leavis, no reviewer of the twenty-volume reprint of *Scrutiny* in its entirety, recently issued by the Cambridge University Press, has failed to mention either the excitement Leavis aroused in his readers and in his students at Downing College or his arrogance, his authoritarianism, and his abuse of those who disagree with him. Both the enthusiasm and the belligerence are essential features not only of Leavis's movement in criticism but of its role in the decades since *Scrutiny* made its appearance, at the bottom of the Big Depression. In many respects the magazine was simply the forerunner of those quarterlies of literary criticism of which several score are now published by the English departments of American universities. This, chosen at random, is a typical table of contents (volume 8, no. 4,

First published in *The New Yorker*, 14 March 1964.

March 1940): "Regulated Hatred: An Aspect of the Work of Jane Austen," "Athalie and the Dictators," "Searchlight on Tin-Pan Alley," "The Poetry of Coleridge," Correspondence, Book Reviews. Most periodicals of this type are of interest only to instructors and doctoral candidates in English studies; the reading public finds them abstruse and tiresome, and practicing authors find them irritating and distracting—Faulkner complained that he could never understand the "deep readings" of his novels produced by the quarterly critics. Published unofficially at Cambridge from 1932 to 1953, *Scrutiny* for most of its life had a press run of seven hundred and fifty copies and a maximum, in its last three or four years, of fifteen hundred. There is general agreement that it printed many original interpretations of Shakespeare, nineteenth-century novelists, poetry from Chaucer to Hopkins. Leavis's most important books, *New Bearings in English Poetry, Revaluation, The Great Tradition* (which gave his version of the high spots in the English novel), and *D. H. Lawrence, Novelist,* reinforced the impression that *Scrutiny* was a strictly literary enterprise. Yet its "new conception of the nature of critical thought," as Leavis described it, had as much resemblance to a calm meditation on the effects induced in the mind by the printed page as one of Francis Bacon's screaming popes has to the *Innocent X* of Velázquez.

The passion of *Scrutiny* lay in Leavis's attitude toward modern life, in his notion of "the literary intelligence," and in his conception of the role of the critic. It was plain from the start that *Scrutiny* had set itself against Progress, democracy, and political liberalism, and that it occupied a sector in the battle line of anti-modernism established by *L'Action Française,* the New Humanism, the classicism-royalism-Catholicism formula of T. S. Eliot, the literary agrarianism of the Old South, and the cultural Fascism of Ezra Pound. In the radical mood of the thirties, to be thus "placed" (one of the magazine's favorite words) was enough to give *Scrutiny* a heavily reactionary cast, despite Leavis's consistent refusal to define his political position. About his outlook toward the modern world there has been no ambiguity; it was summed up in the question he hurled at C. P. Snow a couple of years ago during his attack on Snow's plea for "scientific culture": "Who will assert," he demanded, "that the average member of a modern society is more fully human, or more alive, than a Bushman, an Indian peasant, or a member of one of those poignantly surviving primitive peoples, with their marvellous art and skills and vital intelligence?" There was no lack of respondents.

What eluded most of them, and provided some justification for Leavis's customary outcries about being misrepresented, is that despite his philosophy of decline and his debt to the ideas of Eliot and D. H. Lawrence, he has never been tempted to return either to ecclesiastical commandments or to grapes trodden by the feet of peasants; apparently he has been too conscious of his plebeian origin to be deluded about the benefits of aristocratic orders. He has stood not for social restoration but for a new secular order. In his tract against Snow he specifically warns his audience against assimilating him (Leavis) among the Romantic Utopians. "I am not preaching," he states, "that we should defy, or try to reverse, the accelerating movement of external civilization . . . that is determined by advancing technology." Leavis hates the modern world, but he wants to ride it and dominate its direction. His new order, though promulgated through literary criticism and not Storm Troopers, has the ominous overtones of a revolution aimed at all existing values, institutions, and personages. (In time these came to include Eliot, too, and finally Lawrence.) He sees innovation as a universal fact and the ability to cope with it as the primary necessity: "The advance of science and technology means a human future of change so rapid and of such kinds, of tests and challenges so unprecedented, of decisions and possible non-decisions so momentous and insidious in their consequences, that mankind . . . will need to be in full intelligent possession of its full humanity." This commitment to the unknown world in formation is not as free of platitudes as might be expected of an author who has just been flaying Snow for his "mess of clichés and sentimental banalities." Also, in conceding that science, an intellectual power that remains a mystery outside of its own realm, sets the pace of our thinking, Leavis has admitted that Snow, however shallow one finds his approach to both literature and science, was discussing a real problem, one that Leavis does not deal with in dealing with Snow. Yet Leavis's statement is a testimonial to a future that differs from the past, a future to be created by contemporary man without much aid from his ancestors: "I haven't chosen to say that mankind will need all its traditional wisdom; that might suggest a kind of conservatism that, so far as I am concerned, is the enemy."

Leavis's wish to change everything extends to his celebrated "revaluations" of the literature of earlier centuries by applying to it principles strictly of our time. René Wellek, professor of comparative literature at Yale, described these revaluations as "the first consistent attempt to rewrite the history of English poetry from the twentieth-century point of view." In his argument with the literary historian F. W. Bateson, Leavis asserted that "the motive [for a proper history of English poetry] would be inseparable from an interest in the problems of contemporary poets." Instead of inherited values, "what we need and shall continue to need not less is . . . a power . . . of creative response to the new challenges of time." If Leavis is anti-modern, it is as a theoretician and practitioner of the modernist search for the new. He asks to be appreciated as a radical; the targets of his criticism are those attitudes and that flabbiness of will and intellect that sap our readiness for innovation. The issue in regard to him lies in the quality of his revolution and the effect of his "outlaws' enterprise," as he likes to call *Scrutiny,* upon the contemporary "power of creative response."

Leavis's vanguard criticism and the policy of *Scrutiny* take their stand on the break with the past that came in both literature and critical method during the early years of the twentieth century. Affirming the intellectual continuity of *Scrutiny* with the *Calendar of Modern Letters,* a British review published between 1925 and 1927, Leavis praises this predecessor for having "recognized unequivocally that a basic change had occurred in poetry" and for having demonstrated a "quick perceptive responsiveness to the new creative life of the time." ("Responsiveness to the new," etc., is pretty close to "creative response to the new challenges of time"; Leavis's theoretical vocabulary is not notable for its richness.) His own responsiveness included following Pound, the Imagists, and I. A. Richards in reading poems in terms of the concreteness and rational coherence of their images; he also adopted Pound's conviction that the way a nation uses words determines its social and political well-being. The source figure for Leavis, however, of both the new poetry and the new criticism was the early T. S. Eliot. *The Waste Land* not only revolutionized poetry for Leavis but established consciousness of the decay of civilization as the measure of literary insight. Eliot's *The Sacred Wood* supplied the chief elements of his critical approach. A statement like this from Eliot's essay on *Hamlet*—"Few critics have ever admitted that *Hamlet* the play is the primary problem, and Hamlet the character only secondary"—came to be applied in *Scrutiny* in as many variations as Lenin's phrase "infantile Leftism" in the polemics of Stalin against Trotskyism. Eliot's insistence on treating the work of literature as literature (*Hamlet* the play as the primary problem) and not as a vehicle for the critic's own theories or imaginings provided the basic axiom of

Leavis's critical "discipline" and of the approach of *Scrutiny* critics.

To many contributors to *Scrutiny,* what counted most in Eliot was the model of literary analysis presented by his essays. Leavis, however, went beyond Eliot in combining wasteland consciousness with literary valuation. It would seem obvious that consciousness of inhabiting a cultural wasteland comes from historical or sociological investigation and comparison, and that to find an author better for possessing such consciousness violates the rule of responding to literature as literature. But Leavis appears to have turned aside this objection with the rather simple sophistry that a keen critical intelligence is an indispensable ingredient of a good poem and that an intelligence of this calibre could not fail to read decay in buildings and on the faces of passersby. The identification of modern literary merit with a specific social vision (continual decline) was the revolutionary tangent by which Leavis set the course for *Scrutiny.* By a single stroke, it introduced into criticism a dogma of subject matter as rigid as those of totalitarian ideologies. In the face of the mandatory optimism of Soviet Socialist Realism or Nazi Strength Through Joy, *Scrutiny* evolved as *the* standard at the root of its "strictly literary standards" the writer's degree of comprehension of the increasing desolation of spirit in the present-day city, the heartlessness of contemporary human relations, the emptiness and frustration of modern work. By this standard, Leavis elected D. H. Lawrence the supreme genius (a word Leavis has never hesitated to use) of our era. The perspective of gathering gloom supplied *Scrutiny* contributors with a definition of what was new in the "new challenges of time." It enabled them to downgrade on aesthetic grounds any literature and art that did not conform to Leavis's disguised politics.

Neither in his critical concepts nor even in his combination

of the ideas of others was Leavis to any great extent an inno-
vator. His strength lay in imposing, with the maximum conviction and over as wide a literary and cultural area as possible,
the point of view he had shaped out of available insights. But in
conceiving his nucleus of beliefs and sentiments as a power capable of revolutionary conquest, Leavis was led to a highly
original result—his dramatic re-creation of the notion of "the
literary intelligence" and, above all, of the figure of the literary
critic. This was his supreme imaginative performance and the
source of the excitement among those who passed under his
influence. To the credo he had evolved from Lawrence and
Eliot, he added the element of moral and organizational pre-
paredness: literary criticism was to be constantly alert to its
consequences outside of literature; that is to say, it was thought
that took on the nature of action. The task he set for literary
criticism was—like the task set by the Marxists, whom *Scrutiny* opposed from the start—not only to interpret books and
other cultural phenomena but to change the conditions under
which both would be produced. In order to act politically,
Pound had to put aside poetry for means that culminated in his
wartime broadcasts for the enemy. Leavis, by contrast, was not
for a moment disposed to yield first place in procuring the results he sought to any medium but literature, be it politics, science, or mass education. Literary thinking and literary
criticism, in his revised form of them, were the most adequate
of weapons.

The fury of Leavis's attack on Snow is thus to be explained as
the riposte to an intolerable attempt to tamper with the creation to which he had devoted his life—I mean the figure of the
literary man as leader. It paralleled exactly his assault in his
maiden contribution to *Scrutiny,* thirty years earlier, on Max
Eastman's *The Literary Mind* and, through Eastman, on the
culture (in quotes) of H. G. Wells. What offended Leavis then,
too, was the writer who identifies human betterment with sci-

ence and technological progress and identifies literature with such minus quantities of the good life as nostalgia, vagueness, and self-indulgence. Then, too, Leavis invoked Lawrence as the type of intelligence far better equipped to grasp the consequences for the individual of the Industrial Revolution than the "complacently Philistine" tribe of Wells-Snow. The inwardness of the author of *Women in Love*—an inwardness that cast a dubious light on the worth of mere material abundance—represented a clarity that was the opposite of the theme of literary muddleheadedness. If further disproof of Snow's stereotype was needed, *Scrutiny* provided it by bringing forth, especially in the person of Leavis himself, a literary mind not to be exceeded in any field in its hardness, its contemporaneity, the definiteness of its assumptions, and its tirelessness in pursuing its objectives—a literary mind distinguished, to use two favorite *Scrutiny* terms, by its "seriousness" and its "discipline."

"*Scrutiny*," testifies Leavis in "A Retrospect," written for the Cambridge reprint, "was a very different kind of enterprise from those subsequent American quarterlies" devoted exclusively to literary criticism. "The difference lay in the charged positiveness of conception and intention with which we were engaged in something more specific, ambitious, and (to the academic mind) offensive than, merely and generally, running an intellectual literary organ." Though nowhere was one more often reminded that the critic's attention must be riveted on the poem as poem, in the context of *Scrutiny* the close examination of texts was actually intended as a training procedure for "something more ambitious"—a means of discovering, concentrating, and augmenting an inner power in anticipation of actual encounters with enemies, in a manner comparable to the sword or archery exercises of a Zen warrior. Walt Whitman had conceived of his poetry as breeding inspired "gangs of cosmos" capable of injecting life and style into American democracy. Leavis's equivalent might be dubbed "gangs of sensibility"; they were not poets but critics and readers. Their first objective would be to wreck the authority in both teaching and publishing of precisely that species of literary mind that passively and with smug self-satisfaction carried the germs of modern decadence, and that Snow futilely hoped to cure by injections of humanitarianism and science. Such was the mind that ruled British universities through what Q. D. Leavis, the "protagonist's" wife, pungently named "the academic club"; it was dominant, too, in the Literary Left, in the offices of the large publishers, in the B.B.C., in the book pages of the metropolitan dailies and weeklies. *Scrutiny* proposed to replace this slack mass, to whom literature was entertainment or a tool of personal or group prestige, by individuals able to transmit "the vital human impulse" celebrated by Lawrence. In her celebrated essay "The Discipline of Letters," Mrs. Leavis envisions how "new and uniquely equipped specialists would be turned out [a dubious phrase for a foe of machine thinking] whose center in literary criticism and training in the methods and disciplines of other specialisms would enable them to work further and further into adjacent fields of knowledge with the most fruitful results." This paean to infiltration indicates that the *Scrutiny* invasion was to capture the realm of learning. But its ultimate design was far grander. *Scrutiny* was, in short, an organ of social revolution. While most of its contributors may have wished for nothing more than to write judiciously about poems and novels, the "we" embodied in *Scrutiny* was occupied with nothing less than an attempt to gain control of British society. Unless this goal is kept in mind, neither the ideas of Leavis nor his style of disputation can be appreciated.

From the start, *Scrutiny* desiderated (to borrow again from its characteristic idiom) power; the word for it was "force." In "A Retrospect," Leavis characterizes it as a "vitalizing force," a "decisive force," a "power to defeat," an entity that "enforced and justified." His chronicle of the hard times of *Scru-*

tiny, forever under the fire of "the comprehensive system" of his enemies, has the ring of the memoirs of an insurrectionary leader. Leavis recounts the inception of *Scrutiny* as an "outlaws' enterprise" at Cambridge (but "in spite of Cambridge"), its success in recruiting the "armed [intellectually, of course] minority," which it forged into a radical "center"; he boasts of the discipline practiced by its members ("We were not using the word 'discipline' lightly") and of their capacity to move outward and become the core of adjacent disciplines ("to take the intelligence trained in 'English' into quite other-than-literary fields"); he describes how through their twenty years of activity the actual Cambridge was overthrown and replaced by "the essential Cambridge" (as the Nazis replaced the actual Germany by the "real" Germany); and he outlines his ultimate strategy, "essential to the conception of *Scrutiny*"—that by means of its example and challenge "a public could be rallied, a key community of the élite (one therefore disproportionately influential) formed and held."

This revolutionary activist spirit, injected into *Scrutiny* by Leavis, enabled the magazine to spread, through its few hundred copies, its "formidable life" throughout the English-speaking world. This spirit was responsible, too, for many of *Scrutiny's* most interesting articles. Q. D. Leavis, whose uninhibited sociological comments made her one of its most memorable contributors, brought out, in denouncing a leader of the British academic establishment, that his charming triviality in discussing books went hand in hand with supporting the smashing of strikes by university undergraduates; both the triviality and the strikebreaking, she contended, were typical devices for preserving the social privileges of "the club." In "Lady Novelists and the Lower Orders," she expressed her disdain, as one "whose class-feeling derives from a less advantageous social origin," for the middle-class assumptions about the working class in Left Wing fiction. As for Leavis himself, who can refuse to consider seriously his continuing theme, which exploded into his barrage against Snow, that one who abuses language with catchwords and banalities is not to be trusted in cultural matters, or, indeed, with any decisions affecting public life? And his denunciations of the hypocrisy of the financially and intellectually well fixed are interspersed with passages of exceptionally warm sympathy for the British working people. His unremitting consciousness of criticism as action lends, it seems to me, intensity even to his purely literary studies; it is as if he sensed in a work, whether it be *Measure for Measure* or *Daniel Deronda*, the energies of willful, living presences that involve him in a contest of minds. Through these encounters, with their atmosphere of issues fought to a finish, Leavis becomes himself a historically vivid presence (which may be the opposite of a reliable literary critic). His much-disputed judgment of *Hard Times* as Dickens' masterpiece was no doubt determined by his responding to its plot as a situation more real to him than any other in Dickens. The essay is an attractive one despite, or perhaps on account of, its being an example of what Leavis most vehemently denies: that his literary opinions are affected by his social attitudes, and that he may be led to admire a work by discovering in it his own line or intellectual pattern. In *Hard Times* he is happy to associate Dickens with Lawrence and to perceive in Gradgrind—the "reasonable" but feelingless utilitarian—a disguised C. P. Snow (the death scene of Mrs. Gradgrind, which Leavis quotes to close his essay, is a superb choice that escapes the pattern).

Leavis conceived of the revolution of *Scrutiny* as an upheaval without a doctrine: the practitioners of sensibility were to owe allegiance to no ideology, philosophy, or religion. They were to constitute, rather, a corps of free intelligences informed by firsthand literary experiences and acting toward a common purpose. He wished, said he, "to prevent the hardening into accepted 'rightness.'" For him the openness and individualism of the *Scrutiny* movement defined it as essentially "liberal." In theory, the minority culture of *Scrutiny* did not differ greatly from Coleridge's, and differed even less from Matthew Arnold's "remnant." *Scrutiny*, however, was a creature of the troubled nineteen-thirties—the decade, to use the phrase of Jules Romains, of "the formation of the bands"—the Leavis's will to establish the authority of his collectivity caused it to take on the tension and totalitarian tenor of that extremist period. There arose in it an increasing pressure for adherence to "the permanent direction at the center," and even to its mannerisms and pet phrases. The no-doctrine ideal realized itself in practice in a set of formulas and verdicts. Pugnacious disputations among contributors appear frequently in *Scrutiny*, but Frank Kermode is justified in observing, in the *New Statesman*, that "there is no discussion, only obscure and angry quarrels." These were consistent with the purpose of *Scrutiny*—"always to maintain a strained posture opposing every description of laxity and ennui and establish the revolutionary system of work and revolutionary tone of life in all fields." (I have lifted these phrases, which to me exactly describe *Scrutiny's* moral stand, from the "Announcement on the Fifth Plenum of the Fourth Central Committee of the Workers' Party of Korea," published in Pyongyang in 1963.) Leavis's diatribes against opponents were intended to silence not only foes but potential doubters within his own ranks. To deplore his rancor and feuding as temperamental idiosyncrasies, products of "Puritanism" or ill treatment, is to overlook the revolutionary affiliations of his rhetorical abuse and its function in stiffening the morale and unity of his followers.

That *Scrutiny* parodied the insurrectionary political parties of the thirties turned the "seriousness" to which Leavis constantly appealed into its opposite; at bottom, it was a program for seizing power through approved readings of John Donne. Leavis was not alone in modelling a literary movement on the organization of political activists. Surrealism, the last of the

Continental vanguard schools, had coalesced in the twenties
into a "center" around André Breton in which purity of doctrine and practice was preserved by excommunications and
splits. *Scrutiny* was precipitated down the same decline. Indeed,
the mixing of art with action philosophies had from the twenties forward become a major innovating factor in literature (Social Realism, Existentialism), as in painting (Action Painting)
and on the stage (the theatre of the absurd). That *Scrutiny* was
too deeply pledged to its nineteenth-century creed of the separation of the "disciplines" to see itself in the crooked mirror of
modernist drift only made its "takeover bid," as the British
critic John Bayley has called it, all the more comic. In the context of power, Leavis's insistence on literary criticism as "central" became nothing more than a weapon against rival special-
izations. One might say that he transformed Lenin's professional revolutionist into a revolutionist of the profession. Such
victories as *Scrutiny* won took place within the teaching profession and as gains for the prestige of the English departments.
They prefigured the enlargement of these departments in the
postwar years and the replacement of the leisurely man of letters execrated by Mrs. Leavis with method-wielding specialists.
Leavis's campaign for the hegemony of literary studies also anticipated the competition of the humanities with the sciences
for their share of college finances.

In his disputes with historians and scientists, Leavis took his
stand on the needs of contemporary creation. As we have seen,
however, he had predefined those needs as a deepening of the
wasteland consciousness. Any other aspect of the revolution in
literature and sensibility that was already well under way before 1932 tends to be treated by *Scrutiny* as irrelevant, wrong-
headed, and aesthetically unsound. Though his modernist
pretensions are the foundation of his claim to significance,
Scrutiny's record in expounding the tradition of the new in art
and letters is deplorable. For him, the revolution in creation

begins with Eliot and ends with Lawrence. The hundred years' upheaval reaching back to Whitman, Poe, and Baudelaire, to van Gogh and the Impressionists, is reduced to a Ten Days That Shook the World. After Lawrence, the banner passes to Leavis. In *Scrutiny,* the twenties become "critical muddle and obscurity," but the writers of the twenties who are attacked in *Scrutiny* are also used to belabor the thirties. The total sum of clarifications of contemporary psychological states, moral and metaphysical dilemmas, indissoluble situations, and experimental assumptions to be found in the thousands of pages of *Scrutiny* would scarcely fill a single volume. If the need of the time was for "a power of creative response to the new," *Scrutiny* met that need by denouncing the most intense "responders" for falling short of the firm standards of the Downing College seminarians. Reviewing Marianne Moore's *Selected Poems,* Leavis confesses that for ten years he had not bothered to cut half the pages of her earlier *Observations* (he doesn't say why observing is less important than scrutinizing); now, persuaded by Eliot's introduction to the new volume, he has made a supreme effort, but "there is not one poem of which I can confidently say that I see the point." Since Miss Moore seems "preoccupied with visual description," Leavis recommends that "she should have chosen some other medium than words" (evidently Leavis thinks that painting is "preoccupied with visual description"). The nub of his response to Miss Moore is the satisfaction he takes in quarrelling with Eliot about the relevance to her verse of the metrics of Hopkins. In another bout with contemporary literature, in the same volume, Faulkner is taken care of by a *Scrutiny* regular, H. A. Mason: "The final comment on these people [the characters of *Pylon*] seems to be that they are not worth the attention the author bestows on them." (What happened to the principle of regarding the novel as primary, the characters as secondary?) Mason's verdict backs up a decision by the Master that "early in *Light in Au-*

gust it should have become plain to the reader that Faulkner's 'technique' is an expression of—or disguise for—an uncertainty about what he is trying to do." (In *Scrutiny,* uncertainty is a crime.) H. B. Parkes, a British-born history professor who represents America in *Scrutiny,* turns philosopher in "The Tendencies of Bergsonism" to instruct the philosopher who inspired Proust and the Fauves that "although intuition is a genuine faculty, it is one which must be employed with caution." In a 1946 issue, the poet of the Cubists, Apollinaire, is abused by one Klingopulos as "a kind of clown in verse, blest with a strong constitution and high spirits but little capacity for interesting experience or for writing poetry"; his images "express not command of experience but the opposite, some pettiness in the impulse to write." Another poet insufficiently in command of experience to satisfy *Scrutiny* is Jules Laforgue, whom Eliot had compared to the English metaphysicals. Though his experiments enabled him to express "the full complexity of his outlook," that outlook itself was "neither complex nor mature." (I'm not sure how this works out; does the critic mean that Laforgue was able to express something that he did not have to express?) His poetry "has a surface complexity which is sometimes little more than a peculiar kind of verbiage" (like the poetry of Moore and Apollinaire, the technique of Faulkner, and—as we shall see—the prose of Joyce). This critic, too, argues with Eliot, this time about the difference between the metaphysical conceit of Donne and the psychological associations of Laforgue. As in Leavis's criticism of Shelley, the flaw in Laforgue turns out to be an intellectual one: lacking the proper base in thought available in earlier centuries, he relies on "personality." But at least Laforgue tried to develop an "outlook." Mallarmé and Valéry did not even try, the *Scrutiny* critic adds. They made "the worship of forms the substitute for an outlook." (That the authors of "Un Coup de Dés" and "La Jeune Parque" lacked an "outlook" could occur only to a *Scrutiny* casuist.) Rilke, in contrast, is praised as if he were a version of Leavis; he had no "philosophy" but a great poetic sensibility. The only item on Gertrude Stein in the *Scrutiny* index, aside from occasional mentions as a bad example, is the review of a biography of her which, even in 1953, finds no better approach to her writings than a discussion of their incomprehensibility. While it was still "Work in Progress," Joyce's *Finnegans Wake* was dismissed by Leavis as "in any bulk not worth the labour of reading," a verdict the New York *Times* editorial page had the good taste to withhold until the volume was published. Employing his usual trick of turning criticism of a work into a dispute among critics, he proceeds to lecture commentators on Joyce about the absence of a "commanding theme" ("command" again) in the still unfinished composition and to introduce his inevitable reference to Lawrence. Since one of Joyce's admirers had compared him to Shakespeare, Leavis invokes historical determinism to show why Shakespeare could be great but writers subjected to modern conditions, including the activities of science, cannot. It is not surprising to find a reviewer in a 1943 issue announcing that "there was something to be said for the Nazi clean-up of German literature."

Scrutiny's presentation of the vitalizing authors of the age, when they are presented at all (Kierkegaard, for instance, is completely ignored), consists of subjecting their works to *Scrutiny's* own academic system, applied in utter ignorance of, or lack of sympathy with, the actual history of modern thinking in the arts. Upon publication of "XXX Cantos," the uses of metaphor were explained to Ezra Pound by *Scrutiny's* official poet, Ronald Bottrall, who had obviously never heard of the Imagist discussions on metaphor versus "fact," and whose prose style by itself should have prevented his manuscript from being presented as anything but a term paper; here, as usual, Hopkins and Donne provide the rule along whose edge a contemporary poet is cut to bits. As a critic, Eliot is a poet among professors;

his *Scrutiny* progeny are exactly the opposite. The anti-modern academicism of *Scrutiny* is distinguished from the older variety chiefly by its revolutionary bad manners, its absurd air of righteousness and intellectual certainty, its greater sophistication in seeking out the victims of its malice. The unanimous devotion of its contributors to a concept of aesthetic "success" is of itself sufficient to prevent their approximating any understanding of twentieth-century creation.

Thus *Scrutiny* failed to discover in the two decades of its existence any new writing in English worthy of serious consideration as art, and since its guiding intellect knew the reason for it in advance, it did not bother to speculate about the absence of such writing. Toward certain contemporaries, Leavis was both savagely hostile and opportunistic—for one, Wyndham Lewis, whom he called "brutal and boring" and whose *Men without Art,* one of the best critical volumes of the thirties, was never mentioned in *Scrutiny*. When, however, Lewis turned against abstract art, he was hailed in *Scrutiny* in terms unexceeded in intellectual vulgarity by Leavis's whipping boy, the Sunday press: "The reason Art has reached a sort of dead end, and . . . that the genuine artist has in a manner of speaking been betrayed, may be attributed directly to the excesses of Surrealism and the Abstract cult. Surrealism in particular has given Art the *coup-de-grace,*" etc., etc. Though books by the leading minds of the thirties and forties were reviewed by *Scrutiny* proconsuls, no writer after Lawrence was ever permitted to affect the magazine's perspective. For Leavis, such men as Kafka, Kierkegaard, and Sartre might as well never have existed.

The significance of *Scrutiny* in the teaching of literature lay not in its elucidation of new values but in its diffusion of a few modernist hypotheses over the whole length of literary history. The Scrutineers read the writings of other centuries as documents that through their technique of interpretation had become suddenly pertinent, as Oedipus had become suddenly pertinent through Freud. New creations could thus be dispensed with. Though the thought would horrify Leavis, *Scrutiny* "modernized" Shakespeare and Chaucer in a manner not too distant from a production of *Hamlet* in modern dress. The effect of its revalued classics was to reduce the distinction between the contemporary imagination and that of earlier periods. The influence in the universities of *Scrutiny's* strangled modernism went contrary to the need of students in the middle of the twentieth century to experience as their own the literature of advanced experiment and search. The ideal it erected was to mimic the virtues of other times, not to compose a work carrying the burden of today. If Leavis's rancor made him a moral ancestor of Britain's angry young men, his literary opinions helped to divert poetry into the arid exercises in traditional metrics that have filled the quarterlies. Through *Scrutiny,* the revolutionary critic became, as in the Soviet Union, the rival and at times the persecutor of the innovating writer. The classroom asserted itself against the studio, the university community against the community of artists. A "correct" way of reading was raised above writing. Pedantic glosses stirred up black clouds between the author and his text: an inevitable phrase in a *Scrutiny* criticism is "What Rosalind is saying is . . . ," "What Touchstone is saying . . . ," followed by words and thoughts that neither is saying at all. As with the Freudians, were it not for the interpreter's megaphone, the speaker himself would not seem so far away. The fervor aroused by Leavis among his students was a passion—different from the poetic— to argue, argue, argue. The Leavis-trained reader of a work strove, one might say, to become its last reader; after him, only his criticism, or the book as reflected in his criticism, was to be visible. In any case, *Scrutiny* gave the literary critic more to do than he had ever had before, as well as a greater assurance in doing it. But it drifted steadily away from its anchorage in Eliot and his ironic balancings of tradition and experiment.

Scrutiny was a protracted action; perhaps the most accurate characterization of that action would be that Leavis embraced the modernist revolution in order to bring it to an end. Today, he would like to see *Scrutiny* resumed, with such changes as conditions in the nineteen-sixties may require, but there is little left for it to do. In its attempt to follow Arnold in making "the best ideas prevail," Leavis's practice went against Arnold's demand that criticism "make an intellectual situation of which the creative power can profitably avail itself." "I am suggesting," charged a British reviewer of the magazine, "that something in the *Scrutiny* tone was actually hostile to the production or the encouragement of literature." In the last analysis, the conviction about modern barrenness could not be reconciled with discovering prolific manifestations of "the creative response." Eliot was right when he advised Leavis that in a world of hollow men the logical alternative was either religion or totalitarianism. Rejecting both, Leavis strove to project into the wasteland the drama of himself and his band heroically arrayed against the forces of pollution. Entirely lacking in his imagination is any sense of the objective drama of modern life, the struggle in it between reality and possibility. Thus, while *Scrutiny* shared the tension of its time, it was as an introverted adventure, a struggle with phantom essences. As one looks back through *Scrutiny's* twenty volumes, its contents seem, for all their straining, curiously drained of time. It is an intellectual nonspace that Leavis has been conquering. No wonder that in the end he can see behind him nothing but shadow victories, as in his unfounded brag about having "established" Eliot and Lawrence and having created a "frightening influence." To quote those Koreans once more: "Today our working people united steel-like around the Party Central Committee headed by Comrade Kim Il Sung are making continued innovation and constant advance to consolidate the successes scored in the scaling of Six Heights maintaining strained attitude and to make preparations for capturing a yet higher summit."

5

The Third Dimension of Georg Lukacs

"everlasting uncertainty and agitation distinguish the
bourgeois epoch from all earlier ones. All fixed, fast-frozen
relations . . . are swept away, all new-formed ones become
antiquated before they can ossify. All that is solid melts in
the air . . ."

The Communist Manifesto

"I have tried to show that these [angst and chaos] form the
essential content of modernism. This vision of the world as
chaos results from the lack of a humanist social
perspective."

Georg Lukacs, The Meaning of Contemporary Realism

I remember Lukacs from the thirties as a Marxist literary critic
who all agreed was a great, original thinker, though no one I
knew had read more than one or two of his pieces. My own
assent to his reputation was based on Lukacs's theory of "intellectual physiognomy," which explained what made characters
in novels and plays profound or trivial. "Intellectual physiognomy" seemed to me the answer to a deep riddle of fiction:
how an Othello or Lear could deliver wonderful utterances yet

Reprinted from *Dissent*, vol. 11, no. 4, Autumn 1964.

be convincingly stupid or raving; while a personage in an "intellectual" novel, e.g., one by Aldous Huxley, might philosophize brilliantly about abstruse issues yet produce an effect of shallowness. "Intellectual physiognomy" went boldly into the relation of intellect to insight, instead of the usual dodge of pitting them against each other. That Othello was endowed with an impressive intellectual physiognomy had nothing to do with his education, his "ideas" or even his mental capacity; it was a quality that descended to him from his author as a kind of family resemblance. Given a Shakespeare or a Tolstoy for his fictional father, an idiot becomes a genius without ceasing to be an idiot.

I don't know how accurate a description this is of Lukacs's idea. I am not even sure, after these decades, that I actually read the article in which it was contained. Perhaps someone told me about intellectual physiognomy and I decided that that's what it meant. Nor did I ever try to figure out what intellectual physiognomy had to do with Marxism, unless it implied that the proletariat as conceived by Marx had, despite its illiteracy, a more profound character than the bourgeoisie and the intellectuals. But the bourgeoisie, too, as they sprang out of Marx's mind would be deeper than they appeared in ordinary experience. . . . At any rate, I have long admired the theory of intellectual physiognomy and its author with it. This admiration was not lessened by hearing from time to time that Lukacs was resisting Stalin's "socialist realism" and that during the Hungarian uprising he was at the age of seventy thrown into prison by the Russians.

The Lukacs who now comes forward in *The Meaning of Contemporary Realism,* written seven years ago and just published in England and in the United States (under the title of *Realism in Our Time*), has nothing to say about intellectual physiognomy nor any concept of comparable originality. He takes his stand as a Marxist foe of modernist literature—Joyce,

Proust, Kafka, Musil—or of modernism in literature, and defends as an alternative, "realism" and the realistic tradition.

Much in the Lukacs we are presently privileged to read cannot be taken seriously; it requires an effort to believe that it was meant to be, though indubitably it was. Such statements as, "Our starting point is really the point of convergence of two antitheses: the antithesis between realism and modernism and the antithesis between peace and war," which line up literary modes on the two sides of current political struggles (are the Chinese modernists or realists?), wake one up to the distance that today separates one's thinking from what has come to constitute Marxism. Given this distance it is futile to dwell on the absurdities, exaggerations and misstatements of fact in *The Meaning of Contemporary Realism;* its very texture is made up of them—e.g., that with Thomas Mann "from *The Magic Mountain* onwards, socialism never ceases to be a central intellectual and compositional (!) element."

Lukacs, it turns out, has also failed to surmount the insensibility of Marxist criticism to the processes by which a work of literature actually comes into being. Creation, he believes (or his critical vocabulary compels him to say), takes place through the "translation" of a "consciousness of reality" into "adequate esthetic form." Thus he complains of the "selective principle which apparently underlies modernist writing" that "it is not a selection applied to the totality of the reality to be described"—as if it still needed to be demonstrated that works of art do not "describe reality" and that their "selective principle" is not "applied" but is an effect of imagination, temperament and the works the author has chosen as his tradition. Lukacs's mechanic's approach to literary creation as the analytical manipulation of facts and situations—"the realistic writer must seek the nodal points of these [social-individual] conflicts, determine what they are at their most intense and most typical, and give suitable expression to them"—raises the suspicion that his good (i.e., cleared of Stalinist perversions) Socialist Realism would result in no better writings than the worst.

It ought to be added that with all due reverence for the pathos of Lukacs's resistance to Stalinism, some of his statements fall short of rudimentary honesty. In his Preface to the German Edition of *The Meaning of Contemporary Realism,* written in Budapest in 1957, he declares his joy at being able at last to speak "openly," then calls for "relentless criticism" with the argument that "only on the basis of such criticism, *as with Rosa Luxemburg's complex legacy,* can Stalin's positive achievements be seen in perspective" (my italics). This abominable coupling of the inspired martyr of German Socialism with the sordid tyrant could have had no other purpose than to display orthodoxy in regard to strains of Marxist thinking condemned by the Party. It took another five years for Lukacs to permit himself a direct thrust at "the disastrous legacy of Stalinism." And though he still gets into trouble, it is for belonging to a wing of Party opinion. Our sympathies for this side in the inner struggle of Soviet development ought not to mislead us into considering him a free mind or into overlooking the weight of intellectual backwardness in his literary opinions.

Lukacs thus turns out to be a thorough disappointment; one did not expect to encounter this much "Marxism" in the great Marxist thinker. The sole interest in the present collection of essays is the angle of Lukacs's attack on vanguard literature, the fact that this attack is made from a premise that welcomes the revolution of the twentieth century. Other anti-modernist critics, say, Bernard Berenson or certain academic "humanists," simply discard this century and its works and glut themselves on the art of other times. As a Marxist, Lukacs is obliged not only to see this radical period as a culmination, he must hold its upheavals to be a good thing. He is stuck with change, and in literature he must ask for more rather than less emphasis on the derangements of the time. If he is to judge modernist works as inferior he must do so not for their failure to measure up to the masterpieces of other centuries but for their inadequacies in dealing with the novelties of this one. That Marxism, like the polemical varieties of traditionalist criticism, for example, that of F. R. Leavis, locates the value of contemporary works in the degree of historical consciousness displayed in them, including the historical significance of their esthetic modes, is of itself almost a guarantee of its pertinence. Criticism by fiction of the historical drama in which we are all cast as actors or as victims, and of which there are no disinterested spectators, is what keeps the novel and the play going in our time above their commercial, academic and propaganda functions. Works deficient in conscious response to this drama, and the psychological, political, cultural, technical issues mixed together in it, are doomed to tiresomeness and triviality regardless of freshened-up mannerisms. We are thus at one with Lukacs to the extent that he examines modern styles from the standpoint of today and tomorrow rather than as incidents in an esthetic totality standing apart from or above time.

In substance Lukacs's objections to modernist productions are familiar to us from other sources. He plays the customary themes on disintegration in Joyce, the nihilism of Kafka and Beckett. The evils of modernist literature he finds to be abstraction, distortion, subjectivism, formalism—traits objected to by all antimodernists from Eisenhower to Pius XII. Lukacs's thesis that "the essential content of modernism is *angst* and chaos" (a thesis which can be refuted without much trouble—where is the chaos in Valéry or Mondrian?) parallels the opinion concerning contemporary *society* held by swarms of elegists of cultural decline, most of them reactionaries who hate the industrial age. The distinction of Lukacs is that his notion of the downward movement of literature is fitted into a coherent theory of social development. He condemns modern art in the name of progress, and in so doing exposes more fully than does any political pronouncement of the Communists what the Communist conception of progress is. And not only the Communist, for as a *liberal* form of Communism, Lukacs's criticism also reflects fairly accurately the cultural outlook of the Left generally and particularly its attitude toward modern art.

In the postwar novel and theater, despair, the "void," "loss of self," have become clichés used to organize episodes, language, images. One can hardly help sharing Lukacs's impatience with glib intimations of an underlying "human condition" that turns real events into mere illustrations of an irresistible sickness. As literary criticism, however, rather than metaphysics, Lukacs's condemnation of philosophies of *angst* and chaos is beside the point; he is obliged to distinguish between pantomimes of despair and its genuine poetry. You do not dispose of Kafka through refuting Heidegger nor through finding a comparable "message" in a grade B movie. This is another way of saying that the issues of criticism cannot be stated, much less solved, in terms of mere abstract disputation. If Marx was right and "everlasting uncertainty" is a trait of the epoch, the effect after a hundred years would inescapably be to deposit a widespread tinge of *angst* in almost every feeling, and "continuous agitation" would have made "chaos" an element of contemporary sensibility. In finding forms for these states *as they are actually experienced,* modernist literature and art would represent not a timeless condition but the condition of the time. Lukacs submerges this problem in the very title of his chapter directed against modern art: it is called "The Ideology of Modernism." As with antimodernists of the Church, the State, the Rotary Clubs, the "distortion," etc., of vanguard forms is seen by him as owing not to the revolutionary character of present-day reality but to the errors of perversity of writers, their faulty "perspective." Adjust this perspective and the social equivalents of distortion (official lies, mass-communication fantasies), abstraction (alienated people, empty relations, things devoid of quality), subjectivism (the collapse and betrayal of ideals), formalism (the regulation of public and private life by impersonal systems) would presumably be overcome. Lukacs's version of dialectical materialism demands that conditions be cured in literature before they are changed in life. Art that takes its shape from the "everlasting uncertainty" is, regardless of its character, mere "naturalism" to Lukacs and inferior to "realistic" works issuing from the mental constructions of "the humanist social perspective." For Marx all that was solid was melting in the air; for Lukacs it has no right to do that in the novel.

Faced with extremist art, all antimodernists raise the banner of "realism," whether it be Catholic realism, the commonsense realism of the liberals and the Left, the "socialist realism" of Khrushchev, the taken-for-granted realism of the mass media and of 95 per cent of U.S. thinking and practice in fiction. Lukacs's discussion of "perspective" reveals that as an alternative to modern styles, "realism" means not the representation of contemporary reality, subjective or social, but its correction through ideological imperatives. For this descendent of the materialistic interpretation of history, social reality has become contingent on thought. In a situation that generates *angst, angst* itself must be driven out by defeating the "ideology of modernism."

What is marvelous about Lukacs is that he has developed a philosophy of resistance to change on no other ground than change itself. "The fact that in the midst of this 'permanent revolution,' this endless 'revaluation of all values,' there were [twentieth-century] writers of major talent who clung to the standards of nineteenth-century realism is, therefore, of ethical as much as of artistic significance. These writers' attitudes sprang from the ethical conviction that though changes in society modify human nature, they do not abolish it." With permanent revolution set in quotation marks, Lukacs has discovered in "human nature" the key for turning Marxism into a species of traditionalism which shores up literature as a trans-historical order against the dissolving processes of twentieth-century development. Whereas in *The Communist Manifesto* the nineteenth-century leaps forward into the twentieth, with Lukacs the twentieth-century crawls back toward the nineteenth. Reality, Old Faithful, is still there in the streets and drawing rooms if only the novelists would put themselves in a position to see it.

All antimodernists, we said, pine for realism. Lukacs wants two: bourgeois critical realism and "socialist" (though not Stalinist). These realisms, he contends, represent the truths of successive historical epochs, but they are connected with and depend on one another. Bourgeois critical realism needs to turn toward Socialism as its goal in order to be able to face the present without sinking into *angst;* "socialist realism" needs to be aware of bourgeois realism behind it in order to be guided by its models and esthetic standards. Both realisms are continuations of the supreme works of earlier epochs; they hold the line of narrative and dramatic art through Shakespeare to Homer.

The test for Lukacs of the realist novelist or playwright is his ability to create solid, three-dimensional characters in contrast to the "shadowy blurs," stylized puppets or unlocated mystics of modernist fiction. Lukacs quotes approvingly the contrast noted by Camus between a character of Dostoyevsky and one of Tolstoy as "like that between a film and stage character" (as silly a distinction as one between a character on a page and one on a stage). Lukacs believes that the malady of shadowiness is getting more serious: already in the time of Zola he observes, it had become extremely difficult to create lasting human types, "the real criterion of literary achievement." Today matters are far worse. But the third dimension can still be achieved through correct perspective: here Lukacs once more recalls Bernard Berenson and his opinion that what made Giotto a great painter was the solidity given to his figures by the new science of perspective. Like Berenson he harks back to the Renaissance for "tactile values" which, Berenson said, will enable us to "realize his [the artist's] representations more quickly and more completely than we should realize the things themselves." If everything solid has melted in the air, it is the job of the artist to put it together again through "the creative role of perspective." "Perspective, in this concrete form," Lukacs assures us, "is central to our problem."

Still, "lasting human types" are getting harder and harder to find in fiction, as on the street. This circumstance weighs heavily on Lukacs's literary judgments. The writers he praises as "major talents who clung to the standards of nineteenth-century realism" include Eugene O'Neill, the late Thomas Wolfe, the late Brecht, early Norman Mailer, who are either not "realists" or something less than "major talents." To oppose, as he does, Thomas Mann as a realist to James Joyce as a modernist is both theoretically absurd and esthetically obtuse. Disregarding the analogical and symbolic structure of *Ulysses* he states that in it "the stream of consciousness technique . . . is itself the formative principle governing the narrative pattern and the presentation of character." Mann's *Lotte in Weimar,* on the other hand, is superior because in it "the *monologue intérieur* is simply a technical device" (what becomes of the unity of form and content?) for exploring "aspects of Goethe's world which would not have been otherwise available," once more the mechanic's conception of the artist's technique as a tool for working on "reality." But the sum of the contrast is Lukacs's cultural conservatism, as revealed in his praise of Mann for upholding literary tradition: "however unconventional the presentation . . . the ancient rules of epic narration are faithfully observed."

Since Mann is the only first-rate twentieth-century writer Lukacs can even pretend to have on his side, and thus the sole ground for believing that "bourgeois realism" is in the running as an important tendency (a chapter in *The Meaning of Contemporary Realism* is entitled "Franz Kafka or Thomas Mann?"), it may be worth pausing on the latter's qualifications as a Lukacs "realist." The very physical setting of *The Magic Mountain* is intended to produce that "chaos" of time and values which Lukacs reprehends as "modernist." Lukacs bends his dialectical ingenuity to separate Mann from his contemporaries on the grounds that he differentiates between characters ruled by subjective and objective time. For Mann, however, the different senses of time represent opposing moral states, neither of which is superior to the other. Mann's organic-mechanical dichotomy corresponds to Bergson's view, which Lukacs repugns, and to the metaphysical split which governs the conversion of data into symbols in *Ulysses* (e.g., an old woman passing by makes Bloom think of the Dead Sea and salt as against a list representing the *élan* of growing things).

As for the solidity of the characters in *The Magic Mountain,* Lukacs's ultimate test of realism, Castorp and Ziemssen, Settembrini and Naphta (said to be a portrait of Lukacs himself) perform not as single figures "in the round" like characters in Balzac or Flaubert; they do their act in antithetical pairs; and they are composed of patterns of "naturalistic" details doubling as symbols, e.g., Castorp's cigars. Frau Chauchat is the personification of disorder—note the rattle of small panes of glass with which she enters the dining hall of the sanatarium and the consciousness of Castorp. The "flatness" of these personae is purposely emphasized by contrast with Peeperkorn, who is blown up to larger than life size, a kind of lumbering deity bumping against the clouds.

To make matters worse for Lukacs and the "third dimension," Mann's other great work, *Joseph in Egypt,* is set in the land of the frieze, and its protagonists are modelled on the serial figures of Egyptian wall painting. Mann makes his intention explicit in the first volume of the novel through a discourse on how the personality of the young Joseph shades into the images in his gallery of ancestors, so that the hero does not know where his history leaves off and those of Jacob, Isaac and Abraham begin. The "realism" thus attained is not Lukacs's "meaning of everyday life" but what Mann calls the "god story." In their indefinite dimensions his characters are closer to those of myth than to Lukacs's nineteenth-century egos, and by the same quality they are affiliated with HCE and Harold-or-Humphrey of *Finnegans Wake* and with Kafka's K, that is, with quintessential modernism.

Having once left the nineteenth century,* Lukacs's "realism" is no longer a descriptive category, but an ideological wish (even Gorky possesses too many expressionist facets to. fit in without doctrinal squeezing)—the wish common to all contemporary "realists," regardless of philosophical, political or esthetic differences, to believe that something is immune to alteration and is *there* to be described, without needing to be constituted anew in terms of its changing relations. Lukacs is seeking in literature what he misses in life: the firmly planted "complete" type. But what is this type except the class man of social formations now in distress? Solidity of character belongs to class society: the solid person of fiction is none other than the solid citizen. A character acquires three dimensions through being set permanently in social space in the role of the aristocrat on the hill, the merchant in the marketplace, the peasant in the field. The density of the Balzacian or Tolstoyan protagonist is the effect of his being cut from a hardened lump of class soil.

Only the members of one social class lack thickness; the proletariat, Marx has informed us, is "denuded." Lukacs sees fictional types as national in substance. "Modern industrial

---

* Lukac's *Studies in European Realism* (Grosset & Dunlap), also published recently in America, with an introduction by Alfred Kazin, comprises such authors as Balzac, Stendhal, Zola, Tolstoy.

labor," Marx replies, "modern subjection to capital, the same in England as in France, in America as in Germany, has stripped him [the proletarian] of every trace of national character." There is another group that is perhaps in an even worse state: the revolutionary intellectuals. But what if the typical condition of man in the mid-twentieth century is that of workers and intellectuals? Instead of the citizen surrounded by his possessions, his family, the stable social landscapes, there appears the fellow employee or the professional who comes and goes. Things are no longer in place and the people seen by the novelist no longer pose against a static background. In that case, to be truly a realist he cannot duplicate the character scaffoldings of *The Human Comedy* (admired by Marx, we might remind Lukacs, for its radical insights into the social formations of the time and not because Balzac was conserving Western literary tradition or belief in "human nature"). The novelist of contemporary social fact achieves imaginative veracity through devising formal equivalents of the *multiple* perspective in which his experience appears: that in which "film" figures flash by in city crowds; in which varying densities of people are established through dealing with them in conferences, cocktail parties, love affairs, the family; that of the self in its metamorphoses and its absence of space which prevent its being grasped except through myth-making. The complexities and discontinuities of modernist fiction are accompaniments of the breakdown of class fixity. Lukacs recognizes this (though again blaming on ideology what has occurred in reality, like Stalin blaming on saboteurs and oppositionists a breakdown in wheat production) when he complains that the wispy personages of contemporary literature "presuppose the elimination of all social categories." A strange complaint for a Communist! Will not the literature of the classless society be populated by ghosts? In which case, ought we not trade in Socialism for Dame Quickly's tavern?

Lukacs has set himself against the transitional person of modern democracy. His "realism" is a literary version of the Leninist program of building the future upon planes of social differentiation which are to be gradually lowered toward a common level under a system of controls, like the locks of a canal. Unlike the medievalist, Lukacs accedes to change in the structure of individuals and their relations; but he accepts it only under the regulation of inherited modes of consciousness in which the class formations of yesterday, or their equivalents, subsist for as long as possible. The anonymous person and anonymous groups struggling for visibility in modern mass society are to be overlooked by literature until a place has been delineated for them by political authority. The mold of man is to be set from above rather than be the product of man's own actions. Similarly, new esthetic possibilities are to be fitted into antique modes—"the ancient rules of epic narration"—rather than be developed as instruments of vision.

Lukacs is unable to see that massively contoured social identities ("lasting types") have been rendered obsolete by the emergence of a world culture beyond folkways or cult, and that modern *angst* is precisely the ambivalent response to the slipping away of established emblems of self. For this Marxist the issue for literature is not its capacity to enter into the range of new human potentialities opened up by the continuous loosening of social forms; as with the metaphysicians of despair whom he condemns, the issue is that beyond the solid types there exists for him nothing but emptiness and chaos.

The fear of nothingness cuts Lukacs off from the grand tradition he is so eager to see continued. It was evident to the author of Ivan Ilych, as to the author of *Oedipus,* that the three-dimensional occupant of social space was a fictional construction, a hollow dummy contrived for the eyes of others, and that in action this made-up shape would crumble—bringing a reversal of the situation and revealing a self belonging to a new order of being. To the dramatic poet individual identity has always been precarious and a pathos. In bringing Ilych, the solid, lasting type, to the fictional execution block Tolstoy was something more than a "realist"—as was Marx when he explained that class societies produce "abstract individuals" under which the real individuals are "subsumed"; in other words, that the social type is the not-self of the individual appearing as a positive shape, while the real self is unknown and awaits disclosure through action. On this theme Kafka would seem to be saying more than any of Lukacs's human-nature-preserving literary emigrants to the nineteenth century.

It worries Lukacs that "socialist realist" dogmatism may cause modernist critics to cover up "the deeply problematic nature of modernism itself." No doubt the problematic is the distinguishing trait of a consciousness truly of this time; this puts new art and ideas at a disadvantage in coping with disciplinarians of proper "perspective." To define modernism as a solution or as a worthy cause is, of course, ridiculous. Yet Lukacs himself introduces into art the war of dogmas when he writes: "We see that modernism leads not only to the destruction of traditional forms; it leads to the destruction of literature as such.* And this is true not only of Joyce, or of the literature of Expressionism and Surrealism." Such opinions are aimed at banishing the incentive to study the masterpieces of our age. They cause the mirror of modern literature to be turned to the wall, so that events take place blindly, while art becomes a copying of monuments in the oversized scale of the "humanist perspective." The net effect is a pervasive Philistinism. For

* Compare the conservative Academician, Kenyon Cox, writing about the Armory Show fifty years ago: "the real meaning of this Cubist movement is nothing else than the total destruction of the art of painting." Poor humanity! To be compelled to endure this same empty threat for decade after decade, from all countries and from all ideologies.

Lukacs modern fiction is an esthetic and moral aberration that has somehow gotten in between the masterpieces of the past and the future. In time, he hopes, this distortion will be straightened out and the familiar proportions be restored. Then reality will be back in force. It is merely a matter of cancelling an epoch of error. Or shall we say, an epoch (our own) of human history?

6

Philosophy in a Pop Key

Understanding Media (McGraw-Hill) has a dry, professional-sounding title, suggesting a handbook on magazines and television for advertising men, in particular those charged with buying space and time. It was written, however, by Professor Marshall McLuhan, director of the Center for Culture and Technology at the University of Toronto and author of *The Mechanical Bride* and *The Gutenberg Galaxy,* whose conception of pop culture is no more conventional than an electronic opera. McLuhan is more likely to write a manual for the angels than for Madison Avenue. *Understanding Media* carries the subtitle *The Extensions of Man,* which alerts readers at the start that more is at issue in this book than the relative merits of news and entertainment packages. We all know that radio, the movies, the press do things to us. For McLuhan they also *are* us: "They that make them," he quotes the Psalms, "shall be like unto them." So *Understanding Media* is nothing less than a book about humanity as it has been shaped by the means used in this and earlier ages to deliver information.

McLuhan's account of the effects of the media upon the

First published in *The New Yorker,* 27 February 1965.

human psyche lies between fact and metaphor. The instrumentalities through which words, images, and other human signals reach us transform our bodies as well as our minds. Our eyes are bulged out by vacuum tubes, our ears elongated by transistors, our skin ballooned by polyesters. ("Clothing and housing, as extensions of skin and heat-control mechanisms, are media of communication.") In his first book, *The Mechanical Bride,* published a dozen years ago and unmistakably inspired by Duchamp's erotic apparatuses, McLuhan dealt with the pop creations of advertising and other word-and-picture promotions as ingredients of a magic potion, "composed of sex and technology," that was populating America with creatures half woman, half machine. "Noticed any very spare parts lately?" he inquired in a subhead of his title chapter. The legs, bust, hips of the modern girl have been dissociated from the human person as "power points," McLuhan claimed, reminding the reader that "the Hiroshima bomb was named 'Gilda' in honor of Rita Hayworth." Man, to McLuhan, often appears to be a device employed by the communications mechanisms in *their* self-development. "Any invention or technology," he writes in *Understanding Media,* "is an extension or self-amputation of our physical bodies, and such extension also demands new ratios or new equilibriums among the other organs and extensions of the body. There is, for example, no way of refusing to comply with the new ratios or sense 'closure' evoked by the TV image."

In McLuhan's *The Gutenberg Galaxy,* the analysis of how the human organism has been remodelled by a single communications medium is turned into a full-scale interpretation of Western history. The outstanding characteristics of life in Europe and America from the Renaissance to the turn of the twentieth century are traced to the invention of movable type and the diffusion of the printed word. The streaming of letters across a page brought into being an "eye culture" that found symbolic representation in *King Lear,* with its blindings and its wanderers stripped naked by the storm. (McLuhan got his Ph.D. in English at Cambridge.) With Gutenberg began the technological acceleration of history that has made constant change the norm of social life. The portability of books, McLuhan says, allowed "alphabetic man" to feed his intellect in isolation from others, thus introducing individualism and the Hamlet-like division between knowing and doing, as well as split personality ("Schizophrenia may be a necessary consequence of literacy") and the conflict between the ego and its environment. The separation of seeing from the other senses and the reduction of consciousness to sight-based concepts were compensated for by the emergence of the world of the unconscious. The fixed position of the reader vis-à-vis the page, says McLuhan, inspired perspective in painting, the visualization of three-dimensional objects in deep space, and the chronological narrative. The uniformity and repeatability of the phonetic bits that make up a line of type strengthened mechanistic philosophies, serial thinking in mathematics and the sciences, and ideals of social levelling, and they were the model for the assembly line. In replacing vernacular with mass media, print generated the centralizing forces of modern nationalism: "The citizen armies of Cromwell and Napoleon were the ideal manifestations of the new technology."

Understanding Media is McLuhan's goodbye to Gutenberg and to Renaissance, "typographic" man; that is, to the self-centered individual. As such, it takes its place in that wide channel of cultural criticism of the twentieth century that includes writers like T. S. Eliot, Oswald Spengler, D. H. Lawrence, F. R. Leavis, David Riesman, Hannah Arendt. *Understanding Media,* McLuhan's most neatly ordered and most comprehensive book, is an examination of how the eye-extended, print-reading individualist of the past five centuries is in our time undergoing metamorphosis under the bombardment of all his senses by new electronic media, the first of which was the telegraph. With the loss of the monopoly of the column of type has come the breakup of its peruser, and with this a landslide of all print-based social and art forms; e.g., the mechanical assembly line gives way to automation, and perspective in painting to two-dimensional, over-all composition. Thus the changeover of media is synchronized with revolutionary phenomena in production and in cultural life and with an extreme crisis of values.

Of all crisis philosophers, McLuhan is by far the coolest. Though his notion of the "externalization" or "numbness" induced in the consumer of today's popular culture accords with Eliot's "hollow men," Riesman's "other-directedness," and Arendt's "banality," he is utterly unsympathetic to any concept of "decline." The collective trance of his contemporaries is to his mind a transitional phenomenon—one that recurs in all great historic shifts from one dominant medium to another. Current unfeeling and anxiety parallel states prevalent in the early Renaissance, when the printed document was replacing the hand-written script. Regarding us all in this light, McLuhan is immune to despair; in his terms, the theory that the modern world is a cultural wasteland is meaningless. What, he might ask, makes the inwardness of yesterday preferable to the shallowness of tomorrow, if both are by-products of more or less effective devices for conveying information? As the phonetic alphabet carried man from tribalism to individuality and freedom, the new electric media are taking him beyond "fragmented, literate, and visual individualism." If man today is part machine, this is not an effect of the Industrial Revolution. Technologies have been a component of human living for three thousand years, and our loftiest feelings have derived from that segment of us that is least ourselves: "By continuously embracing technologies, we relate ourselves to them as servo-mechanisms. That is why we must, to use them at all, serve these objects, these extensions of ourselves, as gods or minor religions. An Indian is the servo-mechanism of his canoe, as the cowboy of his horse or the executive of his clock." In line with Toynbee (the idea of the Eskimo as a merman, the cowboy as a centaur, is his), McLuhan has superseded Marx's "fetishism of commodities" with a fetishism of the medium to explain the forms of belief by which men have been governed in various epochs. Societies in which the sacred played a greater role than it does in ours were simply those ruled by media of communication more primitive than the visual. "To call the oral man 'religious,'" McLuhan observed in *The Gutenberg Galaxy*, "is, of course, as fanciful and arbitrary as calling blondes bestial."

McLuhan, then, is a modernist to the hilt; his own "sacred" touchstones are Cézanne and abstract art, the new physics, *Finnegans Wake*. His is the kind of mind that fills with horror the would-be conservator of values (a Leavis, a Yeats, a Lukács). He is not tempted in the slightest to dig in at some bygone historical moment. Accepting novelty as inevitable, he is not only a modernist but a futurist. In his latest mood, he regards most of what is going on today as highly desirable, all of it as meaningful. His position is to be inside change; he is given over to metamorphosis on principle. The present worldwide clash between the new and the old arouses him to enthusiasm, since "the meeting of two media is a moment of truth and revelation from which new form is born." It is this appreciation of innovating forms that distinguishes McLuhan from other writers on popular culture. Instead of discovering menace in the chatter of the disc jockey and the inanities of the commercial, or relief in New Wave films of in Shakespeare and ballet on TV, McLuhan probes beyond the content of the media to the impact of each medium itself as an art form. What takes place at any moment in the rectangle of the comic strip or on the screen of the TV set may not be worth serious reflection. But as you look, or look and listen, in the particular way demanded by the comic strip or the television image, something is slowly happening to one or more of your senses, and through that to your whole pattern of perception—never mind what gets into your mind. Hence the first axiom of *Understanding Media* is "The medium is the message." Radio tells us about bargains in second-hand cars, the great books, the weather, but the ultimate effect of radio is that, day after day, it is displacing reading and reintroducing on a new, technological level the oral communication of preliterate societies—or, as McLuhan calls it, "the tribal drum." The effect of a tale differs depending on whether we read it, hear it, or see it on the stage. McLuhan therefore ridicules the reformist idea that changes in programming could alter the cultural mix now produced by the popular arts. "Our conventional response to all media, namely that it is how they are used that counts, is the numb stance of the technological idiot. For the 'content' of a medium is like the juicy piece of meat carried by the burglar to distract the watchdog of the mind. . . . The effect of the movie form is not related to its program content." In fact, McLuhan suggests that one medium always uses another medium as its subject matter: "The content of the press is literary statement, as the content of the book is speech, and the content of the movie is the novel." Whether or not this is so in every case, it provides a suggestive description of much contemporary art—for example, that of Rauschenberg, who through photographs and silk-screen reproductions makes news the content of painting.

A remarkable wealth of observation issues from the play of McLuhan's sensibility upon each of today's vehicles of human intercourse, from roads and money to games and the computer. After *Understanding Media,* it should no longer be acceptable to speak of "mass culture" as a single lump. Each pop form, this work demonstrates, has its peculiar aesthetic features: the comics, a crude woodcut style; TV, a blurred "iconic" image shaped by the eye of the viewer out of millions of dots (in contrast to the shiny completed image of movie film). A further aesthetic complexity of the popular media pointed out by McLuhan lies in their division into "hot" and "cool." The hot medium, like radio and newspapers, is aggressive and communicates much information, while the cool, like TV and the Twist (also open-mesh stockings and dark glasses), is reticent and tends to draw its audience into participation. The varieties of aesthetic influences by which modern man is showered ought to dissolve the belief, prevalent among intellectuals, that today's man in the street, in contrast to the peasant or the bushman, has been cut down to a bundle of simple reflexes.

Responding to the man-made forms that flow continually through our senses, McLuhan arrives at happy conclusions for the future. No, man is not being impoverished by packaged cultural commodities. On the contrary, it was the split personality created by the book who was deprived of sensual self-realization: "Literacy is itself an abstract asceticism that prepares the way for endless patterns of privation in the human community." Though the shock of the sudden passage from mechanical to electrical technology has momentarily narcotized our nerves, integral man is in the process of formation. For the first time in history, the media are providing us with extensions not of one or more sense organs but of our sense structure as a whole, "since our new electric technology is not an extension of our bodies but of our central nervous systems." The mechanical age is departing, and with it the division of man within himself and his separation from his fellows. "Synesthesia, or unified sense and imaginative life, had long seemed an unattainable dream to Western poets, painters, and artists in general. They had looked with sorrow and dismay on the fragmented and impoverished imaginative life of Western literate man in the eighteenth century and later. . . . They were not prepared to have their dreams realized in everyday life by the aesthetic action of radio and television. Yet these massive extensions of our central nervous systems have enveloped West-

ern man in a daily session of synesthesia." Instant
communication through the electric media, McLuhan goes on
to argue, is ending the age-old conflict between city and country; by "dunking entire populations in new imagery" and
bringing them together in the "global village," it is eliminating,
too, the conditions that make for war.

In sum, McLuhan has built a philosophy of history on art
criticism, which he has directed not at styles in literature, painting, or architecture but at the lowly stuff of everyday life. In
doing this, he has also sought to recast the meaning of art and
literature since the Renaissance by finding in Shakespeare,
Pope, or Blake "galaxies" of meaning related to the aesthetics
and metaphysics of print. He has experimented with form in his
own writings; that is, he has tried to function as an artist. *The
Mechanical Bride* was a kind of early pop art, with a layout like
a museum catalogue and with headlines, clips of advertising
art, comic-strip boxes. *The Gutenberg Galaxy* and *Understanding Media* regard the human habitation as an enormous
art pile, a throbbing assemblage of things that communicate,
and they try to make it comprehensible by means of a mosaic of
exhibits and comments that the author's "circulating point of
view" has assembled from widely separated fields; McLuhan is
attempting to imitate in his writing the form of the TV image,
which he describes as "mosaic." The effort to develop an open,
expressive social-science investigation in place of the customary
learned research report may in time produce important results;
McLuhan's version of this new form has the virtue of allowing
the author to pick up bits of observation (e.g., that girls in dark
glasses are engaged in "cool" communication) that are usually
excluded, and it also enables him to bring into focus a remarkable spread of information (e.g., the measurement of time by
smell among the ancient Chinese and among modern brain-
surgery patients). McLuhan's concern for style tempts him into
discharges of epigrams, wisecracks, and puns. These have

abated in *Understanding Media*, but the chapter titles are still haunted by gags ("Money: The Poor Man's Credit Card," "The Photograph: The Brothel-Without-Walls"). Some of this wit is low-grade ("Movies: The Reel World") even if we consider bad puns to be in keeping with the pop spirit. However, formulas like "If it works it's obsolete," to suggest the rate of change in media, and "Today, even natural resources have an informational aspect," more than balance the account.

McLuhan, then, is a kind of artist, and his quick leaps from datum to axiom ("Take off the dateline, and one day's paper is the same as the next") are often aesthetically pleasurable. In his communications-constructed world, the artist is the master figure—in fact, the only personage whom he differentiates from the media-absorbing mass. The artist, McLuhan believes, anticipates the changes in man that will be wrought by a new medium and through his work adjusts the collective psyche to it. Thus the artist provides an antidote to the numbness induced by changeover. Painting has long since gone beyond being a merely visual medium; praising someone for having a "good eye," as if a modern painting were an object to be taken in by a single sense, is tantamount to praising him for being out of date. A Kandinsky or a Mondrian is actually apprehended through a "resonating interplay" of the whole keyboard of sense and consciousness; no wonder that eye-trained people continue to ask, "What does it mean?" One of McLuhan's most valuable contributions is to help dissolve the craft-oriented concept that modern art works still belong in the realm of things contemplated instead of being forces active in "the unified field of electric all-at-onceness" of tomorrow's world community.

Unfortunately, despite his insights into form, McLuhan's organization of his own ideas is far from first-rate. As a composition, *Understanding Media* is often out of control; "circular" perspective becomes synonymous with going round in circles. Endlessly repetitious, the book, for all its rain of bright intuitions, creates a total effect of monotony. This repetitiousness probably reflects McLuhan's uneasiness about his ability to make himself clear. For there are in his thesis inherent ambiguities. Given the advanced nature of the electric media, the implication is that older forms, like the book and the stage, are obsolete and that film and comic strip are the art forms of the future. In clinging to a sense extension (the eye) that has been surpassed, the novelist is a reactionary—except for the beatnik who gives readings in coffeehouses. Even being an individual is retrogressive, so turn the dial and slip into the new global kraal. Much as McLuhan lauds the artist, he has pitted the pop media against him, in disregard of the fact that the masterpieces of this century have been paintings, poems, plays, not movies or TV shows. The point is that while McLuhan is an aesthete, he is also an ideologue—one ready to spin out his metaphor of the "extensions" until its web covers the universe; if clothes are media, and trees and policemen are, too—if, in short, all of creation "speaks" to us—McLuhan is discussing as media what used to be called "Nature," and his notion of the "sensuously orchestrated" man of the future is a version of the pantheistic hero. He is a belated Whitman singing the body electric with Thomas Edison as accompanist. Yet to expect Adam to step out of the TV screen is utopianism of the wildest sort. For McLuhan, beliefs, moral qualities, social action, even material progress play a secondary role (if that) in determining the human condition. The drama of history is a crude pageant whose inner meaning is man's metamorphosis through the media. As a philosophy of cultural development, *Understanding Media* is on a par with theories that trace the invention of the submarine to conflicts in the libido or the decline of the handicrafts to the legalization of interest on loans.

"Usury," Ezra Pound wrote in the *Cantos,*

> rusts the man and his chisel
> It destroys the craftsman, destroying craft;
> Azure is caught with cancer.

McLuhan has taken with deadly literalness his metaphors of the media as extensions of the body and of a nervous system outside ourselves. "Man becomes, as it were, the sex organs of the machine world, as the bee of the plant world, enabling it to fecundate and to evolve ever new forms." His susceptibility to figures of speech leads him to describe possibilities of technological innovation as if they were already achieved facts. In his world, money and work are things of the past; we live on credit cards and "learn a living" as managers of computers, and the struggle, backwash, surprise of real events are somnambulistically brushed away. The chilly silence of science fiction reigns over a broad band of McLuhan's temperament.

These deficiencies might be decisive were there to arise a McLuhan "school" of cultural interpretation through media analysis. If one judges McLuhan as an individual writer, however, what remain paramount are his global standpoint and his zest for the new. As an artist working in a mixed medium of direct experience and historical analogy, he has given a needed twist to the great debate on what is happening to man in this age of technological speedup. Other observers have been content to repeat criticisms of industrial society that were formulated a century ago, as if civilization had been steadily emptied out since the advent of the power loom. As against the image of our time as a faded photograph of a richly pigmented past, McLuhan, for all his abstractness, has found positive, humanistic meaning and the color of life in supermarkets, stratospheric flight, the lights blinking on broadcasting towers. In respect to the maladies of de-individuation, he has dared to seek the cure in the disease, and his vision of going forward into primitive wholeness is a good enough reply to those who would go back to it. *Understanding Media* is a concrete testimonial (illuminating, as modern art illuminates, through dissociation and regrouping) to the belief that man is certain to find his footing in the new world he is in the process of creating.

7

Thugs Adrift

The hijackers radioed to officials in the Dubai control tower that they were "awaiting instructions," but they did not say from whom or where.

Report in Newsday, *August 1973*

Like the story of the hung-up hijackers, that of Watergate is a mystery dealing with sources of instruction. In whose mind did the idea of the break-in originate? Who authorized it? And who passed it on as an order to those who executed it? Witnesses testified at the Senate hearings that they were simply "carrying out an assignment" which in their view seemed, at least at the time, within the normal range of their duties. John Mitchell, Herbert Kalmbach, Anthony Ulasewicz, and other White House–connected persons refused to admit that they had done anything wrong, though considering the events in retrospect some now believed they ought perhaps to have behaved differently. Ulasewicz, the ex–New York cop who initiated complicated methods for having paper bags full of one-hundred–dollar bills fall into the hands of Watergate defendants, saw himself as strictly a "tool." But Kalmbach, Nixon's lawyer, from whom

Reprinted from *Partisan Review*, vol. 40, no. 3, Summer 1973.

Ulasewicz received his assignment, said he was also acting on instructions and also saw himself as a tool. The tool and the tool of the tool each agreed separately that he had been "used," which is what tools are for. But neither Ulasewicz nor Kalmbach could say by whom they were used. The Watergaters acted within what they kept calling, with evident pleasure at playing soldier, a "chain of command." In the sum of the hearing's testimony, however, the chain led nowhere. At most it consisted of two or three links—e.g., Dean, Kalmbach, Ulasewicz—reaching down from the empty air. Erlichman even denied that he had advised Kalmbach as a friend that it was "proper" to raise money to help the defendants, though Nixon said later in his press conference that people were always raising money for defendants. Mitchell denied that he had listened to Liddy. With Erlichman and Haldeman every fact that connected one action with another was smashed against a stone wall of denial or forgetfulness. These men empowered to say the last word had authorized nothing, given no instructions.

Nixon himself advanced the theory that no human instructions were necessary. Hunt, McCord, the Cubans had acted in response to the voice of history. They had absorbed the vibrations of lawlessness generated in the 1960s by antiwar demonstrators, hippies, and civil rights activists. Reacting against these outrages, they had become lawless themselves—a case, to follow Nietzsche, of gazing too long into the abyss, so that the abyss gazed back into them. Thus corrupted by the enemy, they became "overzealous" in behalf of their cause: the reelection of Richard Nixon. History pointed them in the right direction but failed to instruct them as to just how far to go. Having overshot their mark, they found themselves surrounded by policemen in the Watergate offices and from then on history had nothing more to say to them.

In his scheme, Nixon made clear, "overzealousness," even in behalf of the most worthy of aims, is conducive to crime, and he condemned illegality on the part of "either side." He did not go as far as FDR did when he told John L. Lewis "a plague on both your houses." Nixon in his statement was not being irritably evenhanded; he was only supporting the evenhandedness of the law. His burglars had fallen in a righteous cause, as had those finest of public servants Haldeman and Erlichman, and the demonstrators certainly lacked the justification of these high-minded patriots. Still, "overzealousness" had produced crime, the crime of getting caught—and the penalty was forfeiture by the criminals of their connection with their ideal, the President. In becoming the means by which plots against the enemy were dragged out into the open, they had themselves given aid and comfort to that enemy. They had forced Nixon's hand, since to approve their behavior he would have had to affirm that a central principle of his policy was that the Democratic Party ought to be destroyed.

Could Nixon have any other view? Since the thirties, the American right has been dreaming of a revolution that would end the system out of which came the "twenty years of treason" represented by the New Deal. Nixon arose out of this dream. Evidence was adduced at the Senate hearings that Haldeman had prepared to revive the myth that demonstrations in behalf of the Democrats were financed by Moscow gold. Someone on the right—was it Goldwater?—had declared that too much zeal (extremism) in the defense of freedom is not a vice, a statement that constitutes a revolutionary manifesto in which law is put in second place behind ideological enthusiasm. But when the program of the radical right was forthrightly presented by Goldwater in 1964, it was overwhelmingly defeated by the electorate. Nixon supported Goldwater, but to him Goldwaterism is another form of overzealousness, in that it invites being caught by the voters. He believes in the right-wing revolution, but he believes in revolution by stealth. His is a *politics of cover-up*. Watergate is the quintessence of his quarter of a century in public life. He has come close to leading the radical right to triumph through presenting its program in the nonradical terminology of Middle American aspirations: support of the Constitution, individual freedom, reduced bureaucracy, grass roots control, prosperity without inflation, world peace, and so on, a list of objectives irrelevant to his real aim—that of consolidating a centralized power—and which his years in office have consistently violated. It is said that Mitchell, Haldeman, and other Nixon intimates hate the term "cover-up." With good reason: it sums up the entire Nixon philosophy of masquerade and concealment as the means of ruling a free country.

In exposing White House inroads into the American system, Watergate has forced Nixon to assert the *right* to cover up. His swollen conception of Executive Privilege is nothing else than a demand to be allowed to run the government in secret: to bomb in secret, to make trade deals in secret, to pressure corporations for campaign contributions in secret, to take steps against a secret list of enemies, to commit secret crimes for the sake of what he chooses to define as "national security." Nixon says that his predecessors also ordered break-ins and wiretaps. Be that as it may, Nixon is the first President of the United States for whom the right to hide his actions is the essence of his office. Everyone else, from the Secretary of State and Congressional leaders down, is spied upon and bugged—the President alone is the invisible seeing eye. Nixon requires Executive Privilege not, as he says, in order to protect confidentiality but to hide the systematic pattern of his moves to concentrate power in his own hands. Executive Privilege puts him in a position to blur parts of the design and thus to make the whole illegible. Nixon demands Constitutional authority to conspire to vitiate the Constitution.

Though he lacks the revolutionary mettle to defend illegality in principle, Nixon declares that he accepts "full personal responsibility" for Watergate. What does this mean? If taken seriously, it is an expression of solidarity with the burglars and an adoption of the break-in as Nixon's own action. He is the instigator, if not by direct instruction then by general encouragement, of acts in this category. Nixon's responsibility is consistent with his idea that the criminals only erred in being overzealous. If Nixon is responsible, history is not responsible; antiwar demonstrators are not responsible; Liddy, Hunt, McCord, and the Cubans are responsible only as Nixon accessories. If Nixon is responsible he belongs in jail with the others. Accepting full responsibility is the stance of the revolutionary leader who asserts his identity with his adherents to the extent of sharing their fate. "I am responsible" means, if you lock them up you must lock me up too. In 1917 the Bolshevik leadership assumed responsibility for the July uprising which they had tried to prevent, in order to shield the revolutionary masses from governmental reprisals, and Trotsky and other Bolsheviks went to prison. Acts of violence perpetrated by Nazis in the days of Weimar were claimed by Hitler as acts of his own. Nixon accepts responsibility for the Watergate crime against the Democrats in order to hold his leadership among activists of the right. But while his vanguard sits in prison, he sanctimoniously assures the public that they deserve to be punished. He takes responsibility, they take the punishment. No wonder it is reported that the Cubans are mystified and enraged. They thought they were acting under the direction of a leader who dared to take his reelection into his own hands. Instead they find themselves abandoned by the master of cover-up.

Nazi thugs knew that their chain of command reached directly to the Fuehrer. By the time leading Nazis were tried at Nuremburg, Hitler was dead. This left a vacuum at the top, comparable to Nixon's ignorance but opposite in its effect on those below. In Jerusalem, Eichmann invoked the missing leader, as had Nazis of all ranks, to argue that he was only a "little man," a "cog in the wheel." All the Nazis were "innocent" because their guilt ascended to Hitler. In the Watergate affair the guilt was not allowed to rise but was shoved down as far from the White House as possible. As the main line of defense, Haldeman and Erlichman were charged with preventing the chain of command from passing through them into the Oval Room. But since no one above them would assume responsibility, they could not claim to be "cogs." The guilt would fall on them. If they were to avoid it, the Watergate "wheel," and other dirty tricks, had to be self-starting.

The techniques for projecting crimes back upon those physically captured while committing them deserve careful scrutiny. The key, as revealed in the fencing of Haldeman and Erlichman with the Senate Committee, is to avoid giving an order, or to give it in a form that allows more than one reading of it (as in Erlichman's memo on the raid of the office of Ellsberg's psychiatrist). By this device Erlichman and Haldeman could create accomplices while staying out of the action. L. Patrick Gray was given to understand that the Hunt files were to be destroyed but no one ever told him to destroy them. To be head of an agency in the Nixon Administration, one had to be able to take a hint, then act on one's own. That the White House desired the action made it "proper" and provided moral absolution. To lack susceptibility to hints, or faith in the cleansing power of the White House, was to be disqualified. Pat Gray was qualified enough to accept the Hunt file and eventually to burn it—and he was rewarded by receiving the nomination to direct the FBI. But poor Gray's faith in the power of the White House to grant remission of sin was faulty—he trusted the President but wondered about the President's lieutenants. Like other Americans he failed to grasp that everything done by the White House represented a single will. As early as July 1972, Gray warned Nixon against his chief aides, and this led in time to his being left to "dangle in the wind." A common myth of authoritarian regimes is that the Czar, the Pope, or the Leader is a prisoner of his subordinates (see Gide's *The Vatican Swindle*), and that if he only knew the facts things would be entirely different. Nixon's "ignorance" of Watergate is a version of this game; John Mitchell presented himself as the Grand Vizier who locked out the President from knowledge that might have damaged him.

White House bosses Haldeman and Erlichman conducted themselves as if they expected all along that some day they would have to account for their actions in a courtroom. Executive Privilege might save them from trial, but if it failed they had to be prepared to save themselves. Thus they functioned, so to speak, as predefendants, ready to meet any accusation regardless of what it might turn out to be. As it happened the crime was Watergate—no doubt, it could have been one of a dozen or even hundreds of others. There are entire fields of this Administration's performance—e.g., Nixon's appointments to regulatory agencies—in which potential scandals are constantly bubbling. Not the least of the contributions of the Senate hearings is their exposure of the system of rules by which Nixon and his associates have been able to evade or blunt charges of incrimination. Understanding the White House processes of maintaining innocence is at least as important as convicting the perpetrators of the break-in and cover-up. Hence, to end the hearings has become Nixon's primary goal in regard to Watergate.

To organize crimes through hints rather than through direct instruction requires that the instigator and his tool shall share a common vision. In *The Brothers Karamazov* Smerdyakov reads the desire for the murder of the father in the mind of Ivan and appoints himself as agent to carry it out. The Nixon collaborators were similarly moved by an essence beyond speech. In regard to Watergate, the planners, the burglars, and the operators of the cover-up lived in the aura of The Presidency—that transcendental entity that in the Nixon Administration had come to reign over the White House. Nixon himself professes to worship this abstraction, which Americans and the whole world are being urged to revere. He withholds the tapes, says the President, not to protect Richard Nixon but to preserve the future integrity of The Presidency. The Chief of State, his staff, the armed forces, the Federal agencies, Billy Graham, Liddy, Hunt, the four Cubans, the American people take on a tribal unity as they kneel before this golden calf. Nixon buys real estate in Key Biscayne and San Clemente: The Presidency transforms it into temple precincts, and public monies are poured into aggrandizing and making "secure" these sacred groves. I know of nothing more offensive to the sensibility of a free individual than the Hollywood-style metaphysics by which Nixon has glamorized his corrupt invention of a Presidency that exists independently of the President. Meditating alone on the beaches of the Pacific or the Caribbean, Nixon seeks inspiration from the Muse of The Presidency, later to return to himself in the company of Abplanalp or Rebozo. The principle of separation of church and state ought to be enforced in Nixon's White Houses. If he wishes to remain as Chief Executive he should be obliged to abjure publicly the superstar Other to which he has been striving to convert Americans. In the United States there is room at the top, according to the Constitution, only for a mortal being—not for a noumenon with measureless powers and endless immunities.

8

Up against the News

"I think," said George Meany, "Gerald Ford is what he appears to be." This metaphysical appraisal could have been offered as an epilogue to Mary McCarthy's *The Mask of State* [Harcourt Brace Jovanovich]. It must have been evoked from Meany by the consciousness that Nixon and his White House had constituted a gallery of false faces, a masquerade. Lawyers, ad executives, experts were actually cadres, armed with "executive privilege," of The Man on Horseback. The Man himself wore the Halloween phiz of a Sunday-school moralist, with his adoring family around him, his dog, his self-communing strolls by the sea, his "fellow Muricans," his "goals," his "work for peace," behind which, as the tapes revealed, was a tough, mentally dissolute King Ubu, with a vocabulary of the gutter and the attitude toward his job of a bum in a burlesque show playing statesman. Haldeman: "Burns is concerned about speculation about the lira." President: "Well, I don't give a (expletive deleted) about the lira. (Unintelligible.)"

Under Nixon (here we're only talking about *him*) "facts"

Reprinted with permission from *The New York Review of Books*, 31 October 1974, © 1974 by Nyrev, Inc.

were a means of concealment. The news media, applying their traditional techniques, could only present a mixture of data and distortion. As Murray Kempton summed it up in *Harper's* last August, "The journalist is, by habit and necessity, increasingly dependent for his rations upon government officials who are more and more inclined to lie." Reporters went on interviewing and reporting what they were told, but honors were bestowed on those who played, or appeared to have played, the role of detective.

The problem was not to gather the "news" but to get behind it or see through it. The laurel-winning word is "revelation." In the July *Commentary* Edward Jay Epstein points out that Pulitzer Prizes this year went to the *Wall Street Journal* for "revealing" the Agnew scandal and to the Washington *Star/News* for "revealing" the campaign contributions that led to the indictment of Mitchell and Stans. The point of Epstein's article is that "reporters at neither newspaper in actual fact had anything to do with uncovering the scandals." If Epstein is right the prizes themselves are a cover-up of the limitations of the press in getting to the bottom of events. Taking credit for discovering the truth, it simply passes along to the public data that have been handed to it. In varying degrees, the news media are part of the system of hiding what is happening by disseminating information about it. The attack on the media by Nixon-Agnew aimed at confining them more completely to this function.

The compost of unassorted fact, hearsay, and official deception produced in connection with any long-drawn-out event, such as the war in Vietnam or Watergate, attains a density sufficient to prevent any objective conception of what is taking place. To form a picture of the whole the mind is obliged inescapably to resort to arbitrary conjunctions of more or less established information (e.g., corpses at My Lai) with more or less logical inferences (they were produced by shooting done under orders, not by accident). As Molotov was quoted as saying sometime around World War II: "The facts are nothing but propaganda"—that is, what counts is the framework of belief which causes the data to fall into place.

The die-hard Nixonites on the House Judiciary Committee entrenched themselves behind the contention that all the evidence on which the majority based their articles of impeachment lacked "specificity." Their position duplicated that of the defense lawyer in *The Brothers Karamazov* who advised the jury that "there is an overwhelming chain of evidence against the prisoner, and at the same time not one fact that will stand criticism, if it is examined separately." Proof can exist only when there is agreement that data ought to be combined according to given rules. "Prior to Mr. Nixon's revelation of the contents of the three conversations between him and his former chief of staff, H. R. Haldeman, that took place on June 23, 1972," asserts the Minority Report of the Committee on the Judiciary,

> we did not, and still do not, believe that the evidence of presidential involvement in the Watergate cover-up conspiracy, as developed at that time, was sufficient . . . in finding Mr. Nixon guilty of an impeachable offense beyond a reasonable doubt. . . . We cannot join with those who claim to perceive an invidious, pervasive "pattern" of illegality in the conduct of official government business generally by President Nixon.

In the human outer space of Wiggins, Sandman, Latta, et al., Nixon's own words were the sole legitimate evidence of his guilt—everything else was mere appearance and subject to whatever interpretation one chose to give it. For a public raised on the news media controversies can only be decisively resolved in the manner of a Perry Mason courtroom drama—by a confession wrung out through cross-examination.

The masses of data and opinion accumulated by the news media surround events with a zone of moral weightlessness in which the attribution of responsibility becomes increasingly far-fetched. As a result, public reaction to the constantly rising mountain of matter labeled "Vietnam" or "Watergate" tends to be an intensified numbness—a state of mind that was recognized by the media themselves in their prediction that Americans would get bored with Watergate if congressional hearings on it were televised in full.

Nixon, too, counted on this boredom in his strategy of calling for a quick end to "wallowing" in Watergate and a return to the serious business of trips abroad and watching inflation grow. Again with an eye on factual overkill as a weapon against truth, he tried to knock out the impeachment inquiry through the landslide of details contained in the tape transcripts he chose to deliver—having buried the public under thousands of pages, Nixon insisted that the conversations had to be considered in their totality, although only some of the tapes were made available, much of them was incomprehensible, and the rhythm of interruptions by unprintables and inaudibles drove the reader to distraction.

If the majority did not get fed up with Watergate—and won't—it is because they have refused to play the game of suspending their judgment while waiting for the final piece of the puzzle to be collected. That public discussion of Watergate became increasingly subjective and "prejudiced" prevented the issue from being sidetracked by disingenuous appeals for "fair play" on behalf of the criminals and their allies. The new facts that kept appearing fitted into the derogatory image of Nixon which his enemies had been holding up for years. If any conclusion was ever objectively verified, it was the antagonism, malice included, felt by those who had watched Nixon's performance since the beginning of his career.

Mary McCarthy has been perhaps more vitally involved than

any other American literary personality in the two large political issues of the past decade: Vietnam and Watergate. The reason may lie in the fact that she spends most of the year in Paris, where an American is held more responsible for America than in America. In 1967 McCarthy went to Saigon, and in 1968 to Hanoi, and she wrote books on her impressions of both places. She reported on the trial of Captain Medina for his part in the My Lai massacre. Reflecting on responsibility for the war, she composed a vigorous polemic against Halberstam's *The Best and the Brightest*. All these writings reappear in *The Seventeenth Degree* [Harcourt Brace Jovanovich], which includes as well an introductory chapter describing circumstances that led to her going to Vietnam. Also issued this year, *The Mask of State: Watergate Portraits* consists of physical and moral-intellectual sketches of the persons who appeared before the Senate committee hearings on Watergate.

Mary McCarthy's books are not histories but eyewitness accounts, and were they only summaries of what she saw and thought at the time they would be swamped under events that have taken place since they were written. Also, as a reporter she has certain peculiarities, chief among which is a complete, self-confessed absence in her of journalistic neutrality, of the pretense of "objectivity" discussed above: in her introduction to *The Seventeenth Degree,* called "How It Went" ("How I Went" would have been more accurate), she makes clear that she did not go to Vietnam in order to learn more about the war but because she wanted to "do something" to help stop it.

Her going was a political action—"I wanted to *move*." She had been daydreaming of one measure after another—tax refusal, sit-ins in factories—that she and her friends could take, and going to Vietnam was a step of that order. To resolve to act presupposes that one is in possession of enough information to form a decision—by implication it asserts that it is possible to have enough information to close the issue. Obviously this state of mind is different from the doctrinal open-mindedness of the professional journalist, as well as the social scientist, for whom there can be no end to data-gathering. One way of putting it would be that McCarthy went to Vietnam not as a reporter but as a writer.

Friends tried to dissuade her from taking on the Vietnam assignment, not on the grounds that books and magazine articles don't stop wars but out of the American superstition regarding specialization—in their view, McCarthy couldn't handle current events because she lacked journalistic training. Aware of her shortcomings as a reporter, she was wise enough to discount them. If she didn't know how properly to interview Ky and Westmoreland—and even found the idea of interviewing temperamentally repugnant—she could look, listen, and converse on the streets, in hotel lobbies, offices, hospitals, refugee and prison camps.

The most serious argument against her trip came from her old friend Nicola Chiaromonte. The gist of it was that the act of a writer is to write, hence McCarthy ought to stay at her desk rather than take off for Saigon. This was a persuasive point, as McCarthy realized, but action sets its own conditions. She was enduring in Paris the anguish, common in our historically conscious epoch, of being aware of atrocity and impending disaster and being powerless to avert them. "How It Went" is an interesting case study of the state of being intellectually stymied yet feeling that "talking while continuing your life as usual [is] not enough."

The typical response to this frustration is a kind of modern acedia—infamy and feared catastrophe are kept at a distance by an indifference that becomes habitual. McCarthy was exceptional in that she continued to be emotionally disturbed over the war, perhaps, as noted, because of her overexposure to European critics of American policy. Trapped between not knowing what to do and the inability to sit still, she found the opportunity to throw herself into the event offered by an assignment from *The New York Review of Books* all but irresistible. In action there is always the chance that something unforeseen will present itself—also by its very nature it generates new material for the participant.

Chiaromonte, a rationalist, who had written a trenchant critique of Malraux's activism, had, according to Mary McCarthy, "a mistrust for action and its theatrics"—apparently, it had not occurred to him that action could also be a means of discovery. In response to her friend's doubts, she marshaled pragmatic excuses for taking the plane to Saigon. Basically, however, getting into the act enabled McCarthy to function without being constantly reminded of the ineffectiveness of what she was doing. Going to Vietnam changed her from a frustrated spectator into a member of the cast, though one without a clear-cut role. In the last analysis, it was on herself that her adventure produced its maximum effect. The climax of *The Seventeenth Degree* comes in the closing pages of the section on Hanoi when McCarthy, meditating on her feelings about America and communism, concludes that she had come not to win a victory for peace but to satisfy a conscience with which she was in the process of becoming familiar. "Nothing will be the same again, if only because of the awful self-recognition . . . the war has enforced."

Concerned as they are with what Aristotle calls "the arts of persuasion," *The Seventeenth Degree* and *The Mask of State* are rhetorical works. "I had the conviction," writes Mary McCarthy, "(which still refuses to change) that readers put perhaps not more trust but a different kind of trust in the perceptions of writers they know as novelists from what they give to the press's 'objective' reporting or political scientists' documented and figure-buttressed analyses." In the medium of rhetoric, style plays an essential part; we are attracted as much by McCarthy's metaphors and witty snapshots—"his words and phrases seem to have been born in a brief case, like the compendious one he carried"—as by her information and ideas. As performance, McCarthy's political writings are as alive today as they were during the events that inspired them. And as *issues,* Vietnam and Watergate are alive too—the attitudes that brought them into being cannot be resolved by new happenings, as someone ought to advise President Ford.

In *The Washington Monthly,* which appears to be some kind of organ of journalism, Mr. James Fallows, one of the editors, attacks McCarthy's newsgathering capacity and, with added vehemence, her apparent lack of respect for finding out the facts. The mood of Fallows's article, "Mary McCarthy—The Blinders She Wears," is reflected in what is presumably a sketch of McCarthy that accompanies it—it is an abysmal work, both as an attempt at a likeness and as a drawing. Had it occurred to Fallows that a drawing, too, says something, he might have hesitated to allow this mean and incompetent caricature to comment on the spirit of his criticism.

Dealing with an impudent outsider who, doubtless through public ignorance, seems to be running off with medals in his field, Fallows is fiercely ironic, as if he spoke from a height to a breathless groundling. His case against McCarthy consists of citing instances in which she dared to speak while being less than fully informed. In a section elegantly subtitled "Glued To Her Seat," Fallows scorns her insufficient legwork, to him synonymous with laziness, and admonishes her that "journalism is a serious business." Relying on what he terms "Pure Sensitivity," she was destined to be confronted with "things that are actually different than they seem" (Meany implied that it was Nixon, not Sensitivity, who faced Americans with things different from what they seem). For Fallows the routines of journalism are sufficient to penetrate these disguises. When, however, Fallows continues, the facts are inaccessible, good reporters "reserve their opinions" (I'll be back tomorrow with

more news), while McCarthy "goes on to interpret the situation boldly and incorrectly."

Fallows counts heavily on his charge that McCarthy took at
face value the antics of John J. Wilson, who represented
Ehrlichman and Haldeman at the Senate hearings—she compared this rasping old reactionary, who yipped at the senators
like a furious lapdog, to Rumpelstiltskin. According to Fallows,
Wilson's rages were not genuine but were put on in order to
scare the senators off his clients. I am not sure if Fallows is
arguing that Wilson is not really Rumpelstiltskin, but unless
this is his contention, McCarthy's comparison would apply—
Wilson looked and behaved like Rumpelstiltskin whether or
not his behavior was fake. Fallows is convinced, however, that
he has McCarthy in a corner—it is "alarming," he sputters,
that she did not "ask a lawyer or even another reporter about
what was going on." The road to truth lies through interviews—and with men, not with angels. Had McCarthy "asked
a lawyer" she might have learned that lawyer's opinion of
Wilson; had she asked a hundred lawyers she'd have collected a
hundred opinions. From "another reporter," she might have
elicited a quantity of gossip, which would have scarcely affected the suggestive metaphor that flashed into her mind when
she looked at Wilson.

Yes, "journalism is a serious business"—and it needs to be
put in its place as a catch-as-catch-can mode of communication
kept at varying distance from the truth by the conditions under
which it operates, by the formats evolved by each medium to
spare its public the need for intellectual effort, by the conventions that spring up in all forms of thought to distort the trans-
mission of experience. Journalism is by now an aging craft, all
but paralyzed by the hardening of its assumptions and pro-
cedures. With a million-dollar corps of reporters in Vietnam,
the war in Cambodia was, as Kempton reminds us, kept hidden

for a year. Fallows can think of no higher function for a writer than to add his voice to that buzz.

As the ultimate insult, Fallows charges that the conclusions stated by Mary McCarthy in her Watergate portraits are not "more provably true than those reached at dinner-table conversations in half the households of America each night." In comparing McCarthy's writing with these discussions, Fallows comes as close as he is able to the meaning of what she is doing. But in judging the great debate of the nation, which held Nixon responsible for Watergate, by the test of "provably true" he loses touch with the world. After watching the Watergate witnesses Mary McCarthy concluded by a process of elimination that Nixon himself had authorized the Watergate break-in—a conclusion that was certainly not "provably true," although it made a great deal of sense and now seems likely to be confirmed by yet unrevealed evidence. McCarthy's political writing does indeed belong to the genre of people talking to one another, not to that of the daily delivery of nuggets speckled with a few grains of fact. What distinguishes McCarthy's discourse is not any secret access to the truth but its high analytical quality and metaphorical reference—as talk it ranks with the best we have.

For Fallows the issue is, what good is talk if it isn't "provably true"? He ridicules McCarthy's attention to style as a species of snobbery—in the news media good writing is a luxury to be partaken of in Sunday editions and the columns of humorists. I take leave of Fallows with the to him no doubt scandalous suggestion that there can be no more valuable contribution to the life of this country than to raise by a single notch the style and imagery of its popular table talk.

If Mary McCarthy does nothing more, she infuses into situations that intelligent people keep talking about the liveliness of an ever-active mind and an alert sensibility—her constantly sparking style makes historical events as tangible to her readers as they are to her, instead of pushing off these events into the dead space of the media. To benefit from her forensic eloquence, in which facts are adduced not for their own sake but as demonstrations, it is not necessary to agree with what she says. My readings on Vietnam, but also my experience as a whole, led me to see eye to eye with her on the rot produced by the American presence in Saigon. The same experience made me more suspicious than she was of the humanity-loving attitudes she encountered in Hanoi—compared with that of communist governments, Washington's "mask of state" is comparatively transparent.

I believe that McCarthy has made a highly valuable, even unique, contribution in her denunciation of America's academic intellectuals who took a leading part in the war. I think she is right in her estimate of "the best and the brightest" when she writes that it is hard "to be impressed, as Halberstam clearly is, by their social and cerebral endowments. . . . What came to Washington was not brains and birth but packaged ideology, a form of overweening stupidity generated in university departments of political science and government, where the 'honed-down intelligence' of a stick like McGeorge Bundy could be viewed with awe." If to Fallows this is nothing but McCarthy's "notorious knife work," it is plain to me that America could do with more butchers and fewer interviewers of great men.

I admire also McCarthy's analysis of the part of language in the character structure of America's villains and men of probity. "Men who had formed the habit of speaking like a letter from a credit company or a summons to appear in court were oblivious of their remoteness from normal communication." But the judge in the Medina case possessed a "speech [that] was surprisingly pure and precise . . . it was probably his concern

for exactitude of language (which some construed as mere fuss-
iness) that helped one feel that he was concerned with getting at
the truth."

To the "half of the households" where Watergate is discussed, I recommend *The Mask of State* for the pleasure of
having an unusually brilliant participant in the family table
talk, as well as a way of measuring how much people noticed
about the witnesses who followed one another on TV. Mary
McCarthy's mastery of the intricacies of the Watergate conspiracy is astonishing in its detail; the running conjectures with
which she tries to get through what the witnesses say to what
they actually know are subtle and imaginative; her verbal can-
did-camera shots and character analyses of Ulasewicz and
Kalmbach, Haldeman, Ehrlichman, and Mitchell are psychologically apt, socially suggestive, and contain the proper pinch
of humor to indicate the inherent farce of these gamblers for
power.

> His [Ehrlichman's] behavior with the courteous old legis-
> lator [Senator Ervin] was so contumacious that the
> hearing-room grew turbulent; there was a general in-
> censed feeling that the senators should not take this lying
> down. I slipped into one of the reveries of the impotent
> and imagined the Chairman signaling to the sergeants-at-
> arms: "Arrest that man." The sneering devil, like Iago (I
> day dreamed), would be hustled out, preferably in chains,
> down to the old prison below the House of Representa-
> tives where persons in contempt of Congress used to be
> held. That was what he deserved, to be kicked back sev-
> eral eras into the antique history of the Republic.

In my view, Mitchell is a much more culpable scoundrel than

McCarthy considers him to be, though I concur that he is a more old-fashioned scoundrel than the White House insiders, hence a scoundrel that fitted less well into the radical conspiracy of which Watergate was an episode and which is now endeavoring to tie together its torn strands.

McCarthy, it seems to me, missed a vital element in the Senate hearings through being out of the country when Patrick Buchanan took the witness stand. Nixon's speech writer openly affirmed the strategy of seizure of power by his minority group and keeping hold of it permanently by incapacitating popular opposition. Faced with this blatant program of sedition lodged in the White House, the senators proved too deficient in historical and theoretical understanding to grasp that what Buchanan was saying could not be reconciled with legitimate American political activity but represented the promulgation of crime. Instead of directing their questions to the ideological conspiracy against representative government thrust into their faces by Buchanan, they indulged in their customary information-seeking queries and seemed to be plaguing the witness with trivialities.

Publicly defeated by this young literary tough, the committee lost heart and public prestige. Only Senator Talmadge scored—having served on a committee investigating foundations, he was able to bring out that whereas the Senate sought to keep foundations out of politics, Buchanan was scheming to turn them into a political tool of the right. Challenged along these lines, Buchanan wavered and backed away. His portrait would have been a valuable addition to McCarthy's masks, and analysis of his testimony could have deepened her interpretation of the motives and meaning of Watergate.

The Seventeenth Degree and *The Mask of State* represent a major effort on the part of a highly developed literary talent to make sense out of the myth matter of our epoch. This enterprise, it seems to me, is basically the same whether it takes the form of novels, theoretical essays, or "reporting." "Men," said Aristotle, "have a sufficient natural instinct for what is true, and usually do arrive at the truth." It is the function of good writing to heighten this instinct and stimulate greater reliance on it.

9

Notes on
Seeing Barry Lyndon

The movies could make their maximum contribution to culture by following the lead of Stanley Kubrick's "Barry Lyndon" in recycling unread literature. Movies based on works that are still breathing—for example, "War and Peace," "Ulysses," "Death in Venice"—have the drawback of presenting themselves as replacements for the originals, and, since they are re-productions in a different medium, are likely to be regarded by the audience as distortions or vulgarizations. Only a graduate student in English, however, would be likely today to have read Thackeray's "Barry Lyndon." Why would anyone else take up time with this item of 19th-century pop entertainment? Years ago, Somerset Maugham, recognizing that such works are not being read, suggested that they ought to be reissued in versions cut down to their plot outlines.

Still, a cultured person should know something about "Barry Lyndon" as a work that constitutes part of his literary heritage, though this knowledge need not be detailed or complete. Kubrick's "Barry" supplies exactly the right amount of famil-iarity—as much as a reasonably attentive reader would have

First published in the *New York Times*, 29 February 1976.

been likely to retain. In short, the movie is a valid substitute for Thackeray's narrative, precisely because it is a "substitute" for something which the audience today doesn't have anyway.

But Kubrick's "Barry" is a lot more than a substitute for an all-but-forgotten tale. The movie also translates the printed page into art for the eye and the ear by coordinating the story with the paintings, music and landscaping of the period. The adventures of Barry, by this time commonplace and thread-bare, are delivered in a faultless esthetic package. If the lead characters are poorly cast, the weakness of their acting is compensated for by their costumes and hairdos. The laggard unfolding of the plot permits one to lose oneself in countrysides that imitate paintings, in classically composed and toned interiors, in the placement and lighting of the figures. Kubrick's salvage job turns out to be a vessel filled with brand new 18th-century treasures. I could have watched "Barry Lyndon" for another two hours without the slightest interest in what was happening to its hero.

The American public today is avid for knowledge of the past, or something that passes for the past, including its art and fashions. Kubrick has done their homework for them. He has read the texts, scoured the picture galleries and art books, listened to the music and compared recordings. He has demonstrated that a confident movie director, not too eager to display his imagination, can be worth a hundred classrooms.

Think of the vein of potential film "properties" that has been opened up by Kubrick's "Barry": obscure novels by George Eliot, Owen Meredith, Disraeli, even Melville's "Israel Potter," to pull out of the air only a few titles. It gives the key to a treasury of livingrooms and parlors, duck ponds, battle formations, romance by the garden gate, fox hunts—all far more civilizing than the unshaven types in current movies who roll around in the grass with bears.

Original, up-to-date scenarios may be more exciting, but

they are not certain to provide much in the way of education, since no one knows how long they will survive. Movies based on unread works by classical authors have the advantage of representing talents that have escaped extinction and thus belong in the common storehouse from which the minds of the living are obliged to draw. Regardless of the interest of the story, the story itself constitutes information that augments the spectator's knowledge. What he misses in pleasure, he makes up for in satisfaction at having earned a mental profit.

Moving pictures are not a good vehicle for original ideas. Images captured by the camera are not sufficiently detached from time, place and natural appearances to match the abstractness of words or mathematical signs. Movie directors sense the intellectual resistances of their medium and confine thinking in movies to references to ideas rather than attempts to develop or apply them. Even the most advanced European moviemakers rarely go beyond name dropping and idea dropping. Fellini, Antonioni, Truffaut relate themselves to thought by quoting, which is a species of scavenging. Avant-garde films stimulate the shock of recognition and generate an aura of profundity by mentioning Malraux or Croce or throwing in a shot of a "Merzbau." In short, like Kubrick's "Barry" they resuscitate the cultural past.

The act of reading a novel is not too dissimilar to that of watching a movie. One sits in a comfortable chair and lets the mind be carried by a stream of images as in a semi-dream. Reading or listening to poetry, or examining a painting, is of a different order; it calls for a heightened alertness. The mixing of media in the movies—dramatic dialogue, color photographs in motion, sound effects, music—produces an exact physical duplication of the novelistic daydream. It keeps the spectator/listener suspended in a universe of sensations, which may occasionally reveal something frightening—the whipping scene in "Barry"—but which does not threaten the witness lounging in his expandable seat.

Regardless of what educators do, the decline of reading is likely to continue. Compared with multimedia relaxations, reading in the future will be preferred for entertainment by the kind of minority that in the past chose chamber music over grand opera. If accumulated literary culture is not to die out with the large public, it must depend increasingly on translation into film.

Reworking old art is a major aspect of 20th-century creation—in painting and sculpture, it is perhaps the dominant approach. Examples are Picasso's recomposed Velasquez paintings, Miró's Dutch masters and, most notorious, Duchamp's obscenely entitled Mona Lisa with mustache and goatee. The resurrected masterpieces tend to contain elements of parody and camp, a way of compensating for the minority status of the fine arts today by flattering their public as insiders.

There is parody, too, in Kubrick's "Barry Lyndon"; the dashing British army officer who falls in a faint when struck by a bullet made of dough. Also camp, as in Barry's marriage ceremony, with its robed priest dwelling on the theme of fornication, and in the beautifully composed funeral procession of Barry's son. On the whole, however, the handling of the adaptation is straight, with just enough caricature to disguise the sobriety of this essentially educational enterprise.

10

The Statue of Liberty

The Statue of Liberty is 90 this year. Since its unveiling in October 1886, it has aroused more intense emotions in more people than any other work of art in America, perhaps any other work anywhere. Most of this feeling was concentrated in the first third of Liberty's existence, the decades when millions of immigrants sailed past her into the gateway of the New World. From slums, villages and ghettos, from poverty, ignorance and tyranny, the "huddled masses" of Europe found themselves saluted at the end of their journey across the sea by the upraised arm of Liberty—"Welcome to Freedom!"

The closing of the period of mass immigration estranged the Statue from its role of inspiring greeter of newcomers. According to Marvin Trachtenberg's extraordinarily thorough account [*The Statue of Liberty* (Viking Press)], the Statue of Liberty is today at the summit of its prestige as the outstanding symbol of America as a whole, but it has also come to be an object of commercial and political exploitation, a version of Miss America, and even of derision. Apparently, monuments have lost their capacity to be lasting embodiments of con-

First published in *The New York Times Book Review*, 3 March 1976.

cepts—though in the light of the constant planting of new Cal-
ders and Moores, I find it difficult to agree that "modernism
appears to exclude authentic monument making." What
Trachtenberg has in mind is that a monument is not merely a
work of art set in a public place—such as an Oldenburg lipstick
or first-baseman's mitt—but a work that is a reminder of some
idea or event that people hold in common. To rule out the
Oldenburgs, perhaps some sense of the august ought also to be
presupposed.

The important point is that a monument and a work of art
are not necessarily identical, nor do their virtues reside in the
same qualities. Trachtenberg is inclined to disparage the Statue,
the creation of Frédéric Auguste Bartholdi, as a sculpture:
"Bartholdi's work for the most part," he writes, "bears little
discernible stamp of formal originality, and resembles the out-
put of a hundred other sculptors—and monument-makers—of
his time." Indeed, a colossal statue, such as Liberty, may by its
very size violate valid concepts of scale. As art, Liberty is the
creation of mediocre 19th-century academicism, but that's only
the beginning of what there is to say about it as a work of art.

The inside of the Statue, for example, is far more interesting
in terms of art today than the figure itself. Describing the math-
ematically determined iron skeleton and the flowing linear patterns on the reverse side of the copper skin that covers it,
Trachtenberg concludes that the effect is that of a kind of "accidental Art Nouveau." On another level, the Statue partakes
of a Pop Art gimmick or toy, in that visitors look out from its
row of windows as through the eyes of a giant, thus "*becoming
the colossus.*" Then, too, the face of Liberty is said to resemble
that of the sculptor's mother.

In sum, Bartholdi's conventional art work of the last century
has more in common with creations that generate myths than
with museum pieces that exemplify achievements in form. Today, Liberty invites comparison not with, say, Rodin but with

vanguard projects, such as Christo's Valley Curtain or Smith-
son's Spiral Jetty, in which the organizational and physical processes of production and the use and transformation of the site
take precedence over the esthetics of the finished object.

One of the virtues of Trachtenberg's study is his grasp of the
importance of beyond-art elements in the realization of the
Statue. "Conventional aesthetic considerations apart," he observes, "Bartholdi's executive competence and formal ingenuity can hardly fail to impress. His strong feeling for site and
scale, image and symbol was, of course, rooted in the French
tradition of planned monumental sites . . . When we descend
to the most concrete of all Liberty's aspects—her structure and
fabrication—it is only to emerge with the strongest admiration
for the skill and perseverance of Bartholdi and his colleagues."

Historically and conceptually, as well as esthetically, the
Statue in New York Harbor has much more to do with France
than with New York or the United States. Trachtenberg's ex-
haustive research lays bare the political, social and building-
project background of the French gift to America. Primarily,
"Liberty Enlightening the World," as the sculpture was originally entitled, was a piece of propaganda art designed to
strengthen Republicanism in France after the fall of the Second
Empire and the demolition of the Paris Commune. The light of
Liberty (the Statue was conceived as also a lighthouse) was
intended to direct its rays across the ocean to sustain the cause
of political freedom. In the imagination of Bartholdi and his
patrons, "the figure loomed so large and bright it could be seen
across the Atlantic"—apparently, one of the less objectionable
ways of meddling in the internal affairs of a friendly nation.

In tracing the evolution of the Statue from its first maquette
in 1870 to its unveiling, Trachtenberg has been obliged to in-
vestigate the political currents of 19th-century France, the biography and temperament of Bartholdi, the history of colossi in
the ancient and modern world, the effects of new technology on

mechanical and engineering methods, the story of how the money was raised in the United States to pay for the base of the monument, the transportation of the statue to New York, and what it has come to mean in our day. In its beginnings, Liberty incorporated a burgeoning cluster of symbols related to illumination, ranging from the Olympic torch runner to Christ as "the light of the world" and the Age of Enlightenment. Trachtenberg pursues each of these as it was embodied in art and entered into, or was dropped from, Bartholdi's design.

Mixed with the symbolism of the torch was the history of female figures of liberty, including the central personage in Delacroix's celebrated "Liberty Guiding the People," and of colossi—plus such fortuitous cricumstances as the placement of the statue in the Port of New York at the moment when the floodgates of immigration were opened. Taken together, the symbols of Liberty were reshuffled into a new emblem; instead of casting its glance back toward Europe, it looked over its shoulder toward the West and toward events to be wrought by naturalized aliens in American history. If the significance of the Statue of Liberty has in our day again been altered, it remains constant in the memory through its association with America's grandeur as "Mother of Exiles."

11

Liberalism and Conservatism

Liberalism is, of course, always changing its content. That is because it is, in essence, not a fixed political or social program or ideology but an expression of generous feelings, particularly toward the poor, the badly treated, and dependent people. Social critics without generous feelings may be right about the history of liberal positions but they are not liberals. When I hear suggestions about "counting the costs" of desegregation or of full employment, or of "moving too fast" in protecting the environment, I find it hard to identify those who urge these cautions as liberals and am rather inclined to regard them as defenders of privilege. If desegregation is uncomfortable, liberalism calls on whites who are opposed to it to suffer the discomfort. Some day through desegregation, all blacks will be as well-educated, refined, good-looking, amiable, and pleasant to have as neighbors as anyone else. More pleasant, certainly, than segregationists, Ronald Reagan, Richard Nixon, "right-to-life" agitators, and enemies of nude bathing.

Liberalism starts with the assumption that "counting the costs" of improving life is made unnecessary by progress—

First published in *Commentary*, September 1976.

those who continue to count do so out of niggardliness. Modern man can afford improvement; he has the resources in wealth, knowledge, and, above all, potentiality (if social impediments are removed) to ease anyone into the material conditions of the middle class and into the good-natured mental state of the liberal. With poverty and ignorance done away with, there would be an end to wars, dictatorships, and so on.

Generosity of feeling is unassailable. The weakness of liberalism today is that it has been losing its clientele through the acquisition of power by everybody, at least the power to make their own demands. No need for generosity of feeling when all are in a position to grab for themselves. Liberalism receives a stunning blow each time it finds itself supporting a social force that is aggressively engaged in achieving gains. Since World War I liberalism has been hit this way again and again—by immigrants, labor, women, young people, blacks—until it now finds itself staggering around with an odd smile on its face, occasionally falling into a fighting posture and going a round of shadow-boxing. When housemaids got 25¢ an hour, the New Deal lady of the house could add a dime to the going rate and agitate for minimum-wage legislation. Try having this feeling for a high-school kid who gets $4 an hour and goofs off to smoke pot between making the bed and vacuuming the rug. Or for the appliance-repair man who charges $46.75 an hour, because, his wife or secretary informs you over the telephone, he considers himself to be "a kind of doctor" (maybe he cures washing machines by listening to their dreams).

Equally destructive for liberalism as the defection of its clients was its support of the Soviet regime in the 30's, as extreme a case of misapplied generosity as any recorded in human history. In their "defense of the Soviet Union," the majority of American liberals ranged themselves on the side of Stalin's tyranny, which was quite capable of taking care of itself, and against its victims—socialists, Trotskyites, dissenters, individuals who refused to lick boots—who were not. What remained of political liberalism was embodied in John Dewey and his Commission of Inquiry that went to Mexico to take testimony from Trotsky concerning the Moscow trial frame-ups. But even at that time they were attacked for being "soft-headed" and "bleeding hearts." Tough liberals knew that the real issue was not truth and justice but the Popular Front Against War and Fascism.

The accommodation to Soviet power initiated the evolution of a liberal who is the opposite of a liberal, a liberal with a political yea or nay but without a commitment to any ideal or social group. From the servitude of Communist fellow-traveling, liberalism passed over to official anti-Communism and service to the FBI, congressional committees, CIA-supported foundations and publishing projects (see my "Couch Liberalism and the Guilty Past" in *The Tradition of the New*, 1959), to end in intellectual fraternization with Nixon-Agnew. The heart of today's new liberalism is caution against being swept by currents of the old liberal generosity and expansiveness.

Conservatism has a philosophy when it is able to contend that advantages in wealth and social position are acquired as a matter of right—God-given, earned through initiative and hard work, or derived through ethnic or cultural superiority. In America today, while inequality is accepted as a fact, it lacks the metaphysical basis provided abroad by superstitions associated with the aristocratic heritage. American conservatism is merely a series of rationalizations for holding onto what one has. Since its kernel is personal hoarding, as a point of view it is a joke. I am being driven through Kansas by a gentleman who describes the region we are in as one of the most beautiful in America, and which is in the process of being acquired by the federal government for a national park. He tells me that when the Secretary of the Interior arrived by plane to inspect the terrain he was chased away at gun point by the owner of the land, one of the state's leading multimillionaires, who threatened to shoot him as a trespasser. A liberal defending the rights of the individual against governmental abuse? A conservative standing in the way of a better life for the people? Soon we pass a huge billboard urging all Americans to protect their freedom by helping to defeat the acquisition of the land as a public park. Defend your right, the landlord is saying, to have me kick you off my land.

New liberalism might go along with this logic, which is not so different from that of Gerald Ford in vetoing the current bill to provide 350,000 jobs on the grounds that federal jobs are not "real" jobs, though he himself has spent his life on the federal payroll.

In an article entitled "Whatever Happened to Liberalism?" Michael Novak wants to know whether a group of new liberals should be called "New Liberals" or "New Conservatives." The answer is contained in the question: both liberalism and conservatism have lost their identities. Shaky because lacking either the liberal or the conservative tradition, all the new lib-con can do is to back away from long-held hopes and ideals by contending that the public, the poor, the ill-treated are less objects of concern than those who have more to lose than their chains. Conservative? Liberal? It is the age of farce, foreshadowed by Marx in *The Eighteenth Brumaire of Louis Bonaparte*.

12

Portraits
A Meditation on Likeness

When I was a kid, there was a side show in Coney Island that featured a two-headed baby. Outside, a barker held up a large photograph that showed a year-old infant in crisp, white baby clothes. The infant had two heads, on each of which was an embroidered cap. The faces smiled at each other, and the heads seemed to be enjoying their unusual companionship. "The camera never lies," shouted the barker, waving the onlookers toward the entrance. Inside, the happy two-headed baby turned out to be a fetus in a jar of liquid. The barker's photograph had, obviously, been a fake.

But although the photograph was not a photograph of the creature in the side show, the impression persisted that it must have been taken of a baby somewhere. Maybe that's why I have remembered it all these years. By its nature a photo belongs to the world of visual fact. The tie to things of this product of a machine is firmer than that of images that are produced in entirety by human beings, such as paintings or sculptures. Regardless of how true or false it is, the camera cannot dispense with an object, even if the "object" be something no more solid than a ray of light. A faked photo is rarely a pure invention; typical fakes, such as those offered in evidence by Senator Joseph McCarthy or circulated in election frauds, are the result of cropping or combining genuine pictures. The camera does lie, but its lies are not made out of whole cloth. The Coney Island baby was most likely produced by pasting an additional head on the photo of a living infant, then photographing that concoction—an early instance of montage.

Photographs have a dual nature, a fact noted in one way or another by most people who comment on photography. A photo is a picture, and only that—an entity in itself, independent of its subject. But it evokes the aura of an external reality, even when no such reality exists. To look at a photo is to see a picture and imagine the pictured. As George Bernard Shaw put it, a photograph "is too true." Avedon speaks of a photo of Humphrey Bogart that hangs on his wall. "It has," he declares, "a life of its own." But to look at the photo cannot fail to bring up Bogart, and Avedon is reminded that Bogart is dead and that "everything has changed." The photo is inseparable from Bogart and from Avedon's sense of how things were in the period when he made the picture. The photograph is anchored solidly in actual time, it is part of a particular interval of the past—certainly more so than a painting. This may account for the appeal of family albums.

The camera falsifies through the credibility of likeness. If it looks that way, that's the way it is. A painting stops short more decisively with what is on the canvas—especially today when everyone is trained to respond to line, color, and form, rather than to lakes or to emperors on thrones. The art in a painting is a generator of distance, both between the painting and the spectator and between the painting and its subject. In contrast, the photograph leads the mind into the actual world—if it is of a nude, it will make one think of women, not art. The difference in the relation to reality is summed up in the notion that painting as an art has been freed of its "literary" aspects by the advent of the camera. "Photography," said Picasso, "has arrived at a point where it is capable of liberating painting from all literature, from the anecdote, and even from the subject." This is a negative way of saying that "stories" are now the province of the photograph.

The delusory power of the camera has to do with the transfer of consciousness from the picture to the thing pictured. Bogart is dead, and "everything has changed," but in the photograph he is present not as a picture but as a living man. In the photograph, "was" is "is." The fabricated likeness augments the materiality of the subject by making him visually present—why else do dictators have their pictures hung in every office and clubroom, and presidents increase their demands for prime time? I have always taken it for granted that portraiture originated as an art devoted to the dead: their images in stone, bronze, clay, and other durable materials kept them secure in the company of the living. Not only was the likeness intended to perpetuate on earth its now semi-divine subject; it was also the representation of his being as a whole, rather than of his appearance in any phase of his life. In their tragedies the Greeks avowed that no man's lot could be truly known until his days were ended—the same rule would be applied in deciding how his face was to be depicted. Since portraits were of the dead, they had to be abstract or generalized, though expressive of extreme feelings. While an individual lives he is engaged in altering himself; thus he is partly composed of undefined areas. Only when he has reached the otherworld of the dead do his image and the consensus regarding his fate become one.

Avedon raises a vital problem about portraying the living. Each sitter, he notes, puts on a performance before the camera in order to get across his conception of himself. "Whenever he poses for me," Avedon wrote of his father, "he smiles and becomes benign, gentle . . . and somehow wise. He's interested in looking sage."

The portraitist, however, has his own vision of the person before him, and his authenticity as an artist and as an individual depends on embodying this image in his picture. Thus a conflict arises between the portraitist and his subject—not merely the resistance of the material that is experienced in art, but a battle of human wills and imaginations, as in practical affairs. Avedon's aging father wanted himself limned as a sage. "My photographs," avers Avedon, "show his impatience."

No matter how deeply the portraitist sees into his subject, he can only represent him in his outer aspects. There is always a side of him which will remain hidden or which the portraitist will choose to overlook. This justifies Avedon's insistence that photographs are "fictions," creations of the photographer. But, unlike the novelist or playwright, the portraitist must round out his character study without the aid of words. This sets severe limits on the degree to which he can depart from visual fact. Against the self-image of the sitter, he can pose an image more in conformity with his own conception, but this image exists solely in potentiality, and the photographer can only hope that it will emerge on his film. The two images, that of the sitter and that of the photo portraitist, are locked in a silent wrestle of imaginations, until they are thrust apart by the click of the shutter. At that moment the issue is resolved, but not necessarily in favor of either of the contestants. In painting and sculpture, the portraitist has the advantage of being able to complete his creation in solitude, in conformity with his own psychological and aesthetic convictions; and in the novel and theater, the author can liberate himself completely from any restraints of likeness. But unless he resorts to darkroom tampering, the photographer is harnessed to his subject. During the entire process of making the picture, he is forced into collaboration, and the truth of his product is bound to depend in some measure on the person pictured in it.

It is in being semi-fictional that photo portraits attain the reality of change and conflict which belongs to the representation of the living.

In portraits of the dead, the fictional aspect is less important, since what has been concealed by the sitter or ignored by the portraitist is now unlikely to emerge and become effective—in short, it has ceased to count. In ancient Egypt, a dead man's friends and relatives were asked by the portraitist to choose his type of eyes, ears, nose, mouth from a chart—the portrait made up of these elements was buried with his body. Actual resemblance to the deceased was not attempted—a hieroglyphic description on the portrait identified him. That is to say, factual truth was assigned to the words, not to the image.

There are many different conceptions of likeness, ranging from that in which conventional forms are matched with the subject's features (as in the Egyptian example) to that which duplicates a visual impression. Picasso conceded that Gertrude Stein did not resemble the portrait he painted of her, but he insisted that someday she would. Like artists of Egypt, police-department portraitists combine physiognomical traits elicited from witnesses to produce portraits of persons they have never seen. But their aim is the opposite of that of the Egyptians; it is to provide the means by which strangers can recognize the subject, not to preserve his identity for eternity in the darkness of the tomb. The police sketches approximate appearances as closely as they can, while the symmetry of Queen Nefertiti's eyes, eyebrows, lips does not occur in nature. Yet there can be no disagreement that the latter is the more lifelike.

The likeness recorded by the camera is a species of naturalistic evidence—that of an eyewitness and presumably one superior in objectivity to human witnesses (which, as we have seen, does not prevent the camera from lying). You do not have to be a primitive to look at a photo and respond, "It doesn't look like him at all," but in time the visual record tends to become conclusive. The camera has made it possible to fool people through facts. The modern public is misled not by fable or fantasy but by information, of which visual information is no doubt the most convincing. Avedon recalls that in the photographs taken for his family album there was always a dog, though the family didn't have a dog. They would borrow one as part of their getup for their pictures, and they would pose in front of a magnificent limousine that didn't belong to them either. By adding these few bits of data to the truth of their appearance, they hoped to delude the world about themselves. "Every one of the photographs in the family album was built around some sort of lie about who we all were."

Having a dog in the photo did not make it a forgery, as would inserting words in a contract; the dog was actually there. Nor were the Avedons impersonating anyone in particular. Their "lie" consisted of embellishing themselves, of applying what might be termed a social cosmetic ("putting on the dog") that would induce spectators to draw erroneous conclusions, and thus to fool themselves. All the physical elements in the photo were genuine—the fraud lay in the eye of the beholder. He could be depended on to be susceptible (in the phrase of Van Deren Coke in *The Painter and the Photograph*) to a "conditioned reflex to the photo as 'truth.'" As the event recedes into the past, misrepresentation through facts becomes increasingly difficult to refute. How prove that people didn't own a dog? Or hadn't gotten a ride in a Packard on the day the photo was taken? For historians, the dog on film is a primary document in the life of the Avedons.

The photo thus becomes more real than the event or person that is its subject. As early as World War I, artists had begun to deal with photographs as, to quote Coke again, "mimics of nature and substitutes for reality." Actual experience is too transitory to be grasped—in imposing stasis on appearances, the photograph duplicates nature with a category of more durable phenomena. The mind becomes habituated to look to the copy in order to be convinced of the original. A riot, a snowstorm acquires an added dimension of solidity when it is duplicated in one or more of the visual media. Avedon summed this up in his remarks on the Bogart photo: "The information in it is self-contained. He's dead. Everything has changed. Everything—except the photograph." The pathos is that Bogart himself appears to have been reduced to a strip of chemically treated paper. That photos have superseded facts has altered our sense of things and has had significant effects on the moral, political, and cultural character of our epoch. The camera has thrust us into a man-made world composed of fictions beheld by the eye and facts about which we are in the dark (for example, TV versions of moon landings). Coke concludes his book with the startling advice that "one can learn more from them [photographs] than from life itself." Apparently, acceptance of the photo as reality (not hearsay) arouses no apprehension. William M. Ivins, Jr., is quoted as reflecting that "the nineteenth century began by believing that what was reasonable was true and it would end up by believing that what it saw a photograph of was true." Supporting Ivins, John Szarkowski declares, in *The Photographer's Eye,* that "the image survives the subject and becomes the remembered reality." Who is to say that there were no two-headed babies in Coney Island in the old days?

The history of portraiture is a gallery of poses. J. Pierpont Morgan, resting his right fist on two leather-bound volumes, stares searchingly out of a dark background into the spectator's eyes. A nude odalisque lounges against a satin pillow, her upraised arm stroking her hair. The king in his ermine cloak stands with his left hand on his hip, his right extending a staff. A Zapotec scribe, his chest and headdress incised with hieroglyphs, is seated with his legs crossed and his hands on his knees. In certain societies, the pose congeals into a mask. An authority on Elizabethan portraiture has propounded the thesis that to the ladies and gentlemen of that period the faces they wore were covers for hidden ones. "Knavery's plain face," says Iago, "is never seen till us'd." In the Conversation Pieces (portraits in customary surroundings) of Hogarth, everyone is an actor: his genius, wrote Sacheverell Sitwell, "was for drama." One could say the same of the age; the candors of the psychological novel were not to appear for at least a century. La Rochefoucauld wrote that at the baths he felt that he was attending a masquerade. In Oriental art, couples engage in complex erotic performances with an unvarying absence of facial expression. Formality, etiquette are species of play-acting; the more formal the society, or the traditions of the caste, the more inflexible its control of appearances. Stable societies consist of an array of types that repeat themselves generation after generation. Nations, social classes, professions, and trades take pride in their historically contrived identities and in the costumes, hair styles, gestures by which they are recognized. Even peasants are not "natural" products of the soil, as was imagined by Tolstoy, among others. The past is a pageant of second selves of man's invention. The desire to be what one is is a late, sophisticated Western ideal, one which—as Paul Tillich's *The Courage to Be* suggests—requires extraordinary efforts.

In the Elizabethan theater, truth and appearances were at war. "Nay, it is," protests Hamlet, "I know not 'seems,'" and he denies that the clothes he wears can "denote me truly." The Renaissance sensibility is concerned with the reality that may underlie the conceits and stratagems of "show." The nineteenth century made the revolutionary discovery that artifice— or, if one prefers, metaphor—is inherent in things; in short, that there is a truth of surfaces. In the Darwinian world, likeness prevails on all levels of organic life—e.g., a microphotograph of a sand fly resembles a lobster. Nature itself uses make-up to fool the eye and to provide clues to unsuspected kinships. The implication is that the aesthetic is everywhere, not merely in the conventions of the individual arts. Meaningful forms subsist on all planes of existence, and wherever they are found—on the sea bottom or in the depths of the unconscious—is but another surface. In the nineteenth century, the secrecy of Being is dissipated into patterns of unprivileged data. "Trace a certain fact in actual life," wrote Dostoevsky in *The Diary of a Writer,* "one which at first glance is even not very vivid—and if only you are able and endowed with vision, you will perceive in it a depth such as you will not find in Shakespeare." In the new Realism the opaque Elizabethan world has been superseded by intertwining networks of incidents, profound and trivial. Reality has been democratized. The core of things has been folded out and laid open to view. "Depth" now depends on the perceptiveness of the viewer. Since there is no essence of reality but only details, "at first glance even not very vivid," representations of things can never be complete. Beginning with Impressionism, paintings are put together as assemblages of clues. Dostoevsky goes on: "It stands to reason that never can we exhaust a phenomenon, never can we trace its beginning or its end." The last word can be nothing more than an aesthetic generalization, and with the invention of the camera everyone becomes a practicing aesthete.

With the elimination of the difference between inner and outer reality, nineteenth-century literature conceived the Split Man, an individual in whom the previously concealed alter ego (Iago's "I am not what I am") rose to the surface and assumed a tangibility equal to that of the original person. The Split Man could be an individual who was two people who did not resemble each other (Jekyll and Hyde), or two visually identical people with opposing natures (Dostoevsky's "The Double"). The reader had no way of deciding which represented the inner reality, which the demonic deception—as he had no way of knowing which was the organic artifice (the painting that grows old in *Dorian Gray*) and which the human aesthetic object (ageless Dorian).

The Elizabethan portrait is finite, finished, near-emblematic, rather than "natural." In the words of E. K. Waterhouse in *Painting in Britain, 1530–1790,* it tends toward "flat pattern, with elaborate dresses and aloof, inscrutable features." In contrast, the post-Darwinian face is "expressive"; the biography of the subject is concentrated in it, and clothes are de-emphasized by sketchy handling or blending into dark backgrounds.

We have seen that the "realistic" portrait, too, is a "fiction," resulting from the conflict between the sitter and the portraitist. But the sitter's fabricated expression is an attempt to present a self-satisfying or socially impressive version of himself; it is not intended to frustrate scrutiny. Nor does the portraitist strive to unmask the sitter but to interpret him. He approaches the subject with suspicion, that of using the occasion for public-relations purposes. He does not, however, suspect him of actually being someone else. It is a question of mascara and eyebrow pencil rather than of a Halloween false face. There is no proof that Avedon senior was less "wise and gentle" than he was "impatient." Aren't the artist's motives under suspicion too? No one today can pretend to have "gotten to the bottom" of anything, but can only insist on having his own say.

In our century, it has become customary to believe that if appearances are deceitful, reality is no less so. The need for masks is no longer felt—faces are enigmatic enough. Nixon had no Mr. Hyde; his alter ego was just another Nixon. Types whose motivations are graspable on sight have become rare even in the theater. In contrast to Elizabethan dissembling, the modern urge is toward self-disclosure, an urge heightened by the promise of psychotherapy that a clean breast will put an end to inner conflict. In practice, self-disclosure proves to be an

endless process, one whose product is a species of fiction, like
the Avedon family album. To rid oneself of all falsifications,
poses, self-dramatizations is a Utopian ideal, very likely left
over from the Romantic striving for naturalness. Today, self-
exposure goes hand in hand with make-up and mannerism.

In the early days of photography, sitters for photo portraits
were posed in the same way as for paintings. Educated photographers depended on canvases they had seen for compositional ideas. In turn, painters depended on photographs for
more accurate likenesses. In most of the painted and photographed portraits I have compared, the photograph is superi-
or in credibility and depth and in uniqueness of expression. The
often-reproduced daguerreotype of Poe is far more mysterious
and intriguing than the etching by Manet, which subsumes the
poet under the type of a successful French papa; and a similar
superiority marks the photos taken of Baudelaire, with the possible exception of the lithograph by Rouault.

Serious painters might in the long run have abandoned portraiture because of the competition of the camera, although
there are qualities that can be achieved by painting that no photograph can match; for example, the rendering of emotion
through color, as in a portrait by van Gogh or Matisse. The
most decisive revolutionary impact of photography came, however, not through its ability to surpass in accuracy the posed
likenesses of the portrait painter. The genuinely momentous
transformation in capturing the human physiognomy was
wrought by the snapshot, which put an end to the need for
posing since poses could be *found* by the photographer and did
not required to be staged. The unpremeditated postures, including those of children, snared by the rapid shutter and increasingly fast films brought about an immeasurable expansion
in the variety of human gesture—and in human self-consciousness. No doubt it was the snapshot that made people
more appreciative of the richness that lay in being natural. Art-

ists, first among them the Impressionists, discovered the aesthetic possibilities of random arrangement in contrast to constructed order. Things, people were found to attain their maximum authenticity when they were present without presenting themselves.

All portraits surprise their subjects in some degree. Individuals have a general notion of what they look like, and this notion tends to be jarred by any particular likeness, almost as if there were a double exposure. "It's a good picture," is the usual verdict, "but the resemblance is off." Portraits are probably most convincing to people who are unfamiliar with the persons portrayed. The snapshot multiplies the quantity of fragmentary or inexact likenesses of each individual to the point where he is assimilable into a universe of light and shadow. Whatever remains recognizable of the photographed object has been rescued from anonymity either by chance or by the skill and discipline of the photographer. "We photographers," said Cartier-Bresson, "deal in things which are continually vanishing." This consciousness can lead logically to abandoning as hopeless the demand for affirmation of individual identity in portraits. The situation is symbolized by Magritte's painting of a gentleman with a huge apple directly in front of his face—which is a companion piece to a photograph of J. P. Morgan with his head completely blocked out by his silk hat.

Optical phenomena are infinite in quantity and each is susceptible to being recorded in countless variations and refractions. Within the endless flood of visual arrangements and rearrangements, the painter seeks an effect of coherence, if only one derived from the habitual reflexes of the hand. Lacking the inhibitions of a nervous system, the camera holds the threat of a mindless accumulation of data, without limit and without purpose, like the accumulation of profit in the economic system in which photography originated. One-man exhibitions of photographs occasionally display the stylistic consistency and formal subtlety of the individual craftsman. Such accomplishments do not, however, alter the fundamental fact that, in the photographic medium, finding can be substituted for making. It is undeniably a factor in the vast popularity of snap shooting that no concept of the subject is needed to take pictures—the thing pictured can be found and refound with each click of the shutter. One can make aesthetic choices from a roll of film shot without a single insight, the way one chooses among pebbles on a beach.

The inauguration by photography of the aesthetics of finding has exerted an incalculable influence on the culture of our time, from the apparently insatiable popular demand for collecting to the innovations in painting and sculpture brought about by incorporating ready-made and found materials.

Finding includes combining. Collage, perhaps the most radical departure in this century from traditional assumptions in painting, arose directly out of the technology of reproduction, which includes photography. Collage was stimulated by the cameraman's bent toward foraging for subjects. In the collage, "finds" consisting of photographic likenesses, real objects, and passages created by the artist are mixed and united in a single dimension. Collage realizes in art the principle cited by Ivins and Szarkowski that the photo is equal in reality to the object or event. In the collage, and in its sculptured equivalent, the assemblage, things are transformed into images and derive their meaning from the new context in which they are set. The visible world is thus conceived as susceptible to unlimited manipulation and readjustment. A Cubist portrait, such as Picasso's of Kahnweiler, symbolizes this liberation from objective solidity, or "things as everyone sees them" (Gertrude Stein), by translating its subject into a complex coordination of physical fragments and abstract shapes. A political equivalent of this domination of external reality by the reconstituting will is to be found in societies governed by revolutionary ideologies.

Finding involves recognition—of particulars that arouse feeling directly (a familiar figure glimpsed in a crowd) or through association (a fruit that resembles a detail of the female anatomy). Theoreticians of photography stress its reliance on selection or choice. Effective photographers know in advance what they are seeking, though this will not prevent them from appropriating images other than those they expect to find. Aaron Siskind found Abstract Expressionist art everywhere—on barns, on rock formations, on stretches of sand. Selection is as vital—and for the same reason—in photography as it is in paintings based on chance, whether composed of found materials, such as collages by Arp or Schwitters, or through automatic drawing or processing, as by Ernst or Masson, or by the thrown paint of Pollock. All these artists find, and only selecting can prevent them from bringing in everything.

Recently, experiments have been made in art consisting of randomly thrown matter in which selection has been abandoned, as in the aleatory music of John Cage, in "scatter" sculpture, and in films made by allowing cameras to record whatever occurs in front of the lens. Finding without selection, however, undermines the concept of finding, which implies the realization of some sort of seeking. The extreme in finding is the flea market and the garbage dump, where something desirable may appear by chance, but which only a dogmatist would present as realizing the logic of collage.

In addition to accident and selection, there is what might be called inspired finding, the advent of transcendental or magical objects or persons, such as the momentous talismans and encounters in legends and in the lives of heroes. Occurrences of this order, sought but not planned, presumably transpire only among those who have psychically prepared the way for them by the search itself, as in the adventures of the Holy Grail. The Surrealists, combing the streets and shop windows of Paris in search of what they called "objective hazards," stumbled over an unusually high frequency of significant "correspondences." There is such a thing as training oneself to be lucky. The shots in the dark of Breton, Arp, and Miró almost always hit a valid mark. "To produce an accident of this sort," said Hans Hofmann of one of his great blot paintings, "one must be in a certain state." There are, in sum, more advanced forms of finding than to bag what is available and choose what one likes. The findings of exceptional photographers occur as the result of exceptional preparations.

Every art has its own moral principle, without which its creations are mere stimulants of sensation. There is nothing to prevent photography from operating on the moral level of the beachcomber, the brothelkeeper, or the second-story man. It is nothing new for the camera to deal with people in public places as potential salvage, to be a source of supply for peddlers of touched-up nudes, to be used to collect testimony in hotel rooms. Lately, it has been argued in court that photographers may appropriate human likenesses as a matter of right. The story of portraits extracted by force is not restricted to mug shots in police stations.

The moral principle of photographic portraiture is respect for the identity of the subject. Such respect does not come naturally in a medium that can without effort produce countless unrelated likenesses of the same object. Light, of which photographs are made, can endow people and scenes with emotional associations that are completely irrelevant to them—a half-lighted face transforms every girl reading into a pensive madonna. To achieve truth, the photographer needs to curtail his resources, which means he must make photography more difficult.

Avedon is a difficult photographer, in the sense that Barnett Newman and Clyfford Still are difficult painters. Like them, Avedon is a "reductionist," that is, one who purges his art of inessential or meretricious elements. Photo portraits of artists, writers, intellectuals, and leaders generally endow them with nobility and thoughtfulness by steeping their features in deepening layers of shadow or catching them in meaningful attitudes. "Personality" is added by drawing on the photographer's repertory of staging devices; the subject is shown with his paintings as background, or peeping around or through a sculpture, or cuddling a cat.

Avedon's camera refuses to confer poetry or distinction on his painters, writers, and other famous personages. It meets each individual head-on; he is allowed only such graces as may come through the vacant stare of the lens. With Avedon the camera seems less a tool of presentation than a source of self-enlightenment. "The photographs," he has said, "have a reality for me that the people don't. It's through the photographs that I know them." He has returned to the posed picture, but only to the extent that his "sitters" (they usually stand) face the lens with an expression of their choice. No snapshots. No taking by surprise, catching people with their mouths full of food or (with the exception of Ezra Pound) opened in a shriek. None of the portraits in this book is made with a "candid" camera. Avedon uses an 8 × 10 Deardorf and a Rolleiflex. "A photographic portrait," he has written, "is a picture of someone who knows he's being photographed." This awareness is enough to distinguish a human being from an object (which is what one becomes in most photos), or from a motif in a pattern. Nor in the Avedons is there a hoaxing for effect by the photographer, though the model may put himself across in any way he or she chooses (for example, in Warhol's Factory). In most cases, the faces of Avedon's subjects are those they came by naturally—all of the Chicago Seven seem to have felt the impact of Avedon's gravity.

Avedon signals the austerity of his portraits by their all-white, flat background. In preparation for a portrait, he develops an intuition of the sitter, then presses the bulb to make his intuition visually concrete. De Kooning, of whom there is a remarkably powerful portrait in this book, told me that Avedon silently set up his large roll of white paper on the shady side of the house, then asked suddenly, " 'Are you ready?' I said, 'Sure,' and he had me stand in front of the white plane. He stood close to me and snapped the picture. Then he asked, 'Why don't you smile?' So I smiled, but the picture was done already, and he didn't take any of me smiling."

Except in varieties of abstract art, paintings in the Western tradition tend to create a visual effect of three-dimensionality. An unfinished portrait, for example, arouses the fantasy that a hidden being is slowly coming into light. In the imagination of the spectator, a painting at this stage is not different from a sculpture. There is no such thing, however, as an unfinished photo portrait—and the all-thereness of the photographic image deprives it of organic gravity.

Avedon's inhibition of the illusionistic rules of the camera— ingenious angles, dramatic lighting, mood-inspiring environments—restores the solidity of the subject, jeopardized by the reign of the surface in modernist aesthetics. His photos also dispense with biographical props (an exception is the armful of Buckley scripts held by William F. Buckley, Jr.), though not with drama, which is inseparable from expression (the photos of Marianne Moore and Ezra Pound), as well as from the lack of it (photo of Robert and Michael Meeropol). Avedon allows his sitters their characteristic disguises, as well as those forced upon them by nature or by their professions, as in his portrait of "John Martin, Dancer," a female impersonator, or of Truman Capote (which conveys the author of *In Cold Blood* but not the giddiness of the comedian of drinking parties).

To portray people as self-conscious subjects is to return to traditional portraiture, in which the appearance of the sitter is composed aesthetically, like a still life, by means of cosmetics, hair style, costume, and, above all, facial expression, before the portraitist applies his craft. Rose Mary Woods packaged herself for Avedon in a blouse crisscrossed with rectangular designs like the labels on a steamer trunk. In the photo of John Martin, the female impersonator, the painted eyes, elongated eyelashes, and obviously artificial hairpiece contrast with the hairy chest and muscular arms to affirm that this is a girl who is not what she seems. Beyond these data, available to any camera, is the look on the subject's face, which presents his dominant state of being as a unique blend of availability and toughness, an ambiguity echoed by the full lips and broad shoulders. One sees through the getup, yet Martin remains a girl—the visual impression is strong enough to neutralize our knowledge. And, of course, why couldn't he be a girl, after all? The hair on his chest might be as artificial as his wig. We are dealing with a photo, a "fiction." Photorealist painters have been fabricating bodies out of flesh-tinted plastics which they adorn with human hair. Let a viewer peruse Avedon's "John Martin" intensely enough and he may discover in himself odd erotic impulses stimulated by the collaboration between the hermaphroditic put-on of the subject and the interpretive art of the photo portraitist. That the theme of sexual doubling is Avedon's and not solely his sitter's is emphasized by the photo of Warhol's Factory—especially the soft, hairless nude, with flowing locks falling below her shoulders, well-manicured fingernails, and a ripe cluster of male organs. No matter how many times one looks at this figure, the astonishment is repeated. Here, the surface seems to leave very little unsaid.

A comparable last-word effect is achieved with the scarred and sutured belly in black leather jacket of Andy Warhol himself. The photo put me in mind of a painting of the cut-up Warhol by the veteran portraitist Alice Neel, with whom Avedon shares what I am led to describe as objective cruelty. Both artists record what has befallen their subjects or what they have done to themselves. With the imperturbable ruthlessness of nature, but without a trace of personal malice, faces, bodies, postures are induced to speak for themselves, and the artist responds, "Amen, that's how it is." Several of Avedon's personae—de Kooning, Herbert Marcuse, Renata Adler, Alger Hiss—show themselves in what seems the acme of self-assertiveness. Their energies are concentrated to such an extent that they almost appear to be moving forward, while Jean Genet slouches into the frame with his head bent, and William Burroughs keeps to a corner of the photo like someone who slinks along a sidewalk close to the buildings.

Avedon takes pictures in flat, artificial light and, more recently, in raw daylight, both of which expose every wrinkle, hair follicle, and skin blemish as vividly as if seen in a magnifying mirror. Among his sitters are persons (Groucho Marx) who, being stripped down to what they are, are transformed into strangers. The clarification of the materials of which faces are made—skin, bone, hair, eyes—at times makes the face itself impenetrable as an animal's. On Lewis Milestone's nose there is a bit of peeling skin, and Jean Renoir could belong to half a dozen species, while he shares with Henry Miller and Dwight Eisenhower a kind of glowing edge, which does not lessen these subjects' materiality. Galanos, a fashion designer, has somehow succeeded in curving his body into the shape of an erect worm. Except for group portraits, Buckminster Fuller is the only subject taken full-size, which sets him back from the foreground of the picture and makes him look smaller. This placement seems right, however, for a man who stands in the universe so firmly with both feet.

The apogee of Avedon's fidelity to objective truth is recorded in the series of portraits of his father. In the seven photos, Jacob Israel Avedon changes from an alert, well-dressed man in his eighties into a hopeless victim of terminal cancer. On the features of the dying man an expression of apprehension deepens into outright terror that culminates in a hopeless appeal (in the sixth portrait), then subsides into resignation. At the height of his desperation, the older Avedon's head seems on the verge of metamorphosis into a petrified skull, like the light-absorbing masks in semi-precious stone of ancient Mexico—in features and strained expression the photo resembles a representation in gold of the Mixtec death god. Here Avedon approaches the ultimate portraiture—that is, portraiture of the dead, in which the individual edges over into the universal. To the question put to him about this series, "What kind of son could it be who would take such pictures of his dying father?" Avedon has responded significantly that the photos represent not his father, or what he felt or feels about his father, but "what it is to be any one of us." It is, of course, this sense of identification that makes the photos so unbearable even to people who never knew Avedon senior.

Avedon's photos aim to restore to his subjects the solidity of being. To this end, he has returned to older aspects of portraiture—one might say he has fought his way back to this art through tides of illusionistic effects made possible by photography and by experiments in the accidental and the unpremeditated. His photos depend entirely on prearranged conditions leading to a final leap into the unknown. Avedon has rejected the limitless fecundity of candid shots in favor of the conscious pose—but shorn of photographic hoaxing through mood lighting and stage props. With him, pose means only that the sitter confronts the camera knowingly, thus wearing a face that is a product of nature and his own act. In the last analysis, the no-comment faces and bodies which Avedon thrusts before the spectator are in accord with the conviction of Giacometti, the most profound portraitist of the mid-twentieth century, that any ultimate portrait is unattainable.

13

Nuremberg and the Corruption of Thought

I

In Marcel Ophuls's *The Memory of Justice,* Stalin is quoted as having proposed shooting 50,000 top Nazis at the end of the war as a beginning of retaliation for their murder of millions. Historical accounts show that Roosevelt and Churchill had also been in favor of summary executions.[1] In time, however, legalistic reasoning prevailed, and a trial of twenty major Nazis lasting almost a year was conducted at Nuremberg. Ever since that four-nation tribunal was assembled, there have been disputes about whether justice was done by it, or whether the Nuremberg Trial was an act of revenge carried out by the victors against the vanquished. If Nuremberg was not an expression of justice, it has been taken to follow that the convicted Nazis were unfairly condemned, that given the pressures on Germany in the Thirties and the abnormalities of war their

Reprinted with permission from *The New York Review of Books,* 20 January 1977, © 1977 by Nyrev, Inc.

1. According to Bradley F. Smith's just issued *Reaching Judgement at Nuremberg* (Basic Books, 1976), Roosevelt's and Churchill's agreement on summary execution of Nazi leaders met with objections from Stalin. Perhaps the trials he had staged in Moscow in the Thirties gave him a preference for this way of disposing of defeated enemies.

behavior was no worse than that of others would have been (as evidenced by the fire-bombing of Hamburg and Dresden by the Americans and British, the atom-bombing of Hiroshima and Nagasaki, the slaughter of the Polish officers by the Russians), and that therefore they deserve sympathy and remorse.

Perhaps I should confess at the outset that I regard commiseration for the Nazis as "human beings" as intellectually degrading and morally degenerate. To me, concern about a square deal for the Nuremberg defendants belongs at best to the kind of sentimentality that led Jean Valjean to rescue the bloodhound Inspector Jouvet who had trailed him for years from execution by the Paris revolutionists. To defend the human status of Elite Corpsmen, whose "heroism" consisted in purging themselves of all traces of human feeling, who stood at the doors of the gas chambers making jokes while prodding children inside, represents, in my opinion, a decadent application of the Christian principle of turning the other cheek and returning good for evil. At least, Jean Valjean repaid good for the evil which he personally had suffered at the hands of Jouvet.

To forgive acts of viciousness suffered by others is the meanest condition into which one can be cast by the feeling of self-righteousness and the wish to relieve the heart of the burden of demanding revenge. To his credit, Hugo had the insight to recognize that Valjean's act of generosity would rebound against himself and in no degree divert Jouvet from his hunter's obsession. In the twilight of Christian charity, the true defender of civilization is not the practitioner of universal forbearance but the unswerving, single-minded angel of reprisal, in whose entire organism there is not a soft spot. No waffling. Catch him and apply the sentence.

The same corrective as Jouvet's to post-Christian decadence and its inexhaustible supply of moral/emotional ambiguities was embodied in Melville's Captain Vere. Billy killed the mate—never mind his innocent state, never mind his lack of intention, never mind accident, determinism, and extenuating circumstances. Hang him. Or you will all go down into the pit. The pit of false sympathy, shallow self-identifications, counterfeit brotherhood, hypocritical sharing of the guilt. Weaken the individual's responsibility for what he has done and society turns into an animal farm.

Ophuls's *Memory of Justice* raises anew the question of whether justice was done at Nuremberg. Today, thirty years after the trial, the behavior of the defendants is to be seen in the light of American violence in Vietnam, French torture in Algiers, atrocities by Algerian rebels against French *colons*. With the historical record crowded with inhuman acts, can the crimes of the Nazis appear as exceptional as they did three decades ago?

While preparing to make this film, Ophuls, it seems, came across a passage of Plato's regarding ideal justice and the thought that men guide their lives by the vague recollection of it. The Platonic concept of perfect justice became the standard of Ophuls's movie. By this measure, which Ophuls makes no effort to define either in Plato's terms or his own, "the difficulty of judging others" emerges as the leitmotif of the film. More specifically, *Memory* is presented as "an inquiry into the relations existing between the history of modern societies and their notions of justice." Intellectually this is pretty hazy stuff, but it is clear enough in its intention to dilute the certainty that the Nazi mass murderers deserved to be harshly dealt with. Other themes discovered in *Memory* also contribute to weakening the Nuremberg verdict of guilty. Have the principles laid down at Nuremberg survived the crimes of the nations that set up the tribunal? If not, upon what grounds can evil be isolated and condemned? Is it actually possible to judge the conduct of a nation or of individuals?

Naturally, by the standard of perfect justice, the difficulty of reaching a verdict that takes into account the unbounded universe of objective fact and subjective motive is insurmountable. The judge ends by judging himself. Moreover, neither the societies under scrutiny nor their concepts of justice have been admirable. By thus dumping modern mankind into a limbo between an indistinct ideal (perfect justice) and compromising historical incidents (Hiroshima, My Lai), Ophuls reaches the conclusion that while the crimes of the Nazis were "iniquitous" the Germans are "just like other people."

In Dostoevsky's *Notes from Underground*, the narrator contends that unless one who is injured reacts directly, the impulse toward retaliation is continually watered down by interpretations of how the offense came about. By the time the inquiry has been pursued to the end (there is no end), nothing is left of the victim's original rage but helpless spite. How much more is this the case when the victim to be avenged is someone else. In the age of science, the Underground Man discovers, the passion for retaliation gives way to sick theorizing. Undoubtedly, there was more cold disputation than avengers' fury at Nuremberg. But why should the emotional inadequacy of the judges and prosecutors be credited to the malefactors, particularly since the inadequacy of the judges is typical of the epoch? Were it not for emotional vacillation the Nazi criminals would not have lived to be tried. The only reason there is complaint about Nuremberg is that there *was* a Nuremberg. Had Goering and his jolly men been shot outright the argument about their guilt would have been closed.

Never was there an instance in which righteous people, if they existed, had more reason than in Germany at the breakup of Hitler's power to spring upon the conspirators and try and condemn them on the spot. In Italy the mob that got Mussolini into their hands dispatched him with suitable ferocity. The Italians purged themselves of the Duce who had forced himself upon them as their personification. A similar purge never took place in Germany. Instead, the Germans, from the highest to the lowest, denied that their Fuehrer was their responsibility, or they acknowledged a guilt so thinly spread out over all as to amount to little more than excessive attention to one's own business. The brightest bit in *Memory,* and the truest, is the interview with the theater man who insists that he was the only Nazi and that the huge crowds at the Hitler rallies consisted of him alone. This difference between the Italians and the Germans is one instance in which the Germans are not, as Ophuls claims, "just like other people."

So, I will be told, you advocate lynching in preference to courtrooms. What about, for instance, the personal or political vindictiveness of partisans when they get the chance to take the law into their own hands? My answer is: the court that deals with capital crimes meets under the frightening shadow of the Furies, whom it must satisfy with it rational alternative. To be a real alternative, it must approximate vengeance in appeasing the soul of the victim or whoever stands in his place. The law, a French chief justice observed in connection with the Eichmann trial, cannot tolerate the scandal of immunity (think of the Nixon pardon). Whenever criminal acts can be performed without retribution, the law court loses efficacy as a civilized substitute for vendetta. If Nuremberg has not served as a deterrent to government-sanctioned atrocities, it is not because if failed to do justice to the defendants but because it fell short of spiritual compensation for the torments of the victims. Societies in both hemispheres have been contaminated by hospitality to inadequately punished Nazis.

Ideal justice cannot be realized, of course—that's why it remains ideal—and one who looks to the ideal ought not to expect to see it applied to actual offenses. For one thing, the accused is always tried for an act he has committed in the past; at the time of the trial he is a different man, biologically, psychologically, and perhaps—given the new experience of being faced with the social formulation of what he has done—even morally. I seem to recall reading that Julius Streicher, the obscene Jew-killer, repented his anti-Semitism while incarcerated at Nuremberg and became an admiring student of the history of the Hebrews. In some degree, punishment is always meted out to a stranger who bears the criminal's name. At the trials of the French collaborators, Sartre and de Beauvoir were troubled by this question of identity: they had known this or that fellow in school—a bright, friendly boy, what did he have to do with this traitor and nasty informer in the dock?

Also, looked at from the other end of the action, would this harmless bumbler on trial be capable of committing his outrages now? In *The Memory of Justice*, Mme Vaillant-Couturier, who had been a prisoner at Auschwitz, after leaving the witness stand walks past the prisoners' box containing Goering, Hess, Jodl, and the rest, and remarks that she suddenly saw them as human beings. A metamorphosis had taken place. The real criminals have been carried off by history and will never return. In their place has been left a group of aging stand-ins, sick and trembling with fear. Judgment will be pronounced on a round-up of impersonators, a collection of dummies borrowed from the waxworks museum. At worst, these feeble, mediocre fellows, "just like other people," could only have been, as they claim, cogs in the death machine somehow fashioned by history.

"But, ah!" cried a voice from the balcony at the Eichmann trial in Jerusalem, "you should have seen him in his colonel's uniform." Yes, the trial is about that other, the creature empowered to dispatch millions to destruction, not this pathetic organism anxiously following the proceedings through his earphones. That fabulous malefactor, though locked forever into an interval of his past, and no longer accessible to the living, cannot be allowed to rest in his perfect refuge.

Justice cannot be attained, only some kind of rough retaliation, which is mostly futile, but without which no incident could be closed and life would be made intolerable by unhealed wounds. The law reached Eichmann and the Nuremberg defendants too late, when they were no longer who they had been. Worse still in regard to ideal justice, were they ever *only* those guilty actors who were being tried? The law judges a person by his deeds, but what man is not more than he does? Whose being, since we live in a socio-historical continuum, cannot be seen as essentially *irrelevant* to what he does? As exemplified by Mme Vaillant-Couturier's seeing the men not the actors and thinking that they looked like human beings, there is a perspective in which the top Nazis, too, not only the Germans, are "just like other people."

A Chicago lawyer who served as a prosecutor in war crimes trials in Bavaria told me that in case after case the evidence established beyond doubt that Wolfgang A— and Otto B— had tortured and murdered concentration camp inmates in cold blood and simply to amuse themselves, but that the same Wolfgang and Otto had been good boys in school, dutiful sons, faithful husbands, devout churchgoers, brave, patriotic Germans, in sum, pillars of the town. As Dostoevsky liked to point out, the human soul has a broad range. A small segment of the psyche of these Bavarian folk, maybe a very minor portion, contained an appetite for viciousness, but if circumstances had not put in their hands the means for satisfying that taste, they might have passed their lives as worthy citizens.

In *The Confidence Man,* Melville describes a type whom he calls the Indian Killer. The Killer is a quiet fellow, who has a good reputation in town for honest dealing and helping his neighbors. One midnight, this peaceful citizen springs out of bed, grabs his musket off the wall, slinks out of the house and lopes off into the woods. He has resolved to "kill myself a few Indians." From that moment on, he is the deadly trapper, cunning and fearless, a landlocked Ahab. Several days later, returning from his expedition with half a dozen scalps in his belt, he steals into his house, goes to bed, and the following morning reappears in town in his usual guise of the model good guy. Since there were no prosecutors to represent justice for the Indians, the Killer's lethal passion could be considered a mere character trait.

To measure the guilt of the good Bavarians was enough to drive the American prosecutors into a fever. When court recessed for the day, they would meet at a bar and put themselves problems such as these: if your Wolfgang murdered eighty people, besides raping and torturing, and my Otto only shot sixteen adult males in spasms of playfulness, is it just that both should receive the same punishment? But what does murdering *only* sixteen mean? . . . Better have another drink.

The Nazis, both before and after their defeat, counted on the ambiguities and limited reach of the law. In their fight for power, they exploited legality at every turn—for example, the Reichstag Fire Trial, all legal and, as the Germans like to say, "proper." The National Socialist Party itself was formed as a law-evading mechanism through its principle that the Fuehrer was solely responsible for everything, hence that every member was only carrying out orders, which he could plead as extenuation—a kind of limited liability company. The psychological effectiveness of this arrangement can be gauged by Goering's feeling of innocence when, upon the collapse of the Third Reich, he drove into the British sector in an open car waving to passers-by and expecting a field marshal's welcome.

At Nuremberg the Nazis were present as wards of legality, all the challenges being directed at the right of the court to try them and at the validity of such novel counts in the indictment as "waging aggressive war" and "crimes against peace." In an improvised court lacking in precedent, and with their responsibility truncated by the absence of their Chief, the heirs of Hitler continued to wield the law as a weapon. But if there are ambiguities about Nuremberg, in addition to those that affect law in general, there are no ambiguities about Nazi guilt. It is time that people of good will stopped mistaking the form of the court for the substance of the act.

II

Movies seem to prosper in an intellectual and moral vacuum.

Luis Buñuel

The impossibility of ideal justice under the law seems to have lured Ophuls into a near-nihilistic bog in which no one is guilty because all are guilty and there is no one who is morally qualified to judge. Among the questions raised by *The Memory of Justice,* one that is probably the most important is missing: on what basis is a maker of documentary movies equipped to comment on historical events and to reach conclusions about crime and retribution? To quote Plato on justice without further analysis is to engage in phrase dropping—the title "The Memory of Justice" is effective not through what it means but through its overtones of feeling, of a kind not dissimilar to a passage of 1920s jazz or a photo of Hitler riding in triumph through Paris. In short, an idea is presented for its aesthetic effect, a sort of brush stroke. Constructed according to this rule, can the documentary be an effective mode of thinking about grand issues?

The movie camera is primarily a machine for collecting visual data. In documentaries these data are augmented by opinions and recollections supplied through interviews. All these—the photo images and the verbal testimonies—are potentially limitless in quantity. Also, all are subject to various kinds of distortion and falsification, for example, through physical resemblances between objects and scenes that are essentially different, and by false and mistaken statements. To avoid bias

Ophuls admits into *Memory* views that differ from his own, in the belief that deformations of the historical picture will correct themselves as more data are added. Admiral Doenitz, for example, is convinced that he has done no wrong, and that speeches he delivered attacking the Jews in no way contributed to the establishment of concentration camps. There is, however, no way of calculating that a sufficient weight of opinion has been piled on the other side of the scale from Doenitz. Nor do we know that any number of denunciations of Germans such as Doenitz could cancel the effect of the admiral's smug self-assurance. Actually, very little is heard in *Memory* from Jews, Gypsies, Social Democrats, and Hitler-haters, though without the victims' hatred of their oppressors the quest for justice lacks substance.

Ophuls has denied that his film intended to "equate" Auschwitz and My Lai—in his view, it merely suggests "comparisons." Ophuls's response could be valid if his medium were able to make this kind of distinction apparent to the movie audience. The moviemaker, however, cannot control the effect of juxtaposition on the spectator. Film shots of piles of corpses create an "equation" between the acts that produced them and those responsible for those acts, regardless of what the filmmaker had in mind. Pictures are less abstract than words, and the impressions they discharge convey blunter messages. An instantaneous connection is established between corpses in a ditch and in the Chicago garage on St. Valentine's Day—the link of gangster violence. No other medium offers greater opportunities for shallow analogies and spurious certainties.

Ophuls originally shot ninety hours of film. Like any report of events, a documentary is essentially endless. At any point in one's life, one could spend the rest of it watching what happened during a preceding fraction. Yet letting the camera run on tells no more than that the world is full of things from this angle or that. Since an uncut film amounts to staring at nature, the reduction of *Memory* to its present four and a half hours was designed to produce an intellectual synthesis—in brief, Ophuls's message that justice is unattainable but that men strive for it anyway.[2] Frankly, I failed to *see* this in the film. What I did see was that the Allies were not morally competent to try the Nazis, and I saw and heard Yehudi Menuhin deliver the concluding statement of the film. This statement—by its positioning as the last word, as well as by its reiteration of the belief, echoed in various ways throughout the film, that judging others was wrong—caused the film to add up to the view that in this imperfect world it was intellectually crude to try the Germans as criminals. I don't know if this is Ophuls's opinion but this is what his film says.

Menuhin is by far the most fatuous interviewee in *Memory*. He was the first artist to return to perform in Germany after the war, his explanation being that since no member of his own family had been put to death he lacked the antagonism of other Jews. And he had a good "Christian" message: no one can judge the criminal but the criminal himself. This Dostoevskian tenet might hold for some isolated Raskolnikov, but for a criminal with a nation of collaborators nothing could be more far-fetched. Goering, Doenitz, and half a dozen others had clearly indicated that for the convinced Hitlerite, and even milder anti-Semites, killing Jews was not considered a crime—the Jews, assuming that so many of them had been killed, were casualties of war, more than expiated by German losses at Stalingrad and by Allied "atrocity" bombings of Hamburg and Dresden. Documentaries splatter bits of evidence but don't add them up, so Menuhin can wait for the Nazis to indict themselves. Menuhin, however, receives support from that noted disseminator of sweetness and light, John Simon, who calls Menuhin's state-

2. If the cutting was to spare the audience from fatigue, the film would have been cut more, since almost five hours of passages unrelated by narrative is also exhausting.

ment that "judgment should really come from within the person who committed the crime" a "sublime conclusion"—and who ends his review with the disclosure that "surely the lesson of the film is that the true enemy is, with rare exceptions, within ourselves." If profundities such as these need to be uttered, decency demands that they be withheld from discussions of Auschwitz.

In a recent issue of *The New York Review*,[3] Gore Vidal charged that in contemporary films "the human situation has been eliminated not through any intentional philosophic design but because those who have spent too much time with cameras and machines seldom have much apprehension of that living world without whose presence there is no art." (Or, he might have added, truth.) In dealing with serious topics, the hubris of filmmakers consists in assuming that skill in handling pictures in an effective manner is sufficient for the procreation of ideas.

Ophuls deals with the momentous issues of Nazi and German guilt within blinders he is not aware that he is wearing. His reconstitution of Western history since Nuremberg draws on journalistic raw materials selected according to a mixture of prevailing catchwords and a sense of showmanship. To the generation of viewers who have grown up since the Nazi crimes were perpetrated, *Memory* presents a dilution of the moral awfulness of the death camps and the killing of civilians and war prisoners, and it trivializes the significance of this vast organized death system by fitting pictures of corpses being dragged to pits into a rhythm of night-club performers, lush landscapes, chatter in sauna baths, and gentlemen reminiscing reflectively at their fireplaces.

3. November 25, 1976.

All about Everything

14

On Violence in Art and
Other Matters

An artist may start with the illusion that he is going to change things through his painting. But he will learn through bitter experience that art will not change anything. In the resulting disillusion he may cease his protest. This is exactly what the history of art since the thirties has been. The artist should understand from the start that political art is not a practical undertaking. An artist does not protest because he thinks that his protest is going to work, but because as a human being it is essential for him to make a statement about things that are humanly intolerable. He can spend his whole life doing it. In other words, one does a thing because it's right and not because it is going to be effective.

During World War II, the Office of War Information hired a great many artists, including people like Ben Shahn and other anti-Nazi artists, to make posters. They made beautiful posters on such themes as security of war information—"Button your lip," "Join the WACS," and similar projects. After the first

Excerpts from remarks by Harold Rosenberg in conversation with Jan van der Marck, director of the Museum of Contemporary Art, Chicago, and artist Bernard Aptekar on the occasion of the opening of the museum's Violence in Recent American Art show. First published in *Artscanada*, February 1969.

year, however, the government decided that the artists' mode of production didn't fit the needs and tempo of the war. The Office of War Information brought in art directors and artists who introduced Madison Avenue techniques of advertising and public relations. Soon there was a flow of effective advertising art. The fine artists were eliminated, and some got sore. I was in the building where they had been working when they were suddenly told that their services were no longer required. They departed, leaving a Coca Cola–type poster with the slogan "the war that refreshes." The only recourse of the artists was to make an ironical statement that from then on the public would hear about the war from Madison Avenue. Sad enough, yet I don't think anyone in his right mind would question that to communicate a message to a hundred and eighty million people, the techniques of Madison Avenue are more effective than the technique of an individual artist making a beautiful poster. The real problem of the artist in regard to politics is that when he satisfies himself he tends to think that somehow this will change the world. This mystique regarding the power of art may be justified in relation to the history of mankind and the general direction of culture. But as a guide in practical situations it can only lead to frustration.

There tend to be three categories of works in political protest exhibitions, such as the *Protest and Hope* show at the New School in New York last year, or the recent Feigen Gallery show in Chicago. The present show [at the Museum of Contemporary Art] is much purer in that it is exclusively involved with the theme of violence. One category consists of works by artists whose aesthetic conceptions have nothing to do with politics, but who as individuals want to express solidarity with the particular gesture of protest, so they participate by contributing paintings that they did ten years ago or two years ago or yesterday. The works themselves have nothing to do with the theme of the project. There were such works by Motherwell,

Frank Stella, and others at the Feigen exhibition, works that said nothing about the subject.

Another category consists of artists who try to adapt their usual mode of work to the theme; for example, there was an anti-Daley artist at Feigen's who imprinted his penis on the canvas. I don't know how he works normally, but obviously he wished to suggest in this instance that someone was a prick. Rosenquist made a kind of statement through cutting up a portrait of Mayor Daley into ribbons. There were others who presented remote symbolic association, like Bill Copley, who had a woman's ass turned toward the spectator, which could mean a lot of things.

Barnett Newman made a work for the occasion that represented the third category: an artist who tries to use his formal vocabulary to make a new statement about the specific situation. This is the most rare. Oldenburg managed it with the drawing of a detached head and with his red hydrants that were directly identified with Chicago. These were works in Oldenburg's style saying something about violence in Chicago. We are talking about the problem of style vis à vis the problem of statement—the political statement. This was the major problem of art in the thirties. Can you make an advanced stylistic and personal work—and at the same time make an objective statement, so that by your style you add something to what has already been said by others? In other words, how do you get art and politics together? Barnett Newman at the Feigen show found a way of using his style to say something that could only be said by him. Now isn't that the ideal way for an artist to make a protest? It is a legitimate work of art and it also makes a statement. Robert Indiana, with his kind of emblematic art, simply has to change the words. He can put anything he wants into it. But he does not augment his statement formally. So it becomes a slogan in a design. I notice that most of the art in this [Contemporary Museum] show is based on pop art. This was also true of the show at the New School. Pop is the one mode today that seems best fitted for political statements because it is so closely related to the mass media.

An artist should be a person who has deep feelings about what's going on in the world. But he also should realise that his role is not to be a political force; that, on the contrary, like the poet, he is related to the medieval clown. He makes free statements, says things that nobody else perhaps would dare to say, and does it with the force that comes from control of his medium. But he should not expect anything to happen as a result. I mean when a clown in a Shakespearean play, for example, makes philosophical remarks that go to the heart of the matter, he does not expect the other characters to turn around and begin to function in a different way. He says what he sees because his role as a clown is to be a representative of the truth. Whoever represents the truth is a clown, intruding into the serious business of mankind. Maybe in the history of the angels it is different; but in the history of mankind the truth-teller is a clown. Now if the artist is sufficiently modest, he will continue to make true statements in order to satisfy himself as an individual; and in this way he becomes an example of what an individual is. But the minute he begins to develop the illusion of power, that he is somehow able to affect events, he is doomed to disappointment and, consequently, will likely find himself ten years later supporting the status quo. Those artists who had notions that they were going to do something big (like some of the Dadaists, some of the Surrealists), that they were going to change the world, have not changed the world and have tended also not to change themselves. But by being sufficiently modest to say, "I see something and I'm going to reveal it and keep on revealing it, because that's the kind of person I am—besides I don't amount to anything anyway"—from this point of view an artist can make great contributions to human consciousness.

Of course, no one knows whether contributing to human consciousness is worth anything. In the nineteenth century it was widely believed that if humanity became sufficiently conscious, it would produce a marvellous society, a wonderful organization of human relations and so on. Today nobody gives a damn whether an idea is valid or not. People have become completely involved in what they consider to be their interests.

Pro or con, the artist must be concerned with politics—I have been insisting on this for twenty years. If art does not engage itself in the struggles of the time, it becomes insignificant and shrinks the figure of the artist. But what these struggles are is by no means always the issues that are most popular.

At the present time the position of the artist as a critic of society is the essential foundation for the continuation of art. There is a dramatic issue involved, for modern modes of art have developed apart from the need to conceive historical events in visual terms. Yet it is absolutely essential that artists should be concerned with such events and with such questions as violence and the question of the future of society, that is, with social problems. The more the artist is aware of the difficulty of making an effective statement within his essentially private medium, the better chance there is that something valid will emerge. The artist has to be a private person. There is no question about that in my mind, and to that extent his social effectiveness is, as noted before, dubious. If an artist today wants to be effective, he must be a part of a larger institutional effort, whether it be an advertising agency or a propaganda agency. This is what the Communists want; this is what the Catholic Church wants; this is what the U.S. government wants. That is, they want the artist to be the aggrandizer of a power which is.

The artist as a rebel is in the tradition of free art. This has been brought out over and over again in modern literature—in

Thomas Mann, James Joyce, Tolstoy, Kafka, or Sartre. The artist is the representative of man insofar as he is an individual. He therefore objects to violence. Or perhaps he celebrates violence. It does not make any difference in his status as artist. For if he celebrates violence, it is as a form of release, and this, too, is the function of the artist. He represents freedom to be a dog, to be a destructive element.

He celebrates the fact that one is a human individual. Individuality is the basis of the meaning of art in our time. This principle has aesthetic connotations. An aesthetic can be derived from the fact that an artist who wishes to celebrate his inner independence will tend to favor a certain concept of line, color, composition. For example, as Baudelaire said, straight lines represent an over-intellectualized approach and are antagonistic to individuality.

In sum, any aesthetic debate and any debate about art and politics must finally take up the question of the reality of the artist and his total idea as a unique human being. One human being, not *the* human being but *a* human being—in his autonomy and his absolute rights. I think that is the ultimate political message of the artist. Whether he is eager to be socially effective, or whether he favors art for art's sake, ultimately this insistence on self is his politics: "I will to say what I want to say." And that is a very strong political position. But of course when I say politics I mean culture.

I think the best artists of the twentieth century are great failures. They can't do what they set out to do, like de Kooning—or to go back to the nineteenth century, like Melville, who said "I wrote this book, *Moby Dick,* to be a great failure." Siqueiros does not believe he is a failure. He imagines he is a hero. I think he is a failure.

The implications of this [Violence in Recent American Art] exhibition are, I think, important for art. I believe that art is going to become more and more political. I feel that it is the only valid direction. There is no place else for it to go, for it has already begun to turn into decoration and entertainment, as we know. I'm not interested in the technological involvement of art. It makes the artist into one factor in a system far too powerful for him. For art, technology is a form of liquidation.

15

Interview with Willem de Kooning

De Kooning I am an eclectic painter by chance; I can open almost any book of reproductions and find a painting I could be influenced by. It is so satisfying to do something that has been done for 30,000 years the world over. When I look at a picture, I couldn't care less for when it was done, if I am influenced by a painter from another time, that's like the smile of the Cheshire Cat in *Alice;* the smile left over when the cat is gone. In other words I could be influenced by Rubens, but I would certainly not paint like Rubens.

I was lucky when I came to this country to meet the three smartest guys on the scene: Gorky, Stuart Davis and John Graham. They knew I had my own eyes, but I wasn't always looking in the right direction. I was certainly in need of a helping hand at times. Now I feel like Manet who said, "Yes, I am influenced by everybody. But every time I put my hands in my pockets, I find someone else's fingers there."

Rosenberg You once said that you could not draw like Rubens because you were too impatient. You said that you could

First published in *Art News,* September 1972, © 1972 by ARTnews, 5 West 37th Street, New York, N.Y. 10018.

draw a foot as accurately as Rubens, but that you didn't have the patience. Do you remember that? that—

De K. I don't remember, but I could very well have said it. I also think that maybe I don't really have the talent for that kind of drawing. I think that certain talents come into being at certain times, but that doesn't make them dead or alive.

R. I suppose nobody in our period could paint a detailed tableau of figures in the manner of the Renaissance?

De K. I think there might be people who could do that. For example, the Spanish painter Sert, who made the murals at the Waldorf Astoria. He was no Rubens, but he was a remarkable painter. He just didn't have as great a talent as Rubens.

R. You think there could be someone like Rubens today?

De K. I would say there is no reason why there couldn't be. George Spaventa and I were open-minded, and we thought there was no reason why, after 40 years of power, maybe one or two Russian artists would be gifted in the kind of painting that the Russian government demanded. We went to the Russian exhibition at the New York Coloseum with open minds. It turned out to be terrible painting—awful; the kind of painting done in this country in 1910 for the *Saturday Evening Post*.

R. Illustration?

De K. Not that so much, because you could say that Rubens is an illustrator too. I felt that making portraits of Lenin and Stalin and workingmen and genre—there was no reason why someone couldn't be very good at it. But they were not good at all. I had thought that maybe after being under pressure, which you slowly get used to, they might have found a way. But it seems that the Russian pressure wasn't the right kind.

R. But that's the idea that there are limits on what people can do in certain cultural situations.

De K. Yes, I guess; to come back to Rubens and to Sert, there must be something in the idea that a certain kind of art can only exist at a certain time.

R. That would be the point, wouldn't it?—A kind of historical pressure works against some forms of creation, though not necessarily in favor of something else?

De K. I take that for granted. But that's why I said before that I am an eclectic painter, and that I could be influenced by Rubens, but I would not paint like Rubens. The smile without the cat. For example, I object strongly to Renaissance drapery. There is so much cloth involved in that period—it looks like an upholstery store. To paint like that would drive me crazy. The drapery covered so many sins. Whenever the painter came to a difficult part he put another piece of cloth over it. That was the style, and it came to a high point . . .

R. You once said you were opposed to any kind of esthetic an artist might have before he produced his work. I believe you were talking about Mondrian and the fact that the Neo-Plasticists tried to work out an esthetic in advance. You said that, at the turn of the century, "a few people thought they could take the bull by the horns and invent an esthetic before-hand." You had the feeling that such a program is a form of tyranny. It interferes with the freedom of the artist.

De K. Well we can go back to Russia. That's probably why good art did not come about there. You can't build an esthetic beforehand. They have canons of art, an Academy.

R. The Russians believe in an Academy, and they believe that art is a definite kind of work for which there are canons. The most admired artists in Russia are called Academicians. But what you were talking about was a modern Academy . . .

De K. I remember that when I was a boy, on a cigar box they had "The Modern Age," the age of freedom and enlightenment, together with the great modern inventions. There was a blacksmith, bare-chested, with a leather apron, and a sledge-hammer over his back, which was considered a modern tool. And the wheel of progress was the biggest gear you ever laid eyes on—it certainly wasn't something that was made by a computer. Those symbols were a Romantic way of expressing the feeling of freedom.

R. Impressionism is very much involved with that—horse racing, ballet, all those things.

De K. I think Cubism went backwards from Cézanne because Cézanne's paintings were what you might call a microcosm of the whole thing, instead of laying it out beforehand. You are not supposed to see it, you are supposed to feel it. I have always felt that those beautiful Cubist paintings exist in spite of the Isms.

R. If you start with an idea . . .

De K. But they didn't. They were influenced by Cézanne and they could never have the patience to do all that again, once they knew what he was doing. But he didn't know.

R. They were influenced not so much by the pictures as by their analysis of the pictures. If you were influenced by Cézanne's pictures you would start imitating his look or style. But the Cubists didn't do that. They analyzed the pictures, and made rules out of what they found in their own minds.

De K. They made a superstructure, and for young people—I'm not being derogatory—for young people that was marvelous. It is unbelievable to think that men in 1910 or '11 could do such fantastic things, yet I don't think theirs was a particularly great "idea." It resulted in marvelous pictures because it was in the hands of fine artists. It depends on who was doing it. As a matter of fact, Cubism has a very Romantic look, much more than Cézanne has. Cézanne said that every brush-stroke has its own perspective. He didn't mean it in the sense of Renaissance perspective, but that every brushstroke has its own point of view.

R. What's amazing is the problems artists in the early 20th century were able to conceive. Instead of painting so that the result would look impressive, they brought to light all sorts of problems. That's what has led to the idea of the desperation of painting. Because if painting isn't desperate—if it isn't in a crisis—why should it have so many problems? Simple responses don't count anymore, or being talented. Modern artists have genius for perceiving problems.

De K. It is interesting that the late Baroque artists were so empty. There is Bernini's Minimalness. He was a virtuoso of genius—terrific. You look at it and it doesn't say a thing. It says nothing about the enormous amount of work. If I ever saw Minimalism, there it was. It says nothing. Like a saint's gesture, looking upwards to heaven . . . It takes your breath away to see that done with such grandeur—and not say anything.

I don't want to defend myself, but I am said to be Cubist-influenced. I am really much more influenced by Cézanne than by the Cubists because they were stuck with the armature. I never made a Cubistic painting.

R. Suppose you have the idea that you'd like to paint a tableau of a tree with people or cats sitting under it. Isn't it true that, while you are painting, you must see yourself come into it? The action of painting has to catch the totality of object and subject. You cannot think it out beforehand. Isn't that why you mentioned Wittgenstein's saying, "Don't think, look!"? Then you go farther, "Don't look, paint!"

De K. That's right! There is this strange desire which you can't explain. Why should you do that? I think I like it because of the ordinariness, so I am free of an attitude, in a way. Of course, that in itself is an attitude, but it would help me in my work, I think . . . The landscapes I made in the 1950s, such as *Park Rosenberg*, were the result of associations. But I had a vast area of nature—a highway and the metamorphosis of passing things. A highway, when you sit in a car—removed . . . Now I'm having the same difficulty. You might say that I'm going backwards by wanting to paint a tableau and not just the mood of it, a kind of double take. In contrast, one might paint something holy, like Barney Newman with his measurements and those divisions of colors (though the word "division" is a bad word). It was fascinating when Annalee [Newman] showed me his studio.

R. You are talking about the linoleum on his painting wall, those squares?

De K. Yes. I had thought that the linoleum would be squared off in feet—1 foot, 2 feet, and so on. So that you could say, this canvas is 8 feet, 6 inches. But I found the squares to be 9 inches, and it's hard to measure by 9 inches. Ten is 1 with a zero. Nine is a mysterious number, because we stop there, and then we repeat the digits. In Europe there is the decimal system, but here the measure is twelve inches, with an eighth of an inch and a sixteenth of an inch. . . .

R. Well, one could do a simple calculation. Ten of those squares would be 90 inches.

De K. Sure. But 9 is also a holy number. There is the mystery about why it is 9—and then 1-zero, and start over again. This is contrary to our usual measurement system.

R. Based on tens.

De K. Everything is based on tens, but then it isn't based on tens but on the human foot. That's 12 inches, and then the inch is divided into the half-inch, and then the quarter inch, the eighth inch. It is a peculiar thing. There is the great invention of the Egyptians of a rope with twelve knots, which makes a right angle—3 + 4 + 5. Barney was interested in the Cabala, I was told.

R. Tom Hess found evidence of that.

De K. Before I knew that I wondered why he bought linoleum with 9-inch squares.

R. You think it was on account of the sacredness of the number 9? Maybe he couldn't find linoleum with 12 inch . . .

De K. Oh, come on. There are so many linoleums with a foot-square design. Or he could have painted one. I wouldn't even paint the squares; I would just make marks on my wall.

R. Why then did he want that linoleum?

De K. Because he wanted it in 9 inches, as a thing to measure with. So I wondered what he wanted the number 9 for. Then, later, they found his interest in the Cabala. That was why, I felt, he wanted 9 inches. He could have had any measurement he wanted. He could have said, "why not?"

R. You mean 9 didn't mean anything to him in particular?

De K. Not particularly. He just liked it I guess. Actually paintings in the dimensions of 9 are hard to place in an ordinary room, because most rooms are only 8 feet 6 inches high. As for me, I like squarish forms. So I make paintings 7 to 8; 70 by 80 inches. If I want it bigger, I make it 77 by 88 inches. That is kind of squarish. I like it, but I have no mystique about it. Also, I like a big painting to look small. I like to make it seem intimate through appearing smaller than it is.

R. Usually, the opposite is the case. Artists want small paintings to look big.

De K. I can see that, if you really make a small painting. But if I make a big painting I want it to be intimate. I want to separate it from the mural. I want it to stay an easel painting. It has to be a painting, not something made for a special place. The squarish aspect gives me the feeling of an ordinary size. I like a big painting to get so involved that it becomes intimate; that it really starts to lose its measurements; so that it looks smaller. To make a small painting look big is very difficult, but to make a big painting look small is also very difficult.

I'm crazy about Mondrian. I'm always spellbound by him.

Something happens in the painting that I cannot take my eyes off. It shakes itself there. It has terrific tension. It's hermetic. The optical illusion in Mondrian is that where the lines cross they make a little light. Mondrian didn't like that, but he couldn't prevent it. The eye couldn't take it, and when the black lines cross they flicker. What I'm trying to bring out is that from the point of view of eyes it's really not optical illusion. That's the way you see it.

In a book on optical illusion there was an illustration with many lines drawn in a certain way. There were two parallel lines, then little lines like this and little lines like that from the other side. The figure looked narrower in the center than on the top and bottom. I don't call that an optical illusion. That's the way you see it. It looks narrower in the center.

R. You see it that way, but if you measured it, it would be different. That's the illusion.

De K. But in painting, that's the most marvelous thing you can do. That's the very strength of painting, that you can do that. It is "optic" naturally, because you have to have eyes to see it. All painting is optic. If you close your eyes you don't see it. But if you open your eyes with your brain, and you know a lot about painting, then the optical illusion isn't an optical illusion. That's the way you see it.

R. The way you see something doesn't mean necessarily that that's the way it is. That business of putting a stick in water so that it looks as if it's broken . . .

De K. Well it is. That's the way you see it.

R. What do you mean, it is broken? If you pull it out of the water it's not broken.

De K. I know. But it's broken while it's in the water.

R. The break is an illusion . . .

De K. That's what I am saying. All painting is an illusion. Mondrian gives you one kind of illusion, whatever you call it, tension . . . He calls it "dynamic equilibrium," or "clear

plasticity." I don't care what he calls it. That's the way you
see it. You have the illusion of this horse. I feel it, but that's
the way I see it.

R. In that case he is an illusory painter in regard to you.

De K. To me, a cow by Courbet is no more illusory than
Mondrian is. I know how it's painted . . .

R. You can do what you wish with a picture. Once after a
meeting with art teachers at the University of Kentucky we
were standing before a large painting of a side view of a cow
in front of a house. One woman said: "Tell me what you see
in this picture." For the fun of it, I began to find all kinds of
images painted into the cow, between its head and its tail. It
turned into a Surrealist painting. The more we looked at it
the more figures began to appear. It became a game—everyone found something—here is a clump of trees on the side of
the cow, there is a river running down the cow's neck. All
this began to appear, as if the artist had actually painted it.

De K. You mean he didn't paint it there?

R. No, they were accidental effects that appeared when you
looked at it in a certain way—as if you were watching
clouds. A human profile emerges, a cathedral, an animal. We
were standing in this idle way and began to see babies and
motorcycles on the side of the cow and around the cow. The
art teachers behaved as if I had given them a kind of magical
lecture, because at first they had seen only a cow and a
house.

De Kooning I know now what you mean. I use that a lot in my
work.

Rosenberg You mean accidental effects?

De K. I don't make an image such as a baby, but I use it. . . .

R. That Abstract-Expressionist painting by Perle Fine that's
hanging in our bedroom is so loaded with images—Arabs,
masked bandits—I can hardly look at it any more. I don't see

the painting, but the cast of characters that has come out of
it.

De K. You know, those figures are very well drawn. If you
asked her to draw a head she couldn't do it that way. That's
the strange thing.

R. You are absolutely right. No artist could do it.

De K. That's the secret of drawing, because the drawing of a
face is not a face. It's the drawing of a face. When you look at
a Rembrandt, it's just an association that there is a man
standing there that makes it realistic. Next to him there is a
black shape. You know it is a man also. But if you look at
that spot for a long time, there is no reason to think that it is
a man. It happens with so many drawings and paintings—in
Chinese art, in all kinds of art—and all the works come
together.

R. What do you mean by coming together?

De K. That they become separated from their period. Chinese
artists did something a thousand years ago, and somebody
else today does something very similar.

R. They are not divided by history.

De K. No division by history at all.

R. What has been going on in the past couple of years? Copying photographs or using actual photographs. Apparently
young artists want to create the feeling of a *mise-en-scène*, a
sort of tableau of people looking at pictures in an art gallery,
or standing around at a party. What do these activities mean
to you? Why should artists make art of photographs, instead
of taking photographs for practical purposes, or for the sake
of sentiment?

De K. Well, such art has a certain psychological effect. It's almost Minimal Art, as if one said, "Never mind what the
meaning is, here it is." This art has a kind of atmosphere, a
psychological overtone that is make-believe. You know it is

painted and yet it looks like a photograph. I don't understand the meaning. The people look ordinary, and the cars
are brand new and look sleeker than the people do, unless
they have a beautiful model in front of them, and then the
model looks sleeker than the car.

R. What's the reason for it? You would expect that works of
this sort would advertise something, or on the other hand
have a political message to tell.

De K. On television you often see shots, as in scenes televised
from Vietnam, that look exactly like painting. If you have
that kind of eye, you may say: "That looks like a Manet." Of
course it's a coincidence. Sometimes a painted portrait looks
like a photograph, and sometimes a photograph looks like a
portrait. There is something fascinating for me about
photography.

R. You don't feel that painting has a particular purpose, or one
that you would like to see it have? You don't care why people paint whatever they paint?

De K. The main thing is that art is a way of living—it's the way
I live. It's not programmatic. When I read *The Brothers Karamazov*, I liked the father the most.

R. I happen to agree that Fyodr Karamazoff is the most important character.

De K. In the end he is really all there, and the others couldn't
break out of a paper bag by themselves. The father isn't a
nice man, but I was painting a picture and all of a sudden it
came to me that I liked the father the most. . . . It came like a
revelation. It hung in the air somehow. A novel is different
from a painting. I have said that I am more like a novelist in
painting than like a poet. But this is a vague comparison because there is no plot in painting. It's an occurrence which I
discover by, and it has no message.

R. You mean your painting is an event?

De K. It is an event, and I won't say it is kind of empty, but . . .

R. An event without an interpretation.

De K. Yes. I have no message. My paintings come more from other paintings. Here is *ARTnews,* and I become fascinated. I could paint the head of this horse. But that would be an abstract painting. There seems to be something constant for me in painting. This man, you could say, is like a Matisse. But this one is made by a Greek, 3000 years ago, and it looks like a Japanese drawing. I don't know how old these things are— I see them with my eyes. The caption says: "The golden age of Greek painting comes to life in this bucolic scene of a herdsman leading his horses" done between 340 and 320 B.C. That's a long time ago. It's fascinating, isn't it, that this was painted 2,300 years ago and you know right away that this is a tree. I am interested in that. It seems it could only happen in the Impressionist period. But once you have Impressionist eyes, you look at those small Pompeian paintings—not the big classical ones—the little paintings with a tree and a rock, and they are almost the same as Impressionism. This is my pleasure of living—of discovering what I enjoy in paintings.

R. Discovering what other people have done, that is like what you have been doing?

De K. Yes, in discovering what other people have done, and that I can do it too. It is like an overtone of my Woman paintings, which are supposed to make me a matricide or a woman hater or a masochist and all sorts of other things. Maybe I am a bit like any other man, but I wouldn't show it off in my paintings . . .

De K. Why do I live in Springs? To begin with, my friends were already there. But also I was always fascinated with the underbrush . . . the entanglement of it. Kind of biblical. The clearing out . . . to make a place. Lee Eastman found a large house for me on Lily Pond Lane, but I know it wasn't for me. There was no underbrush—it had been taken away generations ago. I like Springs because I like people who work. Snob Hill is really nice, too, but the trees have already grown up there and it looks like a park—it makes me think of people in costume and Watteau. As I said, I had friends in Springs and visited them and that made me decide to move in.

R. Has working in the country affected your work? Everybody seems to think that it has.

De K. Enormously! I had started working here earlier, and I wanted to get back to a feeling of light in painting. Of course you don't have to have it, but every artist has it. Léger has a light. It's another kind of light, I guess; it's hard to go into that. I wanted to get in touch with nature. Not painting scenes from nature, but to get a feeling of that light that was very appealing to me, here particularly. I was always very much interested in water.

R. You were interested in light on Tenth Street, too, where the light is, of course, quite different.

De K. On Fourth Avenue I was painting in black and white a lot. Not with a chip on my shoulder about it, but I needed a lot of paint and I wanted to get free of materials. I could get a gallon of black paint and a gallon of white paint—and I could go to town . . . Then I painted the Women. It was kind of fascinating. *Woman I,* for instance, reminded me very much of my childhood, being in Holland near all that water. Nobody saw that particularly, except Joop Sanders. He started singing a little Dutch song. I said, "Why do you sing that song?" Then he said, "Well, it looks like she is sitting there." The song had to do with a brook. It was a gag and he was laughing, but he could see it. Then I said, "That's very funny, because that's kind of what I am doing." He said, "That's what I thought."

R. You mean you had the water feeling even in New York?

De K. Yes, because I was painting those women, and it came maybe by association, and I said, "It's just like she is sitting on one of those canals there in the countryside." In Rotterdam you could walk for about 20 minutes and be in the open country. Of course in that time it still looked like the Barbizon School, the idea of farms and . . .

R. But then you did *Gotham News* and those rough looking cityscapes.

De K. I started doing them later. Then slowly I got more and more involved with being here in Easthampton, and it came to me that one has different periods in painting. There was a certain time when I painted that men series . . .

R. In the 1930s?

De K. Yes, but it was all in tone. The *Glazier* was influenced by Pompeian murals. I was often with Gorky when I saw those murals, and he couldn't get over the idea of painting on a terra-cotta wall like the Pompeians were doing. I had that yellow ocher, and I painted a guy on the yellow ocher and the wall was really like the yellow ocher, a flat thing. It was never completely successful, but still it had that feeling. Then slowly I changed, and when I started to make those landscapes, I had the idea of a certain kind of light from nature. The paintings I was doing of men had another idea of light, not like on a wall . . .

I knew that if I made some kind of shapes with certain tones or values of paints mixed in paint-cans, instead of having ready-made colors from art-store tubes, that I would be stuck. But if I began arbitrarily, then I would have to find a way to come back with an answer. I don't know if you get what I mean.

R. Well, say some more about it.

De K. Arbitrarily, I made those bright flesh colors. All I needed was white and orange to give me an ideal, bizarre flat color, like the color on Bavarian dolls. I made it completely arbitrarily. Then for some reason or other—I forget the details—the idea was that I was going to make a liver color, and the liver color I picked out was the color of the liver when it was cooked and sliced as I remember it from Holland. That was a kind of grey-brownish color and to get it I had to mix about six different colors. It was an uncomfortable color to work with, and I wanted to be kind of stuck with it. It did me a lot of good because it was like a tone; something you can't lay your hands on; almost like a kind of light on a roof. It seems colorless, like a dazed kind of light. It can be a dark color or a light color. You can make it shade in between things. If you have a light of so-called bright colors, you can make them tones in between. It shapes up to the doings of it.

R. Was this color one you used in the landscapes?

De K. That's right. I even carried it to the extent that when I came here I made the color of sand—a big pot of paint that was the color of sand. As if I picked up sand and mixed it. And the grey-green grass, the beach grass, and the ocean was all kind of steely grey most of the time. When the light hits the ocean there is kind of a grey light on the water.

R. And that was related to the liver?

De K. Well, it came out. I kept forgetting about it, but I was in a state where I could start with that. I had three pots of different lights, instead of working with red, white and blue like Léger or Mondrian . . .

R. Instead of the colors you had tones!

De K. Indescribable tones, almost. I started working with them and insisted that they would give me the kind of light I wanted. One was lighting up the grass. That became that kind of green. One was lighting up the water. That became that grey. Then I got a few more colors, because someone might be there, or a rowboat, or something happening. I did very well with that. I got into painting in the atmosphere I wanted to be in. It was like the reflection of light. I reflected upon the reflections on the water, like the fishermen do. They stand there fishing. They seldom catch any fish, but they like to be by themselves for an hour. And I do that almost every day.

R. You do that?

De K. I've done it for years. As in your lecture about the "water gazers," do you remember, in the beginning of *Moby Dick?* When Ishmael felt desperate and didn't know what to do he went to Battery Place. That's what I do. There is something about being in touch with the sea that makes me feel good. That's where most of my paintings come from, even when I made them in New York.

R. How does the figure come in? How do you relate it to the light of the landscapes.

De K. I started all over again in the sense of painting those women I painted on Fourth Avenue and on Tenth Street [in 1950–55]. I went back to it here. When I made *Woman Sag Harbor* [1964] I just titled it that, because I go to Sag Harbor and I like the town and I frequently have this association. While I was painting it I said to myself, "That's really like a woman of Sag Harbor, or Montauk, where it's very open and barren." I started to make them more in tone. You can see that; in brightness of light, which makes me think I have some place for her.

R. In those tones?

De K. Yes, in those tones. There is a place there. When I say Montauk . . . Oh, I could find other places. There is no difference between the ocean beach nearby and at Montauk, but I have an association because I go there quite often. Particularly in the off-season, in the late fall, or even in the wintertime. It would be very hard for me now to paint any other place but here.

R. The light of course, is quite different in the wintertime, isn't it?

De K. It gets very pure. Blue skies and very pure light. The haze is gone. Some of my paintings have that light and develop that haze.

De K. If you have nothing to do and want to meditate and have no inspiration, it might be a good idea to make a sphere.

R. Out of what?

De K. Out of plaster. It's easy. You can add to it, you can sandpaper it. But you mustn't use calipers or any other instrument. You could never make that sphere because you would never know.

R. You mean, you wouldn't know when you had produced a perfect sphere? Or you wouldn't know how to go about making it?

De K. You can imagine yourself doing it. Let's say you make it about 12 inches, but you don't use a ruler. It is very hard to know what 12 inches is without a ruler.

R. Do you want it to be a sphere of a certain size or just round?

De K. Well, you could start to make it 12 inches. Then you turn it around and say, "Gee, I have to sandpaper this a little more." Then the next time you say, "I have to add a little more here." You keep turning it around and it will go on forever because you can only test it by eye.

R. If you didn't feel that you had to add or subtract, would you be convinced you had a perfect sphere? I mean, if you got to the point where you felt there was nothing you could do to it. Then it would be a sphere, wouldn't it?

De K. Yes, but that can never happen.

R. You don't think one would ever get that feeling?

De K. No, because a sphere is social. If they give you a ball bearing, you know it is absolutely right?

R. You would take their word for it.

De K. Most things in the world are absolutes in terms of taking someone's word for it. For example, rulers. But if you yourself made a sphere, you could never know if it was one. That fascinates me. Nobody ever will know it. It cannot be proven, so long as you avoid instruments. If I made a sphere and asked you, "Is it a perfect sphere?" you would answer, "How should I know?" I could insist that it looks like a perfect sphere. But if you looked at it, after a while you would say, "I think it's a bit flat over here." That's what fascinates me—to make something I can never be sure of, and no one else can either. I will never know, and no one else will ever know.

R. You believe that's the way art is?

De K. That's the way art is.

16

Art and Technology
A Dialogue between
Harold Rosenberg and
Benjamin Nelson

Interviewers: Robert Boyers, Dustin Wees

Q. To begin, is it any longer possible to speak of truth and beauty as in some intimate way involved in the contemporary visual arts?

Rosenberg Truth and Beauty are ideas that used to go together—everyone remembers their coupling by Keats. The 19th century broke the connection, because it considered truth to be scientific, hence unrelated to beauty. We have inherited that attitude, indeed, we have discarded the concept of beauty altogether—and along with it the idea of truth, too. Truth still has some reality in the world of art—though we prefer restrictive adjectives, such as "authentic," to describe an image of what has actually occurred. By contrast, the idea of beauty no longer means anything. It is one of those transcendental concepts which lost its reference when the world of contemplation was replaced by that of action and history.

Edited transcript of a public session conducted at Skidmore College in the fall of 1972 under the auspices of *Salmagundi*. First published in *Salmagundi*, Summer/Fall 1974.

Nelson When Keats said that truth and beauty are one and that was all he knew and needed to know, he was actually talking, not as Lionel Trilling supposed, about the nature of desire, and the beauty of the energy of desire; he was talking in Platonic terms: truth and beauty were one because they were in fact at once truth, beauty, and goodness; that is, whatever was, whatever has being was at one and the same time true, beautiful, and good. Now when Harold Rosenberg talks about the diremption of beauty, he is talking about the diremption of the old world, which did its conceiving in very different terms. Beauty was conceived as contemplative, yet it was also active, involved in existence. They have since become separate from one another, and I think, Harold, when you talk about the stress on action these days, you're of course talking about our current way of seeing the world. When you talk about truth as propositional, again you're talking about a world that has undergone many profound changes.

Rosenberg So we're talking about the world since the industrial revolution.

Q. Is this idea of truth as inevitably relating to some kind of historical necessity forcing us in the present to judge quality only in terms of what we can predict or explain, in terms of past or future? If art, in particular, seems to be involved with technology, do we find it more truthful than art which is not?

Rosenberg Well, that may be a point of view, but I don't know whose point of view it is. Those who seek an identification between art and technology apparently feel that technology has become the truth of history, that is, that in order for human civilization to advance, mankind must take on the characteristics suggested by the presence of technology. So an attempt is made to bring everything into the purview of technology, including art, philosophy, and even morals. The question is whether one wants to yield to that point of view.

It is a very persuasive point of view. The modern world is constantly being reformed by new kinds of technology, whether it has to do with instruments of war, or the moon shot, or new electronic devices. So it's safe to expect that art associated with technology will to some degree overcome its lagging character, which may now be described as the activity of a single person using old apparatus, such as a pencil and paper. My own feeling is that new technology itself begins with a pencil and paper—for example, in sketching a new plan or formula—so I don't go along with the idea that you have to have an electronic keyboard to get an idea. But that may be a reactionary prejudice.

Q. The insatiable demand for revolutionary innovation has to do with the rhythms of the cultural commodity market, as you remind us time and again in your writings. But to what degree are serious artists affected by this insatiable demand for revolutionary innovations? Is it possible to say that there are still gifted artists who resist these demands?

Rosenberg The question isn't so much whether there are demands for the new, but rather, what is really advanced, what is new? Now, I like to think of this: in the forward sweep of technological development, a great many phenomena of human life are passed over, and artists often pick up what has been passed over. I can't think of anything more simple-minded than to believe that to go along with the pace of technology, or the pace of the market, is necessarily to advance—because mankind is also concerned with many kinds of submerged feelings and motives. What do we do with these? Leave them out there behind? Much of modern art is related to recapturing experiences that have been passed over by Henry Ford. If Ford and General Motors really represented the farthest reach of man's imagination, we wouldn't need any art at all. We'd just buy a new car, and know all we needed to about ourselves. But Proust digging up his past is newer than this year's model.

Q. Newness with another kind of concern, though, with another kind of object. That is, Proust's newness was inevitably a by-product of his concern to penetrate to the levels of human experience which—

Rosenberg . . . had been passed over. I think it was Valéry who said that what others failed to see, Proust divided.

Q. You've spoken of the setting in motion of previously uncontrolled and undiscovered powers of the mind by a work of art. You say that in this sense every artist is a naif. Could you explain what you mean by this term, in what sense it is possible for an artist in a technological culture to remain a naif?

Rosenberg This is related to my reply to your previous question. The artist looks for forces within himself that have not been rationalized by society and its vocabulary. In other words, the artist tries to touch the actual phenomena of his life. This is of course very difficult to do, because to look at any phenomenon is to run into a formula for it, as in saying "this is a glass." How difficult it is to know what actually happens when you look at a glass! Cézanne, for example, realized that to look at a glass if one is a painter, is not to grasp the total object but to begin a series of glances from the glass to the canvas. How many times does a portrait painter look at you, in order to paint your portrait? Picasso had Gertrude Stein do 90 sittings. What was he doing all that time? Anybody who looks at Gertrude Stein, sees Gertrude Stein. You look and look and look, and have endless experiences, each different. In the past artists did that too, but they weren't so aware of what they were doing. They thought, "that model is sitting there, and I'm here." They applied the formula of their schools, which told them how to do the head, the shoulders, and so on. But the modern artist knows he'll grasp it; he knows perfectly well that it's impossible to draw that woman. Keep at it as long as you like, you wind up making a mess. Picasso finally made a mess that resembles the living Gertrude Stein whose portrait he was painting. From that he may have derived the idea that perhaps that's what the Africans were doing. His next step was cubism.

Q. Do you think artists are much more aware, or self-conscious, about the process of what they're about?

Rosenberg There's no doubt that modern art is a form of anxiety, and anxiety is the result of self-consciousness. It's what Picasso said about Cézanne, that he was an anxious person. He raised questions about apples, what could be worse than that?

Q. Speaking of this anxiety, there seems to me an obsession among many artists that there be no division in their work between art and life, and the obsession has produced many novels on environmental detail. Would you attribute this to developments in historical consciousness, or would you say that it has other roots, deeper roots, perhaps?

Rosenberg When artists talk about relating art to life, or making an identity between art and life, they think they're getting closer to life, usually. Nobody wants to be just an artist. They want their art to be a conduit into life. I find that it works the other way. People who want to put their lives into a work of art discover that instead of experiences they have ideas about art. In all cultures until our own there was a sense of a supernatural realm, a realm where dwelled ideas in the Platonic sense, or gods or demons—another world not like our own. Art was related to that other world. Through art the other world was pictured like this one to some degree. For example, the Renaissance discovered that figures of the past could be painted as if they were living persons. Artists painted the madonna to look like a woman and the infant saviour to look like a baby. In the early Renaissance paintings, the babies look like old men. But after a while real children began to appear. Still, up through the 18th century, there remained the idea that art belonged to another world. In a way it did—since art was made for aristocrats, for the church, for the court; it did not belong to the world of the everyday. A revolution came about in the 19th century when artists began painting portraits of men wearing black business suits. No more togas, suits of armor—not even a peasant's costume. Cataclysm. No more separation between art and life. Art discovered realism. Every movement since Impressionism has been described as a new Realism. Whether it's de Stijl, Minimalism, Surrealism, it's always "realism." Our age doesn't know anything but reality. It may not know much about that, but it doesn't know anything else. We have nothing but reality.

Nelson It occurs to me that one who wishes to explore the relationship of "art" and "reality" has to ask questions about the relations between art and all the elements that at any given time shape the structures of consciousness. From this angle it seems to me necessary to remark that before "art" came to have the ambiguous relation to reality of which Harold speaks, there had been developments in sensibility, philosophy and the sciences which had very powerful after-effects within "art." One central development was the awareness that reality could not be described so simply as one once believed.

With Kant and after Kant, there was a sense that one could never really comprehend ultimate reality totally and fully; it was in some sense noumenal, not phenomenal, and any effort to describe the phenomena fell short. All perspectives, no matter how numerous and varied, failed to give us the "thing in itself." I think this was a very fundamental part of the evolving structure of consciousness.

Now along with this, there is a sense, which I consider to be very critical, already apparent in a man like Leibniz, that there needed to be devised a sort of algorithm, an abstract language-calculus, which might give one, if not a real depiction of so-called object reality, at least some clue to all the possible forms that any reality might take. Then Hegel came along with the notion that reality is never made available to us in an instant, but is always undergoing very complex processes and always surpassing itself. At some point in the 19th century, there came the feeling that all of our efforts to describe ordinary reality would necessarily carry us beyond any conception of it as composed of objects related to one another in any space, whether Newtonian or any other.

These and other very critical issues for the whole structure of experience were posed by these changes in root images and ideas. The historian, trying to demonstrate how we constituted our world through our own arts and sciences, became a component of this new image of fact. We were after some clue to new realities that could be freshly constituted through art and technology, the assumption being that these were no longer absolutely anchored in or expressed by any particular reality that we now had before our eyes. Now that is indeed what is the case in the sciences, and the arts and sciences from a certain point of view seem to me to share in this common sensibility. If we think of asking about technology, in this wider sense, it is because, for better or worse, there is a thrust towards the supposition that in some way all of us are engaged together not simply in the delineation of sociology but in the re-creation of reality, or in fact of the new world, which is what really happens in the arts and sciences. There was a *perspectival* revolution. Rimbaud proclaims this in his *Season in Hell;* he announces that he can in fact—and will—constitute a *new* world.

Q. But do you feel that that's characteristic of the contemporary visual arts?

Nelson Yes, I do, but I am pointing to an even larger matter. I am suggesting that what we were talking about is a structure of consciousness that comes to coalesce or crystallize out of a lot of complex experiences. We end up with the supposition that it is the task of art not simply to depict the world but to constitute it. Technology is a semi-conscious way of talking about this, and of course the activities that go under the heading of technology are often very far short of the vision; but still there is the vision.

This sense of reality doesn't appear for the first time in the 19th century. There are Renaissance artists, technologists and scientists who already had such a vision. I think that the 20th century has had it to a very great degree—and only too often in distorted forms. In brief: I don't think it's the commodity market alone that wholly accounts for the constitutive vision. The Commodity market trades on the vision, but my sense is that it is the structure of consciousness which underlies the constitutive vision—and it is this which finds expression in our images, ideas, and acts. We here—all of us—are in a measure committed to our own necessary involvement in the re-creation of our worlds, believing that we can—and must—create new arrangements out of our times and spaces. Many suppose—I am now speaking of myself—that if we so choose, we can—and must—turn day into night, fuse or confound the public and private. This is all now part of a general sensibility.

Rosenberg Let's translate that into cruder terms. Gertrude Stein, in her little pamphlet about Picasso, had a rather simple formula which in a way is probably what bothers the public about modern art. That formula is this: she said that Picasso's art was not interested in "things as everybody sees them." He was interested in working out the way things are. You say the artist reconstitutes reality, the scientist reconstitutes reality, the psychoanalyst reconstitutes reality—everybody is reconstituting reality. In order to reconstitute reality they have to reconstitute the system by which they deal with reality. Picasso makes a cubist portrait, and when you look at it you can't identify a face. Later, you pick out the watch chain, the nose. It turns out that the reality of the sitter is the reality of the painter. Let's tie that into other fields, for instance, Sociology. The sociologist builds a set of categories, a system by which he reconstitutes reality. Going back to Stein's formula, his system consists of "things as everybody sees them." The sociologist's reality is a reality reconstituted by everybody. One might say that in that case reality has disappeared. Or one might say it consists of capsules of methodologies, or processes, like the reality of industry. The industrial system turns out things for the industrial system. If one asks, "What do we need it for?" the answer is, "Industry needs it." What do we need art for? Art needs nothing, so it is a combination of great insight and complete confusion. As a result, conferences are conducted in the hope of returning to reality somehow. When everyone in the world has become a member of the same profession, reality will have disappeared altogether, and there will be a Utopia of panel discussions.

Q. I've often thought about Buckminster Fuller in these terms, as one who has gathered together a great deal, who has projected the creation of an environment based on gathering together. Would you comment on that at all?

Rosenberg Buckminster Fuller is a marvelous person, and when we listen to him we are swept away, mostly by his sincerity. And he is also a good man in the 19th century sense, that is, he would like to see everybody eat and sleep. He also has the terrific advantage at the present time of there being no program for intellectuals to advocate in politics. Twenty years ago his lack of confidence in politics led many people to be antagonistic to him. But since no one now has any confidence in politics his prestige has risen enormously. I even found myself defending him in a colloquium against someone who wanted to know why Fuller wasn't interested in politics. Yet there is nonsense in the minimalism of Bucky too. For example, he likes the set-up in a space ship, where the astronauts lie in a kind of seat in which they sleep. They eat things handed to them by a mechanical arm, and the food itself is processed into capsules so they can swallow it without bothering to chew. In Bucky Fuller's opinion this was marvelous. For the first time, in his opinion, man is in control of his environment. People are put in there, and they function. It gives us a model for the future distribution of resources. I said to his assistant McHale, "Bucky seems to have forgotten about dungeons. They're controlled environments, too." Mankind is peculiar. People want to waste things, to move around, to have more room than they need, more food than they can stand. Bucky Fuller feels that the world ought to be redesigned—after all he's a designer. He wants to redesign the world so that everybody can fit into it. But it's obvious that a lot of people don't fit into the world, and even if they did they wouldn't fit in the right way. Perhaps they ought to be lying down. Fuller is another instance of specialization: he solves a problem but he doesn't solve *our* problem.

Q. Do you worry about possible political consequences of these plastic realities, these totally controlled and programmed environments that people like Fuller, and on another level Mondrian and other artists, have spoken about?

Rosenberg Don't talk about these things as if they're in the future. They already exist among us. People are always criticising high-rise slums, for example. You have a rationalized utilization of space. In New York's East side there are dozens of houses built within a small compass with a great many families living in them; they fit the module idea. But the people break the plumbing and mess up the halls, and there is crime, you have to get more policemen, the police build guardhouses and the place turns into a prison. That this would happen was argued a hundred years ago—by Dostoyevsky, for instance. Fuller is an old-fashioned rationalist with humanitarian impulses. A very good man, one can't be against him, but one can't agree with him either. One can only agree with him as long as he's an aesthete, as long as he has no power.

Q. Do you have much to do with artists who are working with reality, trying to reorganize the total environment?

Rosenberg There's one thing that bothers me: whenever I go to a technology show, nothing works. There was a big show of art technology in Brooklyn Museum a few years ago, and everything was out of order. Environmental art never seems to work, at least not for very long. But no environment ever seems to work either. Machine art is just as expressive if the machinery is out of order. Environmental artists don't mean to be romantic but that's the way it turns out.

Q. What about the developments of things like these junk machines, which deliberately break down and which deliberately suggest the irreconcilability of art and human nature on the one hand, and the technologized environment on the other?

Rosenberg You're thinking of Tinguely?

Q. Yes, that sort of thing. Is this inevitably a kind of sentimental reaction, a rearguard action of some sort?

Rosenberg That's another old idea, that an artist reflects the technological environment by showing it to be a wreck. There's a painting of Max Ernst I've always liked which is called "Airplane Garden Trap," it's a painting of an airplane, a monoplane of the early 20's, which has come down in a garden and has begun to develop roots and shoots. It is turning back into an organism. After all, the stuff that's used in technology originally came from nature in some form or other, and we have fantasies that it will all go back and turn into grass again, or milk, whatever they made it out of.

Nelson I was just wondering whether it might not be interesting to speculate about what possible alterations might be occurring. Take the sphere of miniaturization in technology, and the extent to which miniaturization of one or another sort might have a very powerful impact on threads of awareness and sensibility.

Q. Could you describe what you mean by the miniaturization?

Nelson All sorts of little machines—some small enough to be carried about in one's pocket; the systematic innovation of machines with greatly reduced components, e.g., transistors. Miniaturized and electronic machines are already in use across the world in field and factory, in production, communication, and so on. There's no doubt whatever that anything that is a tool can be put to varied uses, noble or monstrous. That is surely true about the symbolic technology we call language. So in considering technology, it's important to consider the entire range of applications and potentials. Some miniaturizations have already had very considerable influence in the spread of awareness. Many of us suppose that there are hardly any limits to what we may come to know, feel, or experience.

It seems to me that there are very few of us who are any longer controlled by the conventional images of the everyday world that we encounter. This is a critical element underlying the reach of contemporary art and science; in one way or another, contemporary art and science serve to defamiliarize the world and propel us to see the possibility for its reconstitution. Of course a heavy price is paid for the quest of

insatiability. We have to face the prospect that as we obey
the summons continually to recreate our world, we go forward into time, dispensing with more and more solace and
comfort—and for that matter anguish. We crave the world
of our imagining, the world of our experience, and the world
that we fancy to be issuing from the sciences. Absence of
limit and vertigo imply each other.

Q. There's a basic point in this which is worth examining a bit.
The defamiliarization that you talk about seems to be taking
place in the arc of our own time more at the level of abstract
idea than at the level of sensuous immediacy. Where in the
past, it would seem, the arts were capable of providing this
defamiliarization experience at a much more intimate level,
in our time, once we've passed the initial experience of exposure, say to a Duchamp or to a Tinguely junk machine, all
further exposure seems to be at the level of idea. So that
when one visits the contemporary art show one is bored by
the progression of the defamiliarizing art objects that have
been provided for us.

Nelson Well, I would simply accept that and say it is an error
to suppose that we have to expect that innovations will be
confined to the spheres hitherto designated as art. Who can
tell just where "art's future" is? But it seems to be evident
that the process to which we refer will go forward in the
sciences, it will go forward in the forms of our activity and
interactivity, it will go forward in the way we actually alter
the character of our own relationships and faces and all the
rest. It seems possible that a certain limit or temporary satia-
tion may have been reached in what has traditionally been
called art in respect to going beyond objects, but in other
spheres that wouldn't necessarily be the case. There could be
a widening of the horizons of what we need to include in the
complex of art, technology and so on. Pollutions of these
insights and inspirations by commercially-based interests or

politically-oriented technologists are surely occurring. I see this as almost inevitably the case. Another critical fact to be noted is that clashing changes in all spheres are currently erupting at different paces and rates. Yet it also appears to me evident that an awful lot of transformation to which we can point is not polluted, and is not wholly controlled by political or commercial interests.

Q. Perhaps pollution is too strong a term?

Nelson I think so, and I think it would be a mistake for us to let ourselves be dominated by the cliché that every thought of technology is a move in the direction of the restriction of human liberty. My reason for talking about miniaturization is that I want to bring attention to a certain fact that many of us are not now grasping clearly enough.

Rosenberg I want to go back to the idea that each field, each profession, each form of study has its own concept of reality. From an academic point of view we can imagine that for the next thousand years there'll be all kinds of ecumenical conferences in which attempts will be made to find common languages in which one field can talk to another. I've been to several conferences of this sort, but nothing ever happens because even within the same art nobody can talk to anybody else. A performance of John Cage or Marty Feldman has one audience, a Bach concert has a totally different one, the opera, a third. If we postulate that this separation is a normal result of the expansion of the human mind, we must assume that it will go on forever. Perhaps some day a sign language will be developed in which it will be possible for people of all kinds of different specialties to talk across their abysses. But that's not likely. When ideas are unable to persuade society, society is persuaded by people without ideas, that is, by men of action. The umpire in the chaos of the mind is doing—and this has been the character of our 20th century society. Let's not let that out of sight. The most violent and brutal events in the history of mankind have taken place within what you might call a scientific and liberal civilization. In short, the frustration of man in being unable to deal with the physical things around him, to know where they come from, what to do with them, how you obtain them, has led to behaviour in which the mind is swept aside. On the one hand we had a fellow from South Dakota who tried to reason with the electorate. On the other hand we had the image makers who kept appealing to the belief that you can trust Dick. "I like Ike"—was a brilliant philosophical idea that swept the country and has prevailed ever since. "I like Ike." "What do you mean by that?" "Never mind what I mean. I like Ike." In an automobile with some ladies, I analysed their conversation; it consisted entirely of statements such as, "I like X_____ bakery," "I don't like that kind of service." "I like apple butter." "I hate loose eggs." Absolutely senseless expressions of preference became widespread, and the notion of preference resolves the academic chaos. Each one simply goes forward in a blind manner unrestrained by any conscious principle.

Q. Would you like to comment about any particular artist that you think recognized your side of the argument?

Rosenberg Art is one of the few things left that a human being can do in which he can completely control the material he uses, whether it's an idea or physical matter. He can work out his aim with what he's able to acquire. He has a piece of paper and pencil, and that suffices. He doesn't have to get into touch with a board of directors or with a committee.

Q. Are you skeptical about the work within a committee? Working within a group of engineers or something?

Rosenberg Absolutely. I have no use for it whatsoever. The engineers are bound to crush the artist. The engineers know what they're doing; the function of the artist is not to know what he's doing. He's looking around. How can he compete with an engineer? You might have an intuition that your car ought to run without gas. Maybe some day it will. But right now you have to use the auto mechanic. The function of art to me is very clear. It's the one opportunity that human beings have within our society to make something themselves and in that way make their own selves. In industry a type is invented and then people are made to conform to the type. People become artists in our society in order to escape being made into something else.

Nelson Harold wants to protest against any and every form of the organization of the imaginative. I don't think I entirely want to go either with his diagnoses or his remedies. Great scientists also are people who, like great artists, are involved with pen and pencil operations and map new worlds. When I was talking about miniaturization earlier I was hinting that an immense enhancement of power and possibility could arise from the fact that any one of us here might have access to new ways of acquiring facilitations or communicating across all kinds of barriers and boundaries. Harold doesn't acknowledge this.

I would also take exception when Harold uses the word artist in what appears to be a kind of transcendental way, to designate someone who is not anchored in any space or time. There are all sorts of artists in different parts of the world creating all sorts of art objects, and they may possibly have some common bonds but they don't necessarily do so. Like others who can become oriented to bureaucratic directives, artists can submit to dictates.

I'd like to say just a word on behalf of a horizon that we haven't really explored, in respect to this relating of the arts and the structures of sciences and consciousness, and the forms of experience. Whether you or I like it, we must accept the fact that for all our stupidities we shall have to be related in some way in helping to do better about a world that is now desperately trying to be born, a world now being born in the midst of the most awful anguish. There is a considerable possibility that that world will never come into being, by the way. The world up to now has only been a geographical expression. There has been no world community or world order. The world has had no history, and we can't even begin to think about its having any kind of language. What can we do, what shall we do, in order to promote the hope that this planet will become increasingly coherent and that as it does so there will not be the trampling of all sorts of aspirations that have a right to a place in this world?

Q. Are you suggesting that it can be a viable function of art to constitute this coherence?

Nelson I believe that arts always work in this spirit when they face the challenges of the times—as they must. Yes, they speak most profoundly not simply of the artist's experience as a craftsman, but of the arts as a vehicle of the most decisive and central experience of the time. I also believe that we don't now necessarily know the forms in which those experiences will take shape. Clearly there have been times when the total image of reality has been transformed, as for example, through the use of linear perspective. Can anyone sum up exactly what effects have followed from that change in the angle of vision? It seems to me that modern and contemporary art at their best have been moving in the direction of yet an expanded cultural—and social—cosmos. Yes, I do believe that.

Rosenberg You like to make predictions. In contrast, my idea of a prophet is someone who sees what is going on now. There is nothing more difficult than to discover the present, and notions about what might happen that are not anchored in what's actually happening, seem to me to be pious generalizations. If you wish to talk about births of new worlds, I must ask you to indicate present phenomena out of which you expect these worlds to arise. You've done that to some degree in talking about miniaturization, and about some technological innovations. I don't accept these as having inherent in themselves any tendency towards a new world. That it may be possible for people to get more information strikes me as totally worthless. Enormous so-called informational media are functioning now, and the amount of information they bring us is negligible. In the 14th century, when people had to travel halfway across the earth to find a book, it was possible to get more information than one gets today. Do you believe you're being informed? By this time the techniques developed by newspeople have so encompassed them that the presentation of a genuine fact is as far removed from them as it is from Mondrian. And I foresee no change in information gathering, only more of the same, which means more and more stupefaction. I think everybody must agree that the American public today is ten times as stupid as it was thirty years ago.

Nelson No, although stupidity dwindles of course, stupefaction seems to be a relatively constant factor in history.

Rosenberg What an out that is. Prove it.

Nelson Moreover at any instant that we take as our vantage point, especially when everything seems to be in the balance, we consider matters from this sense of the awful preponderance in our presence of all kinds of trends we dislike. Now one of the critical elements in this picture is that in the spheres of spirit, intellect, and so on, we have also had an incredible revolution of rising expectations. Precisely because all of these new technical means lie at hand, and all of these new possibilities abound, we are unbelievably impatient at the increasing stupefaction of our time. But the truth is that "subject populations" have long been stupefied in many societies without any notable chance of entering into wider awarenesses. Nowadays individuals and groups across the globe—including ourselves—are becoming increasingly aware of worlds that were once closed to them and to us. The newest achievements of the sciences and the newest options are not coming into our ken. The parliament of man is growing. From my point of view we here tonight are part of that parliament. I don't consider it at all odd that we spend so much of our time in "palaver." Frankly, I hope that we continue to have more "palaver" rather than less. The cultural authority of the parliament grows and I think that is the way cultural irradiations occur across the world.

Unhappily we don't readily see the effects of cultural irradiation very often. It takes time for very central changes to occur, and it is because the cultural irradiation is as decisive as it is now that political forces are as regressive as they have become and so many other groups are as committed to the intensified stupefaction of their contemporaries. But they don't succeed. They may succeed in this election, or that election, but they cannot in fact succeed. For that reason I do feel it urgent that we do consider these wider problems of technology, science, art, and human values, from the point of view of how man's hopes and possible failures may be very profoundly affected for better or for worse, and I think both have to be considered together. Forgive me for making that long speech, but I just had to tell the story as I see it.

Rosenberg Amen.

Nelson Amen. I know that we agree on that.

Rosenberg By way of elaborating what Ben has been saying, I would add that art is one of the ways in which individuals can develop themselves while making connection with ideas of the past. What Ben says is true, that we tend to underestimate the effect of people developing themselves, and I think that's the fundamental idea of art, the one that continues to allow us to survive. Socially, art today has no meaning, because one man, working with his own ideas and trying to find some kind of appropriate image, is completely out of keeping with the industrial or technological outlook. My conviction is that a society, no matter how efficient and even humanitarian, in which there are no individuals is not a human society—in the 19th-century metaphor, it's an ant hill. Now, art has become more and more difficult precisely because it has become more and more difficult for individuals to exist. I don't mean to say that this activity has only to do with painting and sculpture. It has to do with all sorts of activities in which individuals are necessary. An individual in order to achieve himself has to have a training ground. He has to work in relation to a concrete situation.

Q. Do you think much about the photographic image? About what television might do, has done, to our lives?

Rosenberg As far as television is concerned I feel it's becoming more and more of a plague, and I must say it makes me sick. I've come to the conclusion that what you do before you go to sleep is extremely important. If you watch television before you go to sleep your sleep is contaminated. You're never going to have a decent idea when you wake up because your dreams will be of a low caliber. And this is very serious. I'm absolutely serious about this. If I had to start all over again I'd try being a sleep expert.

Q. But I think the new realists' works have been very much influenced by this kind of photographic dream.

Rosenberg We have all been influenced by everything.

Q. I mean the new realists. The people that specialize in caricature.

Rosenberg You mean those photo realist paintings? Those great big close-ups? One must develop a resistance to what is called popular culture. I don't see any reason for capitulating to this stuff. People have been terrified by the psychiatrists into thinking that kids brought up without comic books would turn into monsters. So they are brought up with comic books and they turn into monsters.

Q. Do you want to talk about McLuhan at all in this context?

Not comic books specifically, but the influence of the media on popular tastes?

Rosenberg McLuhan I've always found amusing. The best thing about him is his style. He doesn't like sequential prose, he's given to puns, he drops hints, if someone catches him up on one he says, "Well, let me tell you this," and changes the subject. I think he's a wonderful fellow to have around. But as a leader of thought—we must do better.

Q. Ben was talking earlier about the reconstitution of reality, and I wonder whether Harold would be willing to particularize a bit further for us what Ben has in mind. Would the artist's reconstitutions perhaps stand as models for the rest of us?

Rosenberg We've been talking, broadly, about the relation between art and technology. Now, we can certainly trace the intersection of art and technology in the Eiffel Tower in the 19th century—that was a great piece of technological art. At the same time, the history of modern art shows a continuing primitivistic impulse. There is the desire to wipe out all confusing systems of thought, and an attempt to develop direct contact with a sensual or intellectual reality. The impressionist movement is exactly that. The artist who had been overcome by technological society discovered that it was possible to go into a field or into the street and paint exactly what he saw, making use, I might add, of a certain degree of scientific sophistication, regarding color, for example. We have had that movement right on through to the present day. Paul Klee, the surrealists, other movements which are sophisticated but primitivistic in the sense that the artist says "I want to behave as if I just got here and knew nothing." Cezanne spoke of "the little sensation," and Picasso wrote a play called "Desire Caught by the Tail." Reality must be caught by the tail, it's getting past you. That's the answer of art to all structural concepts, with which we are overloaded. Catching "la petite sensation" takes work, like learning to sneak past your innate grammar in order to write a good sentence. Sentences roll out, any newspaperman knows how to write sentences. But to say something takes a lot of work, and that's the work of art, to make it new, not in the sense of a social novelty, but in the sense that it has actually happened, and put it down.

17

Recent Paintings by Philip Guston

Rosenberg Philip, you know the big problem of your painting as far as the public—well, we don't know what the public thinks—but as far as the reviewers are concerned, the big problem is their appearance of crudeness. They look as if they were all bashed up. Now do you regard that crudeness as a positive quality or as a sign of indifference to qualities which are usually tempting to be dealt with in a finished way?

Guston The only answer I can think of is that years ago, it was reversed. In the fifties when I was doing certain pink pictures—people would talk about a certain beauty, how seductive they were—it was thought they weren't crude, you see. And speaking of whether I had planned this beauty, I remember in the late fifties when the work started getting blockier and heavier John Cage, who liked the work of the early fifties, was very upset and he said, how could you leave that beautiful land? I agreed with him. I mean, it was a beau-

Edited conversation between Harold Rosenberg and Philip Guston, based on a talk given at the Boston University School for the Arts by Harold Rosenberg. Reprinted from *Boston University Journal*, vol. 22, no. 3, Fall 1974, by permission of Trustees of Boston University.

tiful land—but I left it. I don't think about beauty, anyway, I don't know what the word is. But, no, I don't plan the crudeness.

Rosenberg But is it a negative thing? Is it that you just don't care about beauty, let's put it that way, or that you want the positive? I guess you've answered the question. In other words, you're not interested in an effect, and it's not simply that you've abandoned the land of beauty.

Guston Exactly. So that when the brush finally goes where it's supposed to go, where it's destined to go, that's it. Some months ago a university here asked me to come and give a slide talk of my work saying that the faculty and students would be most interested in hearing me explain why and how I moved from abstract painting to figurative painting. I declined, and giggled to myself when I read the letter because in the late forties and early fifties I would get invitations to come and give a slide talk and explain why and how I changed from figurative painting to abstract painting. (Laughter.) So you can't win, I mean it's impossible to explain.

Rosenberg You can't win, but you can keep on talking. (Laughter.)

Guston No, you can keep on painting.

Rosenberg Let's start with the idea that you don't care anything about beauty. But I've noticed that the composition of these paintings is quite careful, even impressively well-balanced. For example, those two smaller paintings called "Smoking I" and "Smoking II" . . .

Guston Yes, two heads.

Rosenberg Are beautifully composed paintings if you got rid of those scrawly lines in the figures. The blocks of color . . .

Guston I don't believe that. For whom?

Rosenberg For the people who like beautiful paintings.

Guston Oh, I see. (Laughter.)

Rosenberg I don't think that you could say that those are care-less or self-developed compositions. Or is that just a habit you can't get rid of?

Guston Well, that could be . . . they're bound to turn into a painting.

Rosenberg That's a problem.

Guston Sure.

Rosenberg What can you do to prevent yourself from doing a good painting? (Laughter.)

Guston Well, you don't start out wanting to do a good painting.

Rosenberg Alright, let's start from there. You don't start out wanting to . . .

Guston No, God knows where you start and how you start. Every painter and writer knows there are private strategies, as Cocteau calls them, professional secrets. Sometimes in painting I keep making "mistakes," (quote "mistakes,") then I realize that what's happening is that I keep scraping out the mistake because it's not meeting certain expectations that I have developed from the last painting and then I reach a point where I follow the mistakes; I mean, the hand wants to go to the left instead of to the right. So at a certain point I become willing to follow and see where going to the left leads and it leads to all sorts of detours, fascinating detours.

Rosenberg Philip, when you say a mistake, don't you really mean something that . . .

Guston Not meeting expectations, really.

Rosenberg Or maybe meeting them. It could be both.

Guston It could be, yes, you're right.

Rosenberg It could be that it looks too much like what you thought it would be.

Guston It could be both, that's right. Sure. Well, you said something at lunch which interested me—as we were talking about critics—and you said that a certain critic of *The New York Times* likes the kind of art, how'd you say it? . . .

Rosenberg He likes art that looks like something that he knows, but not quite.

Guston Yes. (Laughter.)

Rosenberg If you want to become a critic for *The New York Times,* the formula is: you're really interested in the depiction of appearances but you know that the camera does that, so you say well, I don't want naturalistic painting, I want a painting that looks like, say, Central Park, but it doesn't quite look like it. So I know that the temperament of an artist has changed the way it looks to the ordinary visitor to Central Park. Then you know that you have a real work of art. (Laughter.)

Guston I didn't have a sense of that. I just thought it was an interesting point. You wrote down some other notes. I'm curious to know . . .

Rosenberg Well, I wrote down three things. One was the question about the crudeness, whether it's positive or negative. We have decided that point. It's negative. That is to say, it's not intended to create an effect of crudeness, it's just indifference to what is normally considered to be beauty.

Guston Now, it was in fact that same question in 1966 when we made that catalogue, that dialogue for the Jewish Museum Exhibition, somewhat the same question came up. Not in the same format but . . . and I brought up the subject towards the end of that conversation which I thought was a crucial one—I still do—is that perhaps part of my process of working is almost to pretend. But you know pretense becomes real after a while and then I'm really in it, and there is no way back. I would imagine what it would be like to paint as if there had never been any painting before. Now that's an impossibility. Naturally I'm very involved with the culture of painting; nevertheless getting involved in the painting means to divest myself continuously of what I already know and this gets you into an area of, well, you call it crudeness, but you see at that point it's not crude to me. I just want to realize a certain subject.

Rosenberg But the concept of crudeness comes up, for example, most perfectly when we talk about folk art, for example. It looks crude, but it has certain qualities—that's the way people who are pro–folk art talk about it. The idea is that somebody has a strong feeling—some farmer or house-painter or signpainter—and depicts the strong feeling but he really doesn't know how to paint, so he makes a terrific painting, only it's crude, and it's technically inept. Now you've been accused of imitating that, that your painting can be inept.

Woman in the audience This is highly sophisticated so what are you talking about? It's really obvious that it's highly so-phisticated so what's all this "crude" bullshit? It's a highly sophisticated development. It's very obvious that the whole history of painting is contained therein so what's all this business about being crude—what is it, a sack of bananas or something? (Applause.)

Rosenberg That sounded very aggressive and passionate. It sounded crude. (Laughter.) Now, in folk art there is the con-cept of crudeness but the idea is only based on the antithesis of academic painting. When you talk about getting to paint like the first person, this is of course a highly sophisticated idea, as when Mallarmé said that the poet is an Edenic per-son—one that comes out of Eden. A first person. And the concept is one of freshness, and of course that's what we like about folk art, that it's fresh.

Guston But that's what we like about some of the modern masters too: Picasso and Matisse and Leger.

Rosenberg And Cezanne, too, even. That is, the idea of freshness is one of the great values in what's called "Modern Art." So in that sense there is no art. Baudelaire in fact made a great distinction between a painting that's complete and a painting that's finished. A painting that's complete can have all kinds of empty spaces around it. A painting that's finished has been tickled to the point where it begins to look like it belongs in a museum and I think that's relevant to what you're talking about. Actually, if you feel like drawing the line thickly without modulation it's a choice that is absolutely as legitimate as any other choice.

Guston Sure, but as a choice it's not that I don't think ahead— I'm trying to imply a previous—it's that it's not even a choice, that is to say I'm at a point where I literally can't do anything else. You see there's no choice, you've been driven to that point. What was once a choice is no more a choice.

Rosenberg I think John Cage suggested that you could prevent yourself from being driven.

Guston That's what my story meant.

Rosenberg He said you could *not* be driven.

Guston That's right, that you could choose.

Rosenberg You made a mistake.

Guston I made a choice.

Rosenberg You made a choice.

Guston But I chose.

Rosenberg Of course if you can't choose you can't make a mistake.

Guston That's right.

Rosenberg You're a victim of mysterious forces.

Guston That's part of the joy.

Rosenberg You want to be a victim of mysterious forces? (Laughter.) You want to choose or not to choose?

Guston I hope to be a victim.

Rosenberg You want to be a victim?

Guston Yes, very much. In fact, it's very difficult to become one; you really have to prepare for that state. Oh, yes. (Laughter.) Were you asking me that thinking I would say no? You know I would say yes.

Rosenberg No, well, I thought you'd also put something else in.

Guston Oh, I see. Any victim that decides to . . .

Rosenberg It's really sublime to think that all you can be is the victim of a sublime executioner. You want to be executed by something.

Guston I don't want to be . . . executed—just so I can continue, being a victim.

Rosenberg We discussed the fact that each time you wanted to be as if you were starting from scratch, like the first man.

Guston That's what I meant, yes.

Rosenberg The Edenic poet. But then how come your paintings look very much alike? You want to start all over again each time as if you were just born and it so happened each time that Guston was born he looked like a Guston who just died! (Laughter.)

Guston I don't think so; to be changed each time may be a necessary illusion that we permit ourselves.

Rosenberg I know every time I write something I feel as if I've gotten into new ground, at least I find myself as completely confused by it as the first piece I ever wrote. And when I'm finished with it it sounds just like the last piece I wrote. I don't think it's an illusion, I think it's a condition.

Guston What I mean by this illusion is that when you are in the work you think you're making a leap, but in truth you may be only, say, an inch worm.

Rosenberg If you're lucky!

Guston If you're lucky. And we really move in time very slowly. Very slowly, although in the heat of it we have illusions . . . which comes from the fact that one picture evolves from the one before. A chain. Otherwise I'd be like someone throwing out a lasso. I don't throw out a rope for a hundred yards and follow it.

Rosenberg Why not?

Guston I seem to be more conservative.

Rosenberg One thing at a time.

Guston It could be a question of personality. At times when I have gone way out, I find I need to come back for that inch.

Rosenberg There was a mystical rabbi who said that a saint was like a thief. He's always active in the middle of the night and he risks his life for small gain.

Guston When a show is put up, when it gets out of the studio, and I see the work on the walls, I have an uncanny feeling that somebody, I don't know who, is writing the plot here, somebody is plotting this, you know.

Rosenberg You mean it was inevitable that you should have done that? You are caught in—what shall we say?—a destiny.

Guston Well, that's making it sound very . . .

Rosenberg Well, a plot is a destiny. I mean somebody has it written in his brain.

Guston Written, yes.

Rosenberg Well, that's what you meant before when you said you couldn't have done anything else.

Guston That's right. I don't have a feeling when I'm painting that I'm just plugging in the holes.

Rosenberg But that's what you mean by the mistakes, too. That it's just a plot.

Guston But the real subject would include the paintings, the images I've destroyed. The manuscripts you've destroyed. It would be fascinating to talk about what one destroys—it fascinates me. Destroying my images. I remember them just as well, sometimes more, than what stays. They no longer exist, but they exist in my mind. So I remember them, they're as concrete as the pictures that remain.

Rosenberg The pictures that remain are related to one another. But would you say that about the ones you've destroyed? You could say that if you had a record of those non-paintings that they could have a similar relation to one another.

Guston I can be very specific. Some of the things I'm painting now, some of the images I'm painting now, I painted and destroyed ten, fifteen years ago, yes. Absolutely. I don't have a photographic record but I just know that that is true. So it's a question of time—being ready, you might say, to accept.

Rosenberg Well, that's not so uncommon. I have for example a painting, an ink drawing by de Kooning which he did in 1948 and which he gave me at the time. Then about seven or eight years later there began to appear some spots . . .

Guston What were the spots?

Rosenberg The drawing was done on a thin show cardboard with ruled squares. The spots began to appear and somebody thought that maybe the paper backing had oil on it. Anyway, we took the frame off; there was an oil painting on the back of the board which de Kooning had obviously discarded. It looked like work he did fifteen or twenty years later, though different, too, of course.

Guston One is never finished with anything.

Rosenberg No, it circles back.

Guston Yes, in fact, some of the new paintings are close to the work of the nineteen thirties. One is never through with that.

Rosenberg Let me ask you this: Do you feel that working now, there is a difference in the degree of freedom of spontaneity of those paintings of yours in the fifties?

Guston Yes.

Rosenberg Very spontaneous? A fresh quality? These paintings look more composed, have preconceived themes.

Guston Well, some of them are . . .

Rosenberg Executed. On the other hand I don't think they're

... necessarily less free and spontaneous. What do you think?

Guston Well, as you know in the early fifties I became very involved in discovering painting as you paint, and this was pretty constant with me over the years. Now in the last six to eight years of painting, I felt like reversing the process, I made drawings for weeks before I started to paint. Why? Well, I felt like it for one thing; I wanted to see if I could do it.

Rosenberg You mean if you could work out a composition completely ...

Guston No, the idea, rather, well, it wasn't so much the composition, but the forms, the subject-content of it, the images. I saw the picture in my mind or in drawings that I made before I painted and the painting usually went very fast with very few changes. It was fascinating to me to do that. But not exclusively so, either. I think that what I've done, I hope, is widen my range. I still will start paintings without drawings and very little preconception. I mean, I know I'm going to have a man lying in bed—I know I'm not going to have three elephants walking there. I know roughly what I'm going to do but I'll start and just plunge in and paint and keep changing areas that need changes. So I do both. It's satisfying to me to know that I can have this range, to not be so exclusively ...

Rosenberg Spontaneous?

Guston Spontaneous. But that's an esoteric obstacle for me. I don't know what spontaneity means, whether it really exists.

Rosenberg Apparently Jackson Pollock felt that the fact that he did not make sketches was a central aspect of his work. That it came into being in the course of trying to paint. You don't think of it that way?

Guston No, it's too simplified a version of the whole thing. I mean I think that Pollock was essential, that he did what he did—every painter does what he does, invents his own technique, so to speak, or method—what he claimed may be his rationalization of it. It may also indicate his own personal struggle, anti-Renaissance. In a sense, Jack came out of late Renaissance painting. I think his early paintings are descendants of El Greco. To speak of spontaneity is too simplified a version. When you study Renaissance painting you can find anything you want to find: you find blotches and spontaneity and spots, especially in drawings, and you can find preconception and years of preparation for a single canvas.

Woman in the audience You've been talking about crudeness. What do you mean by that?

Rosenberg Well, look at the show afterwards. That's the best reply, because you'll see that the contours and the way it's painted show no great interest in a finished or elegant canvas. What's the opposite of crude?

Audience Refinement.

Rosenberg Alright. These paintings are not very refined.

Woman in the audience Are you talking about the paintings or are you talking about the subject?

Rosenberg I'm talking about the handling, that is, the form, the way details are treated. For example, there are plates of French fried potatoes that really don't look like a good . . .

Guston Meal.

Rosenberg Well, a good ad. I mean you'll never sell any French fries. They wouldn't give you an appetite for French fried potatoes. They might give you an appetite for paintings.

Woman in the audience Are you trying to say that what you mean by crudeness is vitality, are you trying to say the paintings have vitality, is that what you're talking about?

Rosenberg What's vitality?

Woman in the audience I'm trying to say, Do the paintings have vitality?

Rosenberg Crudeness is not a synonym for vitality.

Rosenberg (to Guston) I think it would be nice if you talked about some of the imagery in your paintings, like pairs of shoes, French fried potatoes, light bulbs.

Guston Well, there isn't really a hell of a lot to say about that.

Rosenberg You have recumbent men. I didn't notice any ladies. Also soles of shoes. I want to talk about those images. Why are they recurrent?

Guston That's a tough one. I don't know. What would you say about that?

Rosenberg Are they unconscious? Of course you did have some of them a long time ago, but also in your last show.

Guston Oh, yes.

Rosenberg You must have some feelings about the use of those light bulbs and . . .

Guston I'm painting, I'm using tangible objects, obviously.

Rosenberg But why those?

Guston Why those? You mean why not, why don't I . . .

Rosenberg I mean you could have a horse instead of an automobile.

Guston No.

Rosenberg As a matter of fact in this show you have no automobiles. In the last show you had a lot of automobiles; automobiles are going, aren't they?

Guston Well, the figures are inside, not riding around. They're in bed.

Rosenberg No, but you have some landscapes.

Guston I don't know. I think what I can say is that six or seven years ago I began painting single objects that were around me. I read, so I painted books, lots of books. I must have painted almost a hundred paintings of books. It's such a simple object, you know—a book, an open book, a couple of books, one book on top of another book—it's what's around you, on the kitchen table, there's a lamp. I don't have that kind of light bulb, but somehow that light bulb recalls something to me. There's something about a naked light bulb, why I don't know. If I talk too much about it I'll stop using it.

Rosenberg You want to continue using it?

Guston No, I don't know whether I want to continue using it. I don't know what I'll do, but I do know that I enjoy the idea of unexotic objects, I like banal simple objects—tangible, touchable. I'm doing a painting and my shoes are on the floor. Man is upright, he walks, he needs shoes—what else do you paint?—I don't paint stripes. (Laughter.) But I don't think shoes are better than stripes.

Announcer I want to take a few questions. A few questions before we break.

Man in the audience I'd like to speak to Mr. Guston. You had a painting exhibition at the school and it was mostly Ku Klux Klansmen. For the past few years you've been working mostly with Ku Klux Klansmen. I notice that in the paintings here you're working with a new image of the sleeping figure. I was just wondering what you foresee about this image as an image. Are you going to explore it as you did the Klansmen or . . .

Guston Yes, they're really very recent, these recumbent figures. Actually, I think of them as the painter in bed. One of them, the one with the French fries, is called "Painting, Smoking, Eating" . . . paint cans on his chest, imagining a painting above him. Thinking now about them, they are mostly about painting, they're paintings about the painter. In the paintings of 1968–70, I also made the hoods into painters. There were pictures where the hoods became artists. My favorite group, the ones I keep, that I find I take out and look at, enjoy the most, are where they are painters. I took one down the other day to show to someone who hadn't seen the work, and I found the first picture I pulled out was where the hooded figure is painting another hood. I also had them discussing art, becoming art critics; I had one looking at an abstract painting.

Rosenberg Are there any where you think of a left political show?

Guston No, I'm not that interested in a direct political interpretation.

Rosenberg But you are interested in politics.

Guston Sure. Everybody's interested in politics.

Rosenberg In the last show, I mean the political experience. I remember you talked about it a lot.

Guston Yes, I was very influenced but what was happening—when the hoods were doing things, beating people there, tying up bodies, patroling, driving around cities. But now I think they're thinking about it. Now they're more meditative about the whole thing. Reflective.

Rosenberg That's why they're lying down.

Guston That's a good statement of reflection, yes.

Rosenberg They're not riding around in an automobile.

Guston It'd be silly to have them . . . I would no more put them in a car now . . . There would be no reason.

Rosenberg So you think times have gotten more peaceful.

Guston Oh no, peaceful, no.

Rosenberg Well, the people aren't running around piling up bodies.

Guston No, well, I was never concerned about illustrating it anyway. I wanted to go deeper into meanings and overtones. Now they're thinking about it all. It's more inside; I have to dig for the images that come out.

18

On Cave Art, Church Art, Ethnic Art, and Art

Rosenberg In regard to the videotape machine, I might point out that every time someone invents a new technological marvel, especially one that takes pictures, it is argued that it marks the end of the line for painting. This has been going on at least since the invention of the camera, and the rate of acceleration of inventions for the production of visual images keeps growing.

In every decade there are artists who refuse to have anything more to do with such primitive materials as canvas, paints, paper, crayons, etc. It is reasonable to expect that mechanisms for picturing things will become more and more wonderful. So you will continue to have to answer the question, why paint, when you can buy a piece of equipment that will produce more remarkable and accurate pictures than can be done by hand?

In a recently published book on the relation between

In 1974 Harold Rosenberg led a discussion at the New York Studio School and invited Philip Guston to join him. The videotape machine that was to have recorded the session failed to work and Mr. Rosenberg began his comments with a reference to technology. This edited version of the discussion was first published in *Art News*, December 1974. © 1974 by ARTnews, 5 West 37th Street, New York, N.Y. 10018.

painting and photography, the work of cameramen of the mid-19th century proved to be far more interesting and expressive than that of portrait painters. A few painters, such as Delacroix and Eakins, used photographs to good advantage, but most were inferior to Brady and other photographers. That produced a serious problem for painting, and one of the answers has been, "Let's forget it. Let's leave catching images in nature to machines, and devote painting to other ends." This has been an argument for avant-garde art. Giacometti, for instance, told me it took him a long time to realize that what he saw in the movies looked quite different from things as they appeared on the street. One day he went to the movies four times, and each time he came out he looked around and verified that he was in a different world. In the end he decided that this proved that the Surrealists were wrong when they argued that the camera had taken over reality, and that the artist need no longer waste his time with the common appearances of things—let him, instead, add a mythical ingredient to reality, in order to make it less boring. Having denied that the camera captured reality, Giacometti concluded that the artist could be boring, but not reality. He turned the tables on Breton by raising the specter of the boring artist as responsible for the boredom of the real world, in place of the artist as the savior from boredom.

Woman I'm going to ask a very broad question. I often think about the origin of painting, and I wonder about the cave paintings and their history.

Guston There are conflicts among anthropologists as to why 25,000 years ago men made images of animals and hunting scenes in caves and elsewhere. The original idea was that the artist was celebrating the hunt or invoking the hunt. In the last 20 years another school of thought has tried to disprove this. Their idea is that the paintings were done for pleasure, and that those who drew the animals were neurotics who satisfied themselves in this way. While the others were chomping on the bones of the beasts they had hunted, the artist burned bones to produce charcoal. There is no way of proving why he did it. Barney Newman was of the opinion that function had nothing to do with it. But why can't it be pleasure as well as function?

Rosenberg I tend to lean toward the magic school. Of course, one might ask, where did those people get the idea that they could hypnotize a bison by drawing a picture of him in a cave? Yet there are plenty of arguments in favor of the magical view: hex pictures, for example, and other means for transfixing an enemy or some divine power. Once you can make them appear where you are, you can force them to do things. Malevich, on the other hand, argued that what counted in icon paintings was esthetics. A medieval Russian, he pointed out, painted the hair on God's beard in exactly the same way as the hair on the devil's tail. For Malevich this was an argument in favor of abstract art. Artists never cared about subject matter, he contended, but only about how things are painted.

Man In what degree is religious art actually religious and in what degree esthetic? How do these qualities come together?

Rosenberg Most crucifixion paintings convey no religious feeling. They are merely images to be placed in cathedrals. An artist with genuine religious feeling in his painting is very rare, even in the early Renaissance. Usually he is engaged in making pictures that society wants to use. While the artist is enjoying himself with ideas or feelings about forms, the public looks at the picture as if it were a representation of some kind of transcendental reality.

Man But what of the artist who paints from an esthetic viewpoint as well as from a religious viewpoint—and in whose work do the two come together?

Rosenberg I was struck by Philip Guston's use of the word "neurotic" for the first person who thought of making a work of art. He might also have been a cripple. The artist couldn't join in the hunt himself, so he figured that he could capture the beast right there in the cave where he was sitting. It might have been cold in the cave, but he was carried away by the hunt and he caught the beast on the wall of the cave. It is said that artists were shamans, neither male nor female, but with the power to invoke spirits. In the magical state there is not much difference between an actual creature running through the woods and one painted on the wall. That identity between reality and the picture is still a very potent factor in art. We are said to live in a secular society, but actually the modern world is more subject to superstition than the caves themselves. We are ridden by mystifications on every level—in our mental operations, in our mode of production, our politics—there are hallucinations everywhere. Clever politicians now count on this. We have media of hallucination, organized and functioning 24 hours a day. An artist who understands this very deeply is Saul Steinberg; he knows that whatever one looks at may be a copy of something else and that a copy may turn out to be the reality. Finally, one becomes satisfied with something called style— and when reality becomes a matter of style, people have lost touch with everything.

One thing that has been fairly well established in recent years about so-called primitive or jungle art is that it was made by professionals. Whether or not they were professional wizards or priests, they were professional painters and sculptors and they worked in a tradition that indicated which powers were secreted in their figures and signs.

For example, the wearing of masks in dances before a battle, or on certain festival occasions, transforms the members of the tribe into something that they are not ordinarily. This is consistent with Philip's idea that art was invented by neurotics, since its fundamental aim was to change the tribe into a psychotic unit carried away by the same ecstasy.

Guston Relevant to what we have been talking about, but also extending it somewhat, I have been struck by the inclusion of so-called "primitive" art in art museums and its removal from the ethnological museums. I once said to Robert Goldwater, who was then head of the Museum of Primitive Art, that when I went to his museum and looked at African fetishes I didn't know what they were about. If I go to the Metropolitan Museum and see Christ on the cross by Tintoretto, I know what it's about. I was struck by the fact that this century has been taking works away from the ethnological museums. African art, Egyptian art, were originally in an ethnological museum, and putting them into an art museum seems to me very significant because it means that we don't have to know what we are looking at. Goldwater said, "You look at beautiful forms." I said, "What do you mean, beautiful forms? I don't want to look at beautiful forms. I want to know what the work means." I think this is a deep argument.

Rosenberg It certainly is.

Guston If we don't know what modern art is about, we might as well put it in an ethnological museum.

Rosenberg We are talking about perhaps 10 different things. One is that Duchamp, by taking ready-mades and putting them in an art museum, was suggesting that we adopt the perspective of archeologists of 200 years from now, who will say, "They made those porcelain urinals in the 20th century." From Duchamp's point of view, everything created or produced in a given society is of equal interest to archeological investigation. There are messages in Greek pots or kraters, why not in spades or urinals? But your studious interest means that you are estranged from them. It is their strangeness that causes them to be put into museums.

The process also works the other way. Take some screw-drivers and cordial glasses from a Woolworth counter and put them in a museum and they become estranged from you. As archeological artifacts they have departed from our time and reappear as leftovers. The present has been changed into ancient history. Exhibiting the urinal in an art museum destroyed the distinction between art and archeology—it was Duchamp's supreme stroke of anti-art. By a futuristic tour de force he turned the present into the past, and thus destroyed the authority of the museum. One could go into a hardware store and *look back*. One could even look back at the latest inventions. What a perspective! The whole world enters the museum as fast as it comes into being. No wonder Duchamp's face took on the look of a profile on an ancient coin.

Some years ago I was going through the Museum of Archeology in Mexico City with the sculptor David Hare, and he became excited about a piece of a cornice from an old temple. "What do you see in it?" I asked. "It's a terrific piece of Cubist sculpture," he replied. I said, "What has Cubism got to do with it? Do we now turn pre-Columbian architects into Cubist sculptors?" But David was right, we have made Cubists out of them. No matter how faithfully we study the past, it turns out to be a projection of our tastes and values. Our tastes loot the past for the 20th century as our museums loot it for North America. This is our culture—to take for our own the forms of all peoples, all times and all places, and to disregard the feelings and ideas of those peoples, times and places.

Another way of putting it is that modern culture consists of two things, grave robbery and esthetics. Our appetite turns all art into modern art. It has taken almost two centuries but at last the past has been consumed. Yet people still ask, "Where are the vanguards?" Then we worry, can't we say something of our own? How do we know who we are when we've gotten through looting the pre-Columbians? Our art-historical esthetes are the deadly enemies of every living artist. Honest people find themselves speaking of the difficulties of contemporary art. To have an idea of one's own, one is forced to fight it out with the history of forms that we have developed into a pattern that allows us to catalogue our treasures from the cave paintings to those artifacts of Duchamp. We're set to swallow them all. We are going to put them all into our culture. Then it turns out that our culture consists of nothing else but esthetics, that is to say, of a mode of appreciation that does away with the past as past and turns all art into modern art.

When I was young I wrote a poem that told of returning zebras to the jungle. I have the feeling that it would be a good thing for the Metropolitan Museum to send all its collections back to where they came from. The pretense of scholarship has been exploded, and as an entertainment medium we can manage with less expensive materials. If necessary they can dig holes outside of Rome or in Peru and bury their loot again. Why do we need to accumulate those old pots?

Guston Let's get rid of modern paintings too.

Rosenberg No, we won't get rid of the paintings. Only those based on museological esthetics. It's part of the absurdity of the museum situation that the museum today dominates the creation of new art.

Guston Again, I was simply remarking on the fascinating phenomenon of the gradual absorption of what was originally the ethnological museum into the art museum. Right now the basements of the nature museums are filled with Eskimo art.

Rosenberg Yes, it looks as if Eskimo art is the next thing that will fill art museum galleries.

Guston That's a phenomenon which our lifetime has been witness to. I think it has a bearing on modern expression.

Rosenberg And on modern society. It is part of the war among the professions to take over new territory. The art historians move in on the anthropologists and ethnologists and take their artifacts away from them by making them popular as art. Then *they* produce the catalogues instead of the archeologists or ethnologists by telling how beautiful the objects are, with reference to examples from Western art.

Guston A fellow did that recently with American Indian objects.

Woman Why are these things called secular art, which they weren't when they were made?

Rosenberg The dynamics of our society lies in the ambition of each profession to become as powerful and pervasive as it can. In the universities the humanities saw themselves suppressed by the social sciences, so they took on the coloration of science in order to recoup their losses through talking about American Indian artifacts as works of art. Art departments were enabled to compete with ethnology without needing to begin a study of Indians. Esthetics has become popular in philosophy in the way logic used to be. In my opinion, esthetics is becoming a major menace to thought in America today.

Guston Why is this happening?

Rosenberg It is the effect of inundating people with images through the mass media. One used to talk of an art public. Today there is no longer a public, only the mass audience. A public makes up its mind about the value of what it sees. An audience either responds or fails to respond. It likes or it does not like, and it gives its verdict by staying or going, that is, by keeping the image or switching it off. The audience, in sum, responds to art by consuming it; its criteria are the same as those it applies in the supermarket.

On the other hand, the contemporary consumer is an expert on low-grade goods, for example, TV shows, so the audience is an audience of critics on a huge scale. He knew that

Nixon was a better daytime-show performer than McGovern, and this esthetic conclusion was enough to give Nixon his rating.

An earlier example was "I like Ike." In the past there were political campaigns on behalf of generals as heroes, strong men. They had done something, they were dependable. All this is swept away in "I like Ike," the esthetic self-assertion of the common man. I respond to Eisenhower, never mind that Stevenson is intelligent, practical, with needed ideals. To hell with him, he's not my style. So politics in America is determined by esthetic preferences—and such an esthetic! If you have a vulgar style, you are a member of the silent majority, and you are going to have representation. At the Watergate hearings the White House witnesses tended to look alike, fauna of the executive suites. The New York cop, Ulascewicz, stuck out like a polar bear.

The same thing appears in art criticism. Here is the aggressive emptiness of the formalist creed that cuts every work down to the same size. Art, it says, has nothing to do with psychology, with the individual, with society. It's a question of linking this work with that one, and if the critic is "serious" he analyzes how a corner of a painting is handled.

One who says, I want to paint a dog or a sphinx, is asked, what have animals to do with art? A good question to have asked in 1870. Now we know that art is a means to reality. Reality is the issue of the contemporary world and therefore of art today. All the clichés of avant-gardism have come to roost in the idea that art can dispense with reality. Do you base art on art or do you base it on experience?

Guston I think there is another alternative. A painter like Ryder or a poet like Melville is neither a formalist nor a realist. Some artists have the capacity for imaginative projection.

Rosenberg Of course reality is not simply a copying of appearances. There is also psychological reality. Action painting is a realistic movement, though in it there are no pictures of things. It is the reality of the artist at the moment that he is painting. This is the most concentrated reality one can think of. But the question arises, are you talking about somebody's experience or about a "contribution" to art? This problem has been especially acute in this country, because after all we didn't invent art. American abstract artists today often behave as if art began with Jackson Pollock. They have given art a new address, and have set it up in business. Artists in America don't have to bother about Cézanne; his problems have been solved. Or at least superseded. We have our own tradition now. All the ideas, visions, sentiment in the art of the past 100 years have wound up in something called the New York School!

Guston In your last book you reproduced a painting that fascinates me. It's called *The Riddle of the Sphinx,* a pilgrim in the desert with his ear to a gigantic monument. You know there was a strong strain in American art and poetry—Melville, Poe—that went in a direction that wasn't that of Eakins' road. Let's say it was the road of Ryder, extremely romantic. These people I am talking about expressed a kind of longing for something else.

Rosenberg I see the artist as someone who suspects that in order to get to reality he has to work his way through layers of forms imbedded in his brain. This is the way he arrives at . . .

Guston The enigma.

Rosenberg At reality. Reality is the unattainable. Take *Moby Dick*. A man sets out to give an account of an incident he read about in a newspaper: the sinking of a ship by a huge whale which was said to be white. Oddly, he starts his tale by telling the reader that he himself was in a bad state. My name is Ishmael. I hung around in the Battery, where lots of men stand looking out over the water. If they didn't dream of immense distances, they would start hitting each other on the head. So Ishmael says, I am one of those water-gazers. Since mere looking did not suffice to quiet me, I decided to ship out on a whaler.

So the story begins. Then Melville turns to literature to tell the reader about whales. The consults encyclopedias and scientific treatises and myths and folklore. He goes on and on. How many different species of whales are there? What size are they? What are they hunted for? What are their mating habits? Where do pregnant females go? What is the structure of a whale? How is he built? Ishmael climbs down into a dead whale and sees that there are all sorts of rooms there. He starts by running away from society in order to avoid violence and he winds up by making a scientific investigation of Cetacea.

This peculiar mixture of objective data with Shakespearian interludes, as when Starbuck walks the deck, speaking mock-Elizabethan phrases, is the American cultural situation. This is reality. I think everybody is doing something like this all the time. They are walking up and down making emotional speeches in false rhetoric while trying to get away from people whom they would otherwise have to brain with a mallet. Melville wants to collect all the data in order to give material substance to their plight. It's all in his book. When you read it you ask, what sort of book is this? And the first reaction is, that's not a book at all.

Many years ago I gave a course on Melville at the New School and a student got up and said, "Your course is different from one I took on Melville last term." "What's different about it?" I asked. "Well, first of all," he said, "you start out with the fact that Melville lived on Fourth Avenue and 11th Street." "I thought that important," I replied, "especially since we are New Yorkers too, and in view of Ishmael's idea of the Battery. But what about your other teacher?" The student said: "He refused to talk about *Moby Dick* at all. Melville to him was *Billy Budd*. The hanging of Billy Budd, was, he said, 'the Crucifixion symbol.' When I insisted on knowing about *Moby Dick* he answered, 'I am not interested in fish.'"

Eakins is a very good artist, I think, though limited by the fact that he is only concerned with hard reality. Look at an object with sufficient intensity, he believes, and you will get to its essence. But who wants to get to an object? True, one wants to get hold of something, especially in America. I can understand that. But to seize reality one must be more like that other kind of nut, Ryder—or Melville or Poe. In other words, art is not about things but about culture, and culture moves from within outwards.

Guston I should like to bring up a question that's been on my mind lately. One of the curses in what's happened in New York in the past 20 years is the internationalization of art. By that I mean that more and more, not only in paintings, but in literature and music too—and I am not talking about regionalism or anything like that, although that doesn't scare me, either—but that the more I go to Europe and see the paintings of the past it strikes me that the place, and the time, and the smell, the flavor, are all essential qualities of a work of art. It's all genre painting. Even Cubism is a kind of genre painting, in a way.

What I am getting at is that I find more and more that what I like is what has a feeling of poetry and is the expression which is of a time and place and region. It is saturated with particularity. Yet, in the last 20 years, when you open an art magazine, some guy in Capetown is painting exactly like some guy in Haifa or Soho. There is no difference. What do you think about that?

Rosenberg At one of the Bienals in São Paulo about 15 years ago I found an Arab who painted Pollocks. Instead of throwing paint he used a compass to mark arcs in all directions. I decided he wanted to keep his connection with Averroes, the great Arab mathematician. Yet he wanted to look like Pollock.

Philip Guston confronts you with the basic questions about art today, which I might have been afraid to raise. Philip, you are flooding the students with basics. Internationalism is a tremendous question.

Hofmann said about 10 years ago, "Art has become international, perhaps too much so." What does this mean? Most of the artists who look the same in Capetown, or in Chile, or Jordan, are working from reproductions. That there are up-to-date illustrated art magazines says a great deal about art today. Art in our century circulates primarily through reproductions. I am convinced that Arab I have been talking about never saw a Pollock. But he saw the art magazines. The art magazines envisage the art of the whole world as existing on a single level. There is something hopeful about this: that the whole world shall have a single language. On the other hand it is destructive, as is any practice of today's universal bureaucracy. Ultimately, when we find location missing, we are talking about bureaucratic art.

Guston Isn't there a loss?

Rosenberg Of course, there is a loss. Bureaucracy makes art abstract, in the most derogatory sense of the term. There are no people, no landscapes, no subjects . . .

Guston That's Esperanto.

Rosenberg Yes, an international lingo. Therefore a lingo without inner life. Esperanto is a language that lacks the accretions of a language that has been used by people. It's a conceptual language disseminated by international bureaucracies. Such internationalists can conceive an avant-gardist negation of art to a degree that no artist could ever dream of, because the artist knows what it takes to do something. But a genuine avant-gardist museum director or critic, such as that fellow who put on the last Documenta in Germany . . .

Guston I was going to ask about that. Have you noticed that these museum directors always come through the other side?

Rosenberg The Documenta show was subtitled "Today's Imagery." It was a mixture of everything—advertising posters, religious kitsch, files filled with esthetic documents, simulated caves and battlefields—there was room in it for anything visible. Not art, but "today's imagery." What has art got to do with that? What is art, Philip? It is a form of inhibition, isn't it? Not every image.

Guston Right. We made a big circle there.

Rosenberg You have to have the idea that you want to draw something . . .

Guston It's a big circle that you made and you have finally come to what is left. All that's left is an itch. That is, you are forced, or want or need to make a mark. That's what you are left with now.

Rosenberg Why would you want to make a mark? Why would you have an itch to make a mark?

Woman I like the idea that it's an inhibition.

Rosenberg It's not wanting to be dissolute. Let's connect it, Philip. You brought up the fact that anthropology has now entered art museums. Past cultures are being incorporated into one total situation. Obviously, then, existing societies are also to be incorporated into one situation—internationalism on a four-dimensional basis.

Guston Could you go back to the reasons why painters should resist it?

Rosenberg You would not resist the expansion of culture. What you resist is the expansion of meaninglessness, since all of these forms can be incorporated into senseless formulas. But wouldn't it be a better perspective to see culture in this century as a culture involved with the cultures of all regions, all peoples, all periods? There are great modern artists who represent this; Picasso, for example, Joyce. These artists have attempted a historical recasting of art, and within this enormous context have managed to affirm their own identities. Isn't this a much better approach than to resist internationalism and try to become regional again?

19

All about Everything

Howard Conant What is your role as an art critic, as you see it?

Harold Rosenberg It is very rare that a critic enlightens anybody but himself. My own activity is a kind of reflection on art and the situation of art—in this sense, it is an extension of what artists keep talking about among themselves. In the studio there is an environment of ideas that surrounds the activity of the artist. As I see it, the critic is valuable insofar as he enriches the environment of ideas in which artists work. Ultimately, this intellectual environment is also that of people who look at artworks and appreciate them. I repeat— the major function of the critic is to improve the intellectual environment in which the creation of art takes place. This is quite different from the function of reviewers, which is to get around to as many shows as they can and to make judgments as to how good or bad the work is. To me, this is a highly

Edited interview based on a question-and-answer session in 1975 at New York University's series of art-critics-in-residence seminars/lectures. Questions were put to Harold Rosenberg by Howard Conant, chairman of the Department of Art and Art Education, New York University, and by the audience. First published in *Craft Horizons,* August 1975.

specialized task, one that I regard, in fact, as fundamentally impossible. I don't know how anyone can go from one gallery to another, look at an artist's work, and say "Give him a B+, or a C, or this guy has flunked." How does the reviewer know what the work is worth? Reviewing is an activity forced on people who need a job. Apparently, the newspapers want it done. The formula is very simple. One goes to galleries, recognizes the art-historical context of the works, then writes a short synopsis of Surrealism, Minimalism, or whatever it is, and points out that this example of this particular type of work is not as good as somebody else's work in the same mode. This is sufficient to make one a full-fledged reviewer, say for the *New York Times*.

HC Since the late '60s, with the student rebellions and the various liberations that took place, one of the nice things that we who teach at universities have noticed is that students feel much more free to ask almost any question. They are not nearly as afraid of authority figures as they once were, and they treat us, in some ways at least, as peers. The next question may sound a bit insulting.

HR Do you mean a peer is somebody you can insult?

HC I guess that frank exchanges are part of it. Here is the question: Do you consider yourself a parasite who earns his living and has made his reputation by hustling, or otherwise dealing with works of art created by persons other than yourself?

HR Before I get to that question of being a parasite, which incidentally I do not regard myself as being, let me talk about this candid interchange which Dr. Conant discovers enthusiastically to have come into existence. I don't believe it's as prevalent as he thinks, especially in public forums. Had it really become a natural thing, he would not have had to assemble his questions in advance. He could simply start the discussion and call for questions and some insolent compatriot would jump up and pose one direct from the shoulder. In regard to feeling free, it's one thing to put a question on paper and have somebody else read it, another thing to get up and ask it of the speaker yourself. I think the question I have just been asked is a valid one, but I don't regard it as an act of courage to have asked it in this way—and I will prove my point by challenging the person who gave the question to Dr. Conant to get up and ask it himself, or herself, if that person is here. If that person is not here, I don't know why not. As to the question, it's a valid question, except for the use of the word "parasite." In a sense we are all parasites, particularly artists. A parasite is a creature who lives on other creatures and, of course, this is true of all of us. Another word in the question which is derogatory is the word "hustling." Hustling has many different meanings associated with different professions. The association of hustling with art critics is something I don't fundamentally object to. What I can't associate myself with is the suggestion of speed in it. That is, a hustler is one who is very active. I am too lazy and always have been to do much hustling in any capacity.

To return to what I do. The question is: "Do you consider yourself a parasite who earns his living and has made his reputation by hustling, or otherwise dealing with works of art created by persons other than yourself?" Now, I can't recall ever having made a nickel from works created by someone other than myself, and I can't imagine making money that way, even if I did hustle. How do I earn a living and how have I made a reputation? To the extent that I have earned a living and made a reputation, I have done it through my own work. Is my work contingent on any artist's work? I mean, in the sense that some critics have made a reputation and a living by promoting certain artists whose work they have been able to acquire on a profitable basis. The artists I admire usually don't need me to publicize them. They are people already of general interest to the art world, and whatever I have to say about them is not going to produce a profit, either for them or for me. Some artists resent my approach. They feel that the function of a critic is to help them sell their work.

Also, there are members of the public who think that the function of the critic is to give them tips on whom to buy, to tell them who is going to be the star of 1980. It would be useful if we could make such predictions. But they will only come true if they are followed up with a tremendous promotional job—if they are what are called self-fulfilling prophecies. A critic who does not wish to become a promotor should not make predictions.

HC Another question . . . should artists teach in elementary schools, secondary schools, colleges, and art schools?

HR I wonder what job the person who asked that question has. If he has a job in an elementary school, I should think he would say, "No." An important consideration is how many hours one has to teach. There is no such thing as a good teaching job for an artist. It takes away too much time. This is what one usually hears from artists who have teaching jobs. It's more to the point to ask whether artists should teach at all, even if the amount of time they spend at it is not destructive. No matter how short their teaching time, at a certain point they must break away from their studios and start talking about art instead of doing it. Also, as teachers, they have got to talk about other artists: They can't just talk about themselves without being very limited. Yet doesn't teaching, even when they do talk about themselves, make them too conscious of what they are doing, since they must convey through words and illustrations a formula for what they may have begun in a spontaneous unintended way.

There are great teachers who are great artists. Also great artists who are great teachers. Paul Klee was a marvelous teacher. His work at the Bauhaus consisted of the most elaborate analysis of the ideas and practices of Paul Klee. Klee proves that, given a certain kind of temperament, there is nothing damaging about teaching. On the contrary, it is hard to think of Klee becoming the kind of artist that he was without his teaching activity. On the other hand, there are artists who are equally eminent and profound who have not taught and would hate to do it. It seems likely that most 20th-century artists, at one time or another, have taught. Most of them must have found teaching desirable, if it didn't take too much of their time.

There is another question here: Should art critics teach? They all do, though they may not teach art criticism but art history, or philosophy of art, or something else related to art. There *are* probably art critics who teach art criticism, but I can't imagine what those courses are about.

HC Here is a question that someone always asks at these presentations: What direction do you think art will take in the next 10 years?

HR I think the question is invalid. One may as well be asked to predict any other aspect of modern life. What happens to the economy, in politics, and in society in general will have a lot to do with the direction art takes. Art does not depend only on its own self. One of the things that is characteristic of our time, and which is sweeping forward with an enormous force, is the internationalization of economics, of communication, and of social problems. We are all aware of the existence of multinational corporations, the oil crisis, and that these affect life throughout Europe and the U.S. It's difficult to conceive that there will be a change in this regard. We may assume that art produced in the next decade will have an international character, if it's to be of any great importance. We may keep in mind as an unavoidable state of affairs that the art of the future will not be local. It will not be national. It will tend, as it has since World War II, to reverberate throughout the world, except where it is excluded by political dictatorships.

Q What issues do you see?

HR The basic issue in art in the 20th century continues to be the relation between doing and thinking, between the ideas in art and the practice of art, or the making of objects. All developments in art since the war have revolved around this issue. A desirable balance has been reached by certain artists between thinking and doing, or thinking and action, as I have called it. In those instances distinguished work has appeared. The tendency, however, is for this balance to be lost. Artists begin to overemphasize the conceptual aspect of art. Right now there is an enormous overemphasis on the craft aspect of art. Many are happy that there are no prevailing ideas in the art world today, because the ideas that prevailed during the 1960s were, for the most part, so narrow, pointless, and debased that it was a relief to see them go. But the reaction against bad ideas does not necessarily produce good ideas. At present, art seems to be in a kind of intellectual vacuum. Better a vacuum than being nibbled to death by petty notions. At the same time, people are uneasy about being able to do anything they want to do.

Q Isn't it true that, traditionally, the critic gets his direction from the art that is forging ahead?

HR Yes, good criticism is normally based on good art—which may or may not be thoroughly understood at the time that it appears. I can't think of a good critic who didn't rely on significant work that was being done. Criticism cannot be elevated into a kind of satellite that runs around the universe all by itself without any art attached to it. What would be the point to it? It would turn into a theoretical bubble.

Since one is necessarily restricted to what is going on, one is subject to becoming despondent. I have been attacked again and again for sounding too despondent. I have failed to achieve enough enthusiasm about what some regard as great avant-garde movements of the past 10 years. Every time I write a book, the *New York Times* manages to find a reviewer who says, "This fellow used to be an important critic, but in the last 10 or 15 years he doesn't know what is going on. We have video art, we have earth art, we have minimal art, and he doesn't like any of it, so there is something wrong with him. He ought to like it."

Q Do you think that when art dealers tell artists what to paint it affects the quality of their work?

HR A very bad situation can produce very bad art. An overpowering of the artist's will by individuals who represent money or some kind of ideology can result in making the artist into an illustrator of other people's ideas. It often seems to me that the present dealer system will have to be transformed if art is to get out of the pit it's in. Dealers keep multiplying and disappearing at a terrific rate. The artist doesn't know what to do without them. On the other hand, how can the artist go along with their needs? A fundamental contradiction has arisen between the needs of the dealer and the needs of the artist. Dealers used to try to get the most prominent artists and were proud to sell what these artists produced. Now dealers say to an artist, "You are not producing enough." Or—"If you make this kind of work, I don't think I can sell it, but if you do this, I could." That's disgusting. The artist who agrees to it might as well get a job in an advertising agency.

Q How do you react to individuals who claim painting is dead?

HR It's obviously dead for them. Years ago, in Washington Square Park, a fellow said to Max Schnitzler, "I have finally decided to give up art." Schnitzler replied, "You didn't decide to give up art. Art decided to give you up."

Q Would you comment on Marcel Duchamp and his influence.

HR Duchamp has recently been attacked as the devil who is responsible for the failure of art to move up a slanting ramp of formal progress. He is accused of being the villain of Modern Art. Actually, Duchamp is one of the most forceful and necessary figures in the art of our time. It's hard to think of somebody being necessary in art, but if there were somebody, it would be Duchamp. It doesn't, of course, follow that because he is necessary, people who have regarded him as their master are necessary. Duchamp himself was very dubious about his followers. In particular, he found that they worked too hard. They produced too many things. When Duchamp himself produced a work, it made a point—and that was it. He then devoted himself to something else. He was not, he said, one of those people who have to make works every day. An artist is supposed to be a free spirit. If he becomes a laborer in art, it's the same as being a laborer in any other field. He is watching the market and meeting its demands. Duchamp didn't like that. When he had an idea, he wanted to put it into some form—perhaps a superficial or jocular form, or an enormously elaborated one, like his last work about gas and waterfalls. Now, as Duchamp pointed out, artists who follow him have not had that restraint. In supplying the market they have become the opposite of Duchamp, who was characterized by austerity of thought. In his view, art in the 20th century ought to be based on ideas. Without ideas it simply consists of commodities for rich people. If an artist wants to make nice-looking things for people to hang in their living rooms, that's O.K. But if he wants to be an artist, he must have ideas. That is a pretty strong message, I admit. Most artists hate this message.

Q What do you think of Hilton Kramer's attack in the *New*

York Times on Sir Kenneth Clark and the Impressionist show at The Metropolitan Museum of Art?

HR I didn't read this attack on Clark. It often seems to me that Kramer wants to clear the world of other critics. To express his program, he ought to find a word equivalent to the Nazi "Judenrein," which meant "purged of Jews." I did read his review of the Impressionist show, and I think it's ridiculous. He attacks the show because it presents "The Impressionist Epoch," instead of being a show that pays tribute to the Impressionists. As a record of the period, the show mingles the works of the great Impressionists with works of people who were their contemporaries but were not Impressionists and were not necessarily great. From Kramer's starved historical point of view, the non-Impressionists could not have had any value and ought not to be allowed to contaminate the Impressionist presence. The reader is meant to see Kramer as a super aesthete who cannot tolerate the disturbance of his sensibility by art that is less than the best. He is so finely tuned that seeing a Manet next to *September Morn* upsets and outrages him. It is as if he had been dipped into a vat of boiling water.

But suppose that to protect the public against being aesthetically violated, you show only Impressionists and only the best of these. The effect is that Impressionism appears as a ready-made triumph in the history of art. It rose up out of the earth. It came out of the Seine. A day arrived and there was Impressionism.

At the Metropolitan, you see what the Impressionist artist was up against; you see what kind of art surrounded him and how powerful his rivals were in the Salon. You derive an idea of the drama of creation—an experience which is far more important than enjoying the aesthetic sensation of looking once again at a Manet you've seen a dozen times.

What is missing in Kramer's view is that he has no appreciation of the enormous difficulty of being an original artist. This is why he demands that the Impressionists be segregated for the delectation of aesthetes and art critics. But such a separation prevents the public from knowing what a tremendous thing takes place when one artist or a few artists manage to create something new. The new cannot be seen except in contrast and in conflict with what was accepted at that time. Today, for example, few people have any notion of how difficult it was for the Action Painters to create what they did. So the opinion that the idea behind the Metropolitan show is bad is the exact opposite of the case, since the show offers an opportunity to become aware how Impressionism differentiated itself from the work around it.

HC I will give Harold a chance to rest his voice by interpolating and taking the prerogative of the moderator to say that if criticism may be looked upon as an artwork, the answer to that last question was a nice example of it.

Q Do you think people are losing interest in art?

HR It occurred to me just this morning that almost everything I read about art is calculated to make it boring. The only way to restore one's interest is to go and look at it. The formulas of modern art writing may be pertinent, they may be profound, they may be revelatory, but whatever they are, they are not interesting. Most of the people who write articles and museum catalogs don't know how to write, and those who cannot write, cannot say anything interesting. They can say, "I went to the gas company and paid my bill," but they can't communicate anything about gas. I don't think art itself can be boring, but one can be bored by it if one keeps seeing it through veils of awkward rhetoric.

Q You were very enthusiastic about Action Painting. . . . I was wondering if you are satisfied with the direction in which it is going.

HR No, I am not satisfied. As a matter of fact, I wasn't entirely satisfied with Action Painting. People began to call me a spokesman for it. I was not a spokesman. There was no spokesman. Practically all the Action Painters, with one or two very important exceptions, denied that there was such a thing. As I pointed out in the original article on the subject, whenever you give a name to what a lot of artists are doing— a so-called art movement—the definition never fits the best artists. It's good for those who pick up the formula, but the best artists escape the formula. It so happened that the best of the Action Painters found it piquant to say that they were Action Painters, but I think that was because the other Action Painters said they were not.

Q Do you see any continuity in modern art?

HR There is always a continuity. Nothing comes from nothing. What we have to be wary about is establishing fake continuities, in which something that is the exact opposite of what it seems to emanate from is masquerading as that thing. There are many examples of that, not only in art, but, more importantly, in politics. There is such a thing, for example, as a fake revolution, a revolution that seems to be in the tradition of, let's say, the Paris Commune, or some other liberating event, and turns out to be, actually, the work of police undercover men. Anyone with political intuitions must begin by seeing the difference between an event that appears to be a continuation of a previous event, but is actually not at all such a continuation, and an event that is a development of that earlier event.

One cannot make continuity into a value in itself. Each phenomenon must be thought about in terms of its own reality, what it is connected with, and just what is the connection.

Q Isn't it one of our problems that the Establishment is interested in any new idea that comes along?

HR I am not sure that the enthusiasm of the Establishment for new ideas is as pervasive as it seems. Throughout the '60s, museum directors, dealers, and collectors were not by any means enthusiastic about all new ideas. They were interested in certain new ideas. One of the jobs which criticism has not yet performed is the analysis of what ideas they were interested in and why. There was an enormous amount of work done by both older and younger artists that never saw the light of day because the Establishment had definitely fixed ideas concerning what art was about and what made it worth showing, and which art was not worth showing.

I wrote pieces about this during the '60s that pointed out how the decade had been defined by The Museum of Modern Art in such a way as to exclude some of the most important work being done. They had a show called "The Sixties," presented, as if to prove my point, in 1968—there were still two years left in the '60s, but MOMA didn't feel the need to bother about what might appear in them. The MOMA already knew what the content of the '60s was and was satisfied to put on a big show of the period from which many people were excluded. I made a comparison between The Museum of Modern Art and Hades, the Greek place for people who were dead. I said, "There are people who are functioning here, but according to The Museum of Modern Art all of them are dead. They have turned into shades, as the Greeks called them. You can see them floating by, but they have no bodies." Alfred Barr replied, "That is unfair. Those artists are shown on the fourth floor." Other times, other places. Anyway, I don't believe that the Establishment is as hospitable to new ideas as you imagine. There is a lot of fighting to be done.

Q How would you define the current situation?

HR No one, including me, seems to know exactly what the situation is. To all appearances, anything that will sell is acceptable as art. The museums have pulled in their horns; they are not involved to the same degree as they were in the past with promotion. For one thing, they don't have the money. Without money, they have been restricted to shows that are either assembled out of their own collections or for which they can obtain money from the National Endowment for the Arts, from the State Arts Councils, and usually from some business firm as well. With these purses they can put on a few big shows a year, but they are no longer prepared to spend enormous sums on young "masters."

As far as the dealers are concerned, they seem totally demoralized. They don't know what is going to sell. They are likely to show almost nothing, but they are most interested in showing old art. Artists who have been successful for years are the only ones in which the galleries have confidence. This produces a situation which is like the '30s, when old art was being shown, but new artists, or artists with new ideas, found it difficult to gain attention.

Q What do you think of a critic who alters the work of an artist over which he has control as the executor of his estate?

HR You are trying to be nice to me. You are giving me an opportunity to attack Clement Greenberg, but your question covers all critics who believe that they are needed to tell the artist how to paint or how to sculpt. Such critics must feel that they are also needed to fix up the artist's work after he has done it. The basic element in this is the belief that the artist is too dumb to know what to do by himself and, therefore, needs to be told to do this and not do that. This is a very widespread belief. It is a belief that can be dangerous and very likely will become more and more of a problem in the future. The great mass of art that is produced in modern countries is developed under orders of art directors. In the U.S. the big production line is, of course, in commercial art. The artist does not work for himself, and he does not determine his own product. He is hired because people like his style; but the intention is that he will be retooled to be useful in this or that advertising campaign.

In the totalitarian countries, artists work on assignments with given themes. Since submitting to direction is so prevalent, both in totalitarian countries and among us, it is not surprising that the system of creation by command should infiltrate what is called fine art—especially when nobody can say exactly what fine art is. And, especially when the guy in the front line is the dealer or the curator. Why shouldn't dealers tell their artist friends, or young aspirants, what to do that will make them more successful than they have been? It's not a bad idea—just the end of art.

Q What is the effect on art, if any, of the drop in prices on Wall Street?

HR The power of money in our society is so great it can easily crush all other values. I don't think any aesthetic values, moral values, even political values can hold up against the crushing power of cash. Anything worthwhile that manages to survive does so with the aid of a miracle. Not that I am opposed to depending on miracles; we are forced to depend on them.

Someone shows up, not to be anticipated, someone, say, like Ralph Nader, who defies General Motors, gets away with it, and becomes a powerful force for values in society. That is what artists have to do. They know they are going to be crushed by money; General Motors is bigger than they are. But they must have faith in miraculous intervention. It's simple: If you assume you've lost the game to begin with, you are in a good position to go on.

Q How do you feel about government subsidies like the WPA?

HR The WPA was a very good thing in many ways. Also, in many ways it was not so good. The government is spending a lot of money on art now, though not, of course, comparable to the WPA. As Dr. Conant pointed out, we are all present in this auditorium because of a National Endowment grant.

If we are going to have a WPA or a government subsidy of art, it ought to be very big, like the WPA. It should even have room for people who are pretending to be artists but who are not really artists. During the WPA, a lot of guys got on the Art Project who weren't painters but became painters, and some were very good. They found themselves in the company of painters and, having nothing else to do, they too began to paint.

Q Could you give us an outline of the structure of the WPA?

HR That would take hours. Enough to say that it was a very elaborate structure. One complicating factor was that the WPA Art Project could never decide whether it was basically a relief project designed to feed a certain number of mouths, or whether it was a project for elevating standards of creation and appreciation in the U.S. There was a constant battle going over this question. Some people in Washington would say, "The Art Project is a cultural undertaking comparable to the building of the pyramids." Others said, "Never mind the pyramids. There are X-number of people who need jobs. They don't know how to do anything else, so let them make art." There was a continuous struggle over these two positions, and the government, including our revered President, purposely refused to resolve the question, which made the WPA Art Project collapsible. If it was intended to feed people, depending on statistics, it could feed fewer people, so a certain number would be fired. On the other hand, those who were working could be urged to work as if they were building the pyramids. The administration kept playing this game with the artists. People in different categories—noncitizens, for example—would be fired. Then they were taken on again. But the WPA Art Project was a great thing. The artists got together, spirit was high, and great things

came out of it. The thing to do is just to spread a lot of
money around. One never knows what will come out of it.

Q Do you think art today is too dependent on ideas?

HR Some works are more ideological than others. There are
works in which the meaning, at least in the first instance, is
inseparable from ideas, so that the work cannot be appreciated by those who lack the mental context in which it belongs. Of course, each work of art is itself and nothing else,
but there is a difference among works in respect to the di-
rectness of their communication. For example, before the
talk, the thinking, the mythology, and the information regarding the paintings of Barnett Newman reached people, it
was virtually impossible for them to appreciate his work.
The spectator saw a canvas with a line down the middle.
Newman was an artist who did stripes. Now, after years of
discussion, including discussion by Newman, people have
begun to attain a somewhat better grasp of what Newman's
paintings mean. This suggests that in regard to any one
painting by an artist, one has to have the idea that applies to
all that artist's paintings like it. One also has to have a notion
as to how they exist in relation to art of the past, specifically
in the case of Newman to Mondrian. One who doesn't know
that will still be seeing nothing but stripes.

But the time comes in regard to particular works when the
public needs consciously to know less. They need not acquire
as much information, because the ideas have gotten around
and been diffused through the general consciousness—people have been told many things that they don't know they
have been told. On a subway today, two women will get into
an argument and denounce each other in elaborate Freudian
terms. Or, in a police report on the radio, the cop will talk
about a "perpetrator" having been "apprehended" and so
on. This sophisticated scientific vocabulary gets to be part of
folklore or mythology. We don't need to know as much

about things that have been around for a long time. But at the beginning you do have to understand them. You can't look a picture square in the eye and be sure you are going to get it because it will look *you* square in the eye.

Q Do you believe that works that involve collaboration are nihilistic?

HR Do you mean that if two people get together it's nihilism? What are you thinking?

Q In the creation of a work of art through collaboration.

HR Oh, you are thinking about collective poems and collective paintings. "The Exquisite Cadaver" of the Surrealists. Why is it nihilistic? It doesn't do anybody any harm. It doesn't destroy anything. It's an experiment to see ESP in print. Some marvelous things came out of that. Someone would draw something dopey on a piece of paper, fold it over, and the next person would continue it in the same style, so that a kind of possibility became visible. It was part of the Surrealists' experiment with the odder corners of the mind. Why do you think it was nihilistic?

Q Do you think there's an avant-garde today?

HR Nobody does, so far as I know, except a few fellows who have been making the same moves for a long time. No, there isn't any avant-garde today. The real question is whether it's possible for modern art to be interesting without an avant-garde. That's a theoretical question that needs to be explored.

Q What kind of balance do you see between Conceptualism in art and handcraft?

HR The Conceptualists are more visible today than other artists because they are talking about something; whereas thousands of people make art, and very good art, but don't say anything. The Conceptualists are the latest talkers in art. And theoretical assumptions go right into the character or style of modern art. So the Conceptualists are on solid ground when they say that the core of spirit of art lies in its concepts, and then proceed to analyze the concepts. Some have come up with the idea that all the premises or concepts of modern art are worn out, exhausted. Hence, there is nothing left to do but criticize the continual use of those obsolescent ideas. But while it's true that concepts are basic in modern art, there is no such thing as a concept getting worn out. Its vitality depends entirely on who uses it. Inventing something that has been theoretically superseded is a perfectly valid creative act. It happens all the time. Art that has been theoretically left behind is constantly inspiring new works, new personalities. The notion that a premise can be exhausted may be applicable in physics, but it doesn't apply in art at all. In art, there is nothing wrong with an old idea. There is nothing wrong with a bad idea. The amount of great art that has been produced out of misunderstood ideas is practically unlimited. On the other hand, a good idea can be absolutely worthless. What is wrong with the Conceptualists is that they have left the doing out of art. Yes, there has to be an idea in it, but the idea is nothing without the doing.

Many artists in our time go over to the other side of art— the craft side. Artists who became disgusted with the endless yakking of other artists, critics, theoreticians, proclaim, "I just paint. I don't know anything about anything. I get up in the morning, put a canvas on the easel, or paste a piece of paper to the wall, and I paint." That's a dumb idea, too, because whatever way one paints, it originated in some idea, which, maybe, the artist thought about. The artist who doesn't think merely repeats in practice old ideas. A genuine artist cannot avoid thinking, any more than he or she can produce works by only thinking.

Q Do you ever have the experience of seeing works of art and failing to react to them?

HR It happens all the time. One of my doubts about art reviewers is that they always present a definite response. At a show of new work I often don't know what I feel about it. Later, I may begin to think about it, and perhaps go back and look again. If some thoughts develop, after a while I may even have an opinion. This takes time. It's a series of stages. You can't walk up to a work of art and say, "This is a monkey; this is a gorilla; this is a kangaroo," which is what the reviewer does. He classifies works as if they were biological specimens. Works of art are not genuinely appreciated that way. The process of recognition of someone else's creative act is extremely complicated. You don't just jump up to it and say, "That's terrific." People gasp about certain sunsets, but that's the end of it. In art, the idea has to intervene at some stage.

Q You refuse to say what the situation in art is today and where art is going. Isn't this copping out?

HR I don't think so. I keep thinking about these matters all the time. I am, in that way, like artists whose work always falls short. All artists know that the art they are working on now is going to be the real thing. This is the time they are going to do it. Then they finish, look at it, and find it's like their other work, so they have to start all over again. If I had the philosopher's stone that you are asking for, I could shut up, which would probably be a contribution too, but I have not yet succeeded in finding it. I keep looking, and the minute I lay hands on it, you will know.

Q Do you see miraculous intervention as taking place in our time?

HR I see miraculous intervention as possible any moment. Absolutely! It's a dogma—you say it because you are going to insist on it, and it may come in five minutes. That's the world art lives in. If you didn't think that, the alternative is awful, because you would have to become involved in politics, in the analysis of society, and the proof that nothing will happen, except something that's lousy. We are tempted to do that, I do it at least as much as other people. I have the habit of pointing out what a hopeless state of affairs has been produced by this or by that. But basically, I am a dogmatist of miracles and so I continue to function. Otherwise, I would have to give up and go home.

20

What Is Art?
An Interview by
Melvin M. Tumin with
Harold Rosenberg

Tumin You've written so much about art that I think if I start
you on your most recent work, we may pick up the main
issues right from the beginning. So I want to turn to your
article on Jasper Johns in the last issue of *The New Yorker*
(December 26, 1977). You start with a quote from Baudelaire, who says, "What is pure art according to the modern
idea? It is the creation of an evocative magic, containing at
once the object and the subject, the world external to the
artist and the artist himself." I take it you quote that
approvingly?

Rosenberg I do, especially in regard to Jasper Johns. The problem was Johns' affirmation of the idea of a work of art which
would in no way include the personality or the temperament
or any other individual aspect of the artist. That is, he was
speaking of a completely objective or impersonal art. This is
a basic misapprehension. So the quotation from Baudelaire
which stresses the dual aspects of a work of art, so as to

This interview was conducted on January 10, 1978. Harold Rosenberg died
in August of that year. The interview was first published in *Partisan Review*,
vol. 45, no. 4, Fall 1978.

reflect both the personality of the artist and the objective world, seemed appropriate.

Tumin That comes as close to your saying what a work of art is as I've ever heard you say.

Rosenberg It doesn't say what a work of art is.

Tumin Well, Baudelaire asks, "What is pure art?"

Rosenberg Well, that doesn't interest me. I'm not interested in pure art. There is no such thing. If Baudelaire wanted to use the term, that's all right with me. I think he meant, What are the requirements in the psychological or, if you wish, the spiritual sense, of a work of art? Or the metaphysical sense? The artist, insofar as he creates a valid work of art, has a magical apprehension of both the objective external world and of himself.

Tumin He has a magical apprehension of himself, as well as of the world?

Rosenberg Of both. At the same time.

Tumin He treats himself as object, as well as the external world?

Rosenberg Well no. Stick to the quotation.

Tumin It says, "It is the creation of an evocative magic by the artist."

Rosenberg That's right.

Tumin "Containing both the object and the subject, the world external to the artist and the artist himself."

Rosenberg That's right. So the work contains both the external world and the artist himself.

Tumin That's obviously not a sufficient definition of a work of art.

Rosenberg It's not a sufficient definition or a definition at all. It's a condition for an acceptable work of art. It could be, you might say, the definition of a perfect work of art. You could regard this magic as totally unattainable, that is, in the Hegelian sense of the subject of the object. But I agree with

Baudelaire that the necessary aim of art is to attempt to see the external world and formulate the subjective experience of the artist at the same time. This is a very important emphasis in art today because of the history of art in America in the last fifteen years. There's been a very great thrust toward one form or another of objectivity, that is, the attempt to eliminate the feelings or subjective impact of the artist. The artist has tried to present himself as much as he could as a figure that you might find in technology or in science. The relationship between technology and art has encouraged the kind of artist who regards himself as a kind of technician or maker of art.

Tumin Why was that impulse so strong? What was it a reaction against? Was it a reaction against a previous kind of subjectivism?

Rosenberg In terms of statements that were made, it was a reaction against Abstract Expressionism—a series of reactions. Among the first were artists such as Jasper Johns, who said, "I don't want to express myself on the canvas, and I'm not trying to evoke on the canvas a mysterious sign. I'm prepared to paint things that everybody knows." Or, as he put it, "*already* knows." And then he produced his paintings of the American flag, and targets, and of numbers, and of letters of the alphabet, saying, "Here is something that has nothing to do with me. I didn't invent the American flag and I didn't invent the numbers."

Tumin You're being very lucidly descriptive of what he does. But I'm trying to press you to say why you think he reacts that way against Abstract Expressionism. What is it that's unsatisfactory about Abstract Expressionism?

Rosenberg Now, that's a big subject. There are many different reasons that artists found for reacting against Abstract Expressionism. One of the basic reasons, it seems to me, was that Abstract Expressionist art implied that the artist was in a continuous state of striving, of attempting to arrive at some kind of vision, and this is very uncomfortable. Before Johns ever appeared on the scene I heard expressions of antagonism on the part of young artists toward, for example, the *angst* of Bill de Kooning. They said, I don't want to spend the rest of my life struggling with art. You know, Bill had said that if he could, he'd spend the rest of his life painting one picture, having in mind the Balzac story of "The Unknown Masterpiece," in which the artist spends his life struggling to realize a single picture. The young artists didn't want that. They wanted to have a career as artists and paint pictures and sell them.

Tumin Are you calling them artists by courtesy?

Rosenberg No, I think they were expressing what are generally regarded as the normal desires of artists. There was something extreme about the Abstract Expressionists. They seemed to lead extreme lives, like Jackson Pollock, or Franz Kline, or Rothko. Somebody has been making the point constantly in the last twenty years that these artists tended to die young, despite the fact that de Kooning is now seventy-four, and Hans Hofmann died at eighty-six. Still there are many examples. There's Kline, there's Tomlin. There's Rothko who committed suicide; there's Jackson Pollock killed in an automobile accident; there's Gorky committing suicide, even though he wasn't exactly an Abstract Expressionist. But the idea is that this was dangerous art. And the fact is that this was dangerous art, that is, the artists were involved in an attempt to change something basic in their lives.

Tumin Are you saying that this is dangerous art, rather than art being dangerous? Or would you argue that art *per se* is dangerous?

Rosenberg You can do whatever you want with art. You can turn it into a commonplace craft. You can turn it into a way of flattering the rich, as in the great days of portraiture. You can paint people's houses and their estates and make them look beautiful.

Tumin But now it seems to me you're getting back to an absolutely minimalist definition of art, one which makes it wholly indiscriminate in terms of what it commands, in terms of any special qualities. Because if it's a something, which we have yet to say what it is, which lends itself so well to so many purposes, what is the "it?"

Rosenberg You can't say that there is the it.

Tumin You said art can lend itself to painting houses.

Rosenberg It can lend itself to anything.

Tumin Then what is the "it" that lends itself?

Rosenberg That's very simple. There is a human activity that has been going on traditionally for 30,000 years, and that activity is therefore well known to human beings, and they call it art.

Tumin What characterizes that activity and distinguishes it from other activities?

Rosenberg Well, for one thing, as they used to say about the herring, you hang it on the wall.

Tumin Yeah, but we know that the herring is not green and doesn't whistle.

Rosenberg That is very often true about paintings, too. But it doesn't prevent them from hanging on the wall, any more than the herring. That is, you can hang any picture on the wall. You can also have social acceptance of certain kinds of images as the only kinds of paintings that are worthwhile, as in the Soviet Union, where they carry certain messages.

Tumin But now you've taken us very far from the Baudelaire statement of the conditions of art. Granted they're not sufficient conditions. Still, they are far more discriminating and restrictive than what you're now allowing art to be.

Rosenberg Don't forget that he said pure art.

Tumin Well, let's leave pure art . . .

Rosenberg Well, wait a minute. The reason why I returned to
the word pure is that he thereby implied that only a certain
kind of art achieved those conditions. He put in the word
pure. I wouldn't use that word. You could substitute the
word authentic, if you like, or anything else. But the point of
the matter is he leaves room with that adjective for all kinds
of other art in which those conditions are not met. It's obvious, then, if anybody knows anything about the history of
art, that a great deal of art was made in shops with shop
techniques. In eighteenth century France there was an enormous production of sculpture for estates.

Tumin For you, then, the word art does not necessarily con-
note anything about excellence or value or worth. You're
saying that it is an activity in which all kinds of people at all
levels of skill or nonskill can participate for all kinds of purposes. However ugly or foul the purposes may be, something
called art may serve all those purposes or may be used for all
that.

Rosenberg Yes, I think that's correct. Because otherwise you
get in a position where the definition would include its own
valuation. That is, if you cut out all those "bad" types of art,
then the word "art" would necessarily mean marvelous art.
In fact, it would be very hard to think of there being a work
of art at all, it would be so perfect. The existence of art depends on adjectives.

Tumin Then you're willing to make the term art almost wholly
nonrestrictive to start with.

Rosenberg Yes.

Tumin And then to discriminate and distinguish various
qualities, dimensions, characteristics, objects, uses, skills,
qualities of art?

Rosenberg Yes.

Tumin So we don't need to worry about what we mean by the generic term art. It's some kind of activity which involves chalk or paint or movement or music or sound or whatever?

Rosenberg That's right. In practical terms, the definition of art—when I say practical terms, I mean not theoretical terms—the definition of art has very often been encouraged by concepts of good art, and therefore the attempt was made to exclude all other kinds of art.

Tumin You want to make art a generic human activity, which is to be distinguished, perhaps, from science, from automobile driving, from gymnastics?

Rosenberg Right.

Tumin That means, now, that it makes sense to say that, given this generic human activity, as in all other human activities, there are levels of excellence, high and low qualities of things.

Rosenberg I want to just get away from excellence itself, because the concept of excellence in art has an almost political meaning. When you talk about excellence you imply that a basic measure in art is purely qualitative, and I don't accept that, because a work of art can be less excellent than another work of art, if you're applying standard A, and, let's say, much more interesting intellectually and much more stimulating emotionally or imaginatively and therefore much more valuable. The concept of excellence taken by itself is an academic idea.

Tumin So we want to talk about the different aspects or dimensions of art which loosely one might say that, if they reached a certain level, you would say that's an excellent level, as against a mediocre level on that dimension, without now talking about the overall excellence.

Rosenberg Overall excellence is an academic term. As I say, it's a very impressive one, and it's being used rather aggressively today.

Tumin You don't object to aggressive criticism and analysis, do you?

Rosenberg Well, I'm making an aggressive criticism of this aggressive term.

Tumin Let's see if we can go after some of the dimensions that you think are important. Let me tell you why I ask this. For better or for worse, people read you very carefully. Lots of people read you, maybe not as carefully as you'd like, but they read you. For better or for worse, you're said to be a very influential person in the world of art. This means that in some sense people are saying that Harold Rosenberg is the kind of person who, if you follow him, he can tell you the difference between a good work of art and a bad work of art. You chronically abstain from ever being willing to assume that posture publicly, although you've been willing to comment about all kinds of things about particular art works. But let's now talk about some of the things that you look for when you're estimating a work of art. One which you mentioned in an unguarded moment was the importance of the idea that the artist is confronting or the problem he is trying to solve. Is that a fair phrasing?

Rosenberg It's perfectly all right. What you have in mind is the aim or intention of the artist. But I don't like the word problem. That's another loaded word because I know that artists have problems. I know that they struggle with various problems. But I don't believe an artist as artist tries to resolve problems. I'm inclined to agree with Picasso when he says he finds, he doesn't seek. There's been a terrible development, as a result of university art education in the last twenty years, in which art has been presented as a problem-solving activity, and believe me some of the problems that have been trumped up we could have very well done without. They're not really problems for artists. They're problems for people who are in universities.

Tumin Then what do you mean when you say one of the criteria you look for when you're looking at a work of art is the idea that the artist has, what he's trying to do, and one of the dimensions of that idea is how important it is?

Rosenberg That's right.

Tumin What do you mean by an important idea? Is it always relevant to the history of previous ideas in the world of art?

Rosenberg The phrases that you add are helpful, at least in the approach I'd like to take. The history of art, especially in the last couple of hundred years, has touched on almost every conceivable form of thought, on physics, on social problems, on psychological problems and all kinds of things regarded as intellectual activities. Now, some of these problems, or areas of thinking and imagination, are basic to human life. Some of them are much less so. For example, it's very important to consider the effects of blue in juxtaposition with red.

Tumin Important for whom?

Rosenberg Well, it's important in general. I mean it's a form of knowledge to understand the optical effects of color.

Tumin Most people in the world could live the rest of their lives without knowing.

Rosenberg That's right. But this is still an important question. That is, optical phenomena are important. A science is devoted to them, and many things have been made and developed as a result of this interest. However, I don't regard it as the most important thing in human life.

Tumin Is the question of categorical imperatives, which comes out of major metaphysical concerns and philosophical problems, a more important problem?

Rosenberg Certainly.

Tumin When you choose the problem of the juxtaposition of blue vs. green, you're choosing a problem which is immediately relevant to the visual arts in some sense. Right?

Rosenberg That's right. They're relevant to the visual arts and to some people they are the field, or area in which the visual arts can make their maximum contribution. I'm about to disagree with that. While it's true that color is a specialization of painting, it's not the greatest thing that painting has ever dealt with.

Tumin What are some of the great things painting has dealt with, the truly great things? God's grace?

Rosenberg God? Yes, traditionally painting has dealt with religious or metaphysical questions. Since these questions are central to all cultures in the past and in the present, too, although they are less visibly central in the present, these metaphysical questions can be said to be the most important questions that art has dealt with. Therefore, to deal with art as if it were exclusively related to color is a reduction of the stature of art. Let me give you an apt example of the answer to this question. If you compare the aims of Barnett Newman and the aims of Josef Albers, the first is involved with the question of the absolute in relation to man, and the second is involved with color relations. This is very clear.

Tumin So one is more important than the other for art, all other things being equal.

Rosenberg All other things can't be equal.

Tumin I knew I would get that. That is, all technique being equal.

Rosenberg They're both very good painters.

Tumin They're both very good painters, but let's say, if you can imagine for a moment all other things being equal, but one painted the best he could paint about the meaning of color and the other painted with an equally good quality about the meaning of absolute *angst*, would you now say that the latter was a better painter because the idea was more important?

Rosenberg But I wouldn't care whether he was a better painter, because you've established that as painters they are equal.

What I would say is that I would be much more interested in the paintings of the one than I would in the paintings of the other.

Tumin I don't want your interests. Would you say that one is more important? Is one more important for art than the other?

Rosenberg I would say so, yes. I would be inclined to agree with Newman, by the way, who said this, that the subject matter of the artist is the most important thing to consider about his work. And if the subject matter could be conceived as having a relation to the experience of the absolute, I would regard that as more important than, shall we say, insights into the relations of blue and pink.

Tumin Can we then have a great painting about a trivial subject?

Rosenberg Well, that's where you run into difficulties of definition. If it's a great painting, it can't be about a trivial subject. Therefore, if a subject seems to be trivial, that is, for example, a bowl of apples, what is important about a bowl of apples?

Tumin The great Cézanne . . .

Rosenberg Exactly. That's not just a bowl of apples. There's something else going on there. I think Meyer Schapiro made the distinction between subject matter and object matter. The object matter there is apples, but the subject matter is something else.

Tumin In the case, say, of Cézanne's apples, what's the subject matter as against the object matter?

Rosenberg Well, as I say, the object matter would just be apples. But the subject matter as far as Meyer, for example, is concerned is infinite. Did you read his article on the apples of Cézanne?[1] He carries these apples off into the tradition of

1. Meyer Schapiro, "The Apples of Cézanne," *Art News Annual*, 34 (1968): 34–53.

apples in art, which is a great tradition. You know, the apples of the Greek goddesses, and the Hesperides, and all kinds of associations with apples, and of course Meyer is in this piece something of a Freudian and talking about virility and various other connotations of apples. So the subject matter there becomes very extensive. Those apples are not just hanging around for somebody to have a piece of fruit.

Tumin So it is not possible to say beforehand that any given subject matter is trivial or important, right?

Rosenberg I wouldn't put it that way because maybe it is possible to say beforehand that certain . . .

Tumin Apples are *per se* trivial, right?

Rosenberg Well, they are trivial perhaps as fruits, but not *per se*. You're twisting language here.

Tumin No, I'm saying fruits *per se* are trivial.

Rosenberg How can you say fruits are trivial?

Tumin Fruits, as against eternal salvation.

Rosenberg Fruit is a part of the eternal salvation. After all, we're all here on account of an apple. You know perfectly well that if Adam had not eaten that apple we would all be immortal, we would be leaping around in paradise, so an apple cannot be regarded as, *per se,* trivial.

Tumin Let's go back to your original distinction in which you said it's quite clear that Barnett Newman's ideas are more important for painting to deal with than Albers' problems, since Albers was concerned primarily with color problems and Newman was concerned more, let's say, with metaphysical and philosophical problems. Now what you're saying is that, on some scale of importance that you can state beforehand, problems of color are less important than problems of philosophy.

Rosenberg Of human existence, yes. I could say that in general, yes. When Meyer wrote his article about the apples of Cézanne, which is not so long ago, it was maybe five years, he was attacked violently by people who felt he was demeaning the art of Cézanne with all this content or context-matter that he attributed to his reading of apples. In other words, there is a very definite vein of thought that holds that art should not be interpreted in terms of content. This has been the biggest fight in the last twenty years in art criticism. It's the same thing, of course, that took place in literature before. The same criticisms have been leveled at Leo Steinberg who makes Freudian, neo-Freudian interpretations of paintings. And some people object very strenuously to this attribution of meanings to paintings.

Tumin Do you?

Rosenberg No. I don't agree with either Steinberg or Schapiro about their particular analyses, but I don't see anything objectionable in their finding rich depths in paintings.

Tumin What do you mean, you don't agree with them?

Rosenberg Well, I don't follow the Freudian mode of thinking to the degree that they do.

Tumin But you don't like that attributional system or the Marxian attributional system, and you don't like the details of the method that those require.

Rosenberg Yes, but I have no objection to anybody who finds them suggestive using them. I think they're all part of criticism, and I think they're legitimate. In other words, I think that Meyer's analysis of Cézanne and Leo's analysis of *Les Demoiselles d'Avignon* are perfectly legitimate ways of looking at paintings.

Tumin What do you mean by legitimate ways of looking at them?

Rosenberg A spectator of a painting has the right to discover in it whatever meanings he discovers in it.

Tumin Now that's reducing that to nothing. You're simply saying that in a democratic society everybody has a right to find what he wants to find.

Rosenberg No, that's not the point. The approach which enriches the meanings of a work of art has value. I think a painting, after all, consists of the aura of interpretations which has collected itself around it over the years and these interpretations add to that aura. It's true that every once in a while people will be stimulated to clean the paintings again of these auras, the same way that you get rid of a lot of varnish, but that doesn't necessarily produce a better interpretation.

Tumin But some of those auras can hurt a painting, can they not? Suppose an aura is wholly misguided?

Rosenberg Well, they all tend to be wholly misguided, and most good paintings are able to endure these blemishes. Otherwise they aren't very good paintings.

Tumin But you would distinguish good auras from bad auras?

Rosenberg That's right, I would. But the bad ones are inevitable.

Tumin But a work of art has a kind of an historical accretion which consists of all the comments made about it, all the contexts in which it has been put, which don't necessarily comment on the goodness or badness, but only specify it as an historical object?

Rosenberg That's right.

Tumin Is that a way of saying what your principal business is? Is it now to discern the current meanings which are being attributed to a particular work of art and to specify them against the background of the previous auras and attributions?

Rosenberg Well, no, you're going too fast. The first part of your question seems like a good one, and I think one of the things that a critic wants to do is to relieve paintings from contemporary murk, from the accumulation of beliefs that have descended upon it, and which no artist meant to be part of his creation. This is a very curious state of affairs in contemporary art. We have painters that have been so over-valued that it is impossible to see that their works are fundamentally ridiculous, or vacuous. We also have a great many people who are ignored because the overevaluation of other painters is always accompanied by the underevaluation of people not like them. So what we have to do in this sense is to create a new balance.

Tumin You said that some painters and paintings are obviously ridiculous. What makes you say that of a painter, *any painter?*

Rosenberg It's ridiculous relative to the value that's been placed upon it by criticism, by acceptance.

Tumin But suppose from the beginning you were willing to say, "This is a ridiculous painting," without there having been a previous assessment of it. Would you be willing to say such a thing?

Rosenberg I wouldn't feel it necessary to say it, because ridiculous paintings normally tend to sink out of sight. But there are occasions when they don't, when they don't follow the laws of nature, but rather the laws of promotion, and therefore they survive with great honors into the present, at which point an occasion arises when it's necessary to disclose their genuine value or lack of it.

Tumin Let's pursue that for a minute. Suppose now a museum decides to hang a painting which you find, for a variety of reasons, outrageous on their part because in your estimation the painting is really a ridiculous work. And let's imagine you're writing and trying to tell the museum and others why you think it's a ridiculous work. What are some of the kinds of things that might make you say it's ridiculous or that it's not worthy to have been hung?

Rosenberg I think you could get a fairly good view of that by going through all the pieces I've written.

Tumin I started out by saying you've written an enormous amount, and so we'll probably be retreading old ground, but I'd like to get it, if we can, on the record. You're quite right in saying, "Look, you want to know what I think about artwork, I've written several thousand pages. Read the things and you'll see."

Rosenberg Especially since you're really asking for a list of the kinds of derogation which I've resorted to on particular occasions.

Tumin Or praise.

Rosenberg No, now we're talking about bad art that's been overvalued.

Tumin But we could just as well be talking about good art that's been undervalued. It would be the same question as to what are the criteria with which you're operating, such as the importance of the idea. A second criteria that you mentioned to me in a previous conversation was the question of whether the medium was appropriate to the idea. So now I want to ask you whether there is some way of discriminating the limits and possibilities of different media for dealing with different ideas.

Rosenberg There's something I don't like about that. There is a very important saying in modern painting which regards the medium of painting or of drawing or of materials used in sculpture as having a life of their own and therefore capable of stimulating the kind of thought which in no other way could be achieved. The fact that this is so is one of the reasons why I'm not enthusiastic about conceptual art. Take, for example, Hans Hofmann, who was very explicit about this. He felt that the artist's basic function, basic resource, you might say, is to animate paint. And the paint itself has a certain life which would bring forth a kind of imagery which could not be achieved in any other way. In short, the medium is the original substance of painting. And it's not a medium in the sense of translating an image or an idea into paint, but is itself the creator of the painting. Now not all painters have that idea, and I don't believe that all painters need to have that idea. That is, it's not a definition of what painting does, what painters do, but it's been a very lively and very productive idea, that the medium itself has inner potentialities and a life of its own, as you often hear in regard to the theater and to novels and so on. There's a point at which the artist has become the tool of the medium, rather than the other way around. This is a mysterious thought which has no place in rational thinking.

Tumin You don't think it can be intellectually discussed to any profit?

Rosenberg I don't see how you could demonstrate this. But nonetheless, I say it's a kind of belief among painters that think paint in itself has the possibility of becoming a thinking substance.

Tumin This is different than saying that the painting of the last twenty years or so has been about painting.

Rosenberg It is different. It's not necessary at all that the painting that will arise out of the self-activity, let's say, of paint will be about painting. It might be about the artist, it might be about the combination of the artist and works of the past. It has been, you might say, a superstition, or belief, or conviction of painters of a certain mode that the medium has an evocative character, as if the canvas thinks. The canvas itself becomes the brain, the imagination. You may say that in art there is an externalization of the mind into the medium.

Tumin What, then, of the idea that the subject matter of much of recent painting has been the act of painting itself?

Rosenberg It's one way in which that thought has been formulated, and it's not incorrect, but it's also not the whole story.

Tumin Would you never as a critic comment about the appositeness or inappositeness of the medium for the problem or the idea?

Rosenberg I wouldn't say, this doesn't really belong in painting, maybe it belongs in a nineteenth century novel.

Tumin You would not say that.

Rosenberg No.

Tumin What, then, of a third criterion: how imaginatively and knowledgeably does the artist realize the possibilities and powers of the media?

Rosenberg I don't think in those terms. I'm a synthetic thinker, that is, I talk about concrete situations.

Tumin If I go through your writing, I can show you you're much more than concrete. There is always implicit, almost explicit, though not usually, a set of operative criteria by which you're making judgments.

Rosenberg That's right, I don't just say I think this painting is good or bad.

Tumin That's right, and you say why.

Rosenberg I say why.

Tumin And you say conceptually why, not just concretely why.

Rosenberg That's right, but if you want to generalize those generalizations, you have to do it. I don't generalize my generalizations.

Tumin But one is permitted to ask whether this is a fair statement of your generalizations.

Rosenberg I don't know. I haven't analyzed which generalization you're referring to. I've been doing this for about twenty-five years, at least, and I can't put the sum total into a few formulas. Let me quote something else Baudelaire said. He used to be an art reviewer, which I'm not. I don't run around as much as he did. He used to review the salons and gallery shows, and he said it often occurred to him that his life would be much easier if he had a set of ideas which he could apply to paintings and he would be able to go into a show and apply his system and come up with judgments of the paintings. He tried to work out such a system and he said it was a disaster because either the system he developed didn't apply to the paintings he saw, or he got so bored with the system he didn't care whether it applied or not. He didn't want to use it. So he said he had to start all over again with each painting he looked at, with each show he looked at.

Tumin But that's pretended innocence and naiveté. He's got a whole history of sophistication. He obviously doesn't start all over.

Rosenberg He starts all over with the totality of his temperament and his sensibilities. He cannot in advance say, I'm going to look at this painting from this point of view in order to arrive at this value. Now, that's what you're asking me to do, and I agree completely with Baudelaire. I have no capacity to do that. I cannot make a set of rules or criteria which will be useful to me when I go to a show. I can't go there with a set of ideas in mind. I don't have those ideas. When I look at the paintings a great many ideas may appear or manifest themselves as of some importance in regard to this particular work. But I have no set of ideas that would be applicable to *any* kind of work. That is to say, the ideas are present only insofar as the experience of the work wants to make them present. Otherwise, I don't know what the work is about. That's why very often I look at works and have no opinions about them. I have to wait until I develop an opinion or concentrate on developing an opinion which comes from a kind of psychological immersion in that work, and then various ideas begin to appear that seem relevant and which also establish what I think about the work. In other words, the judgment that I arrive at is the result of an activity carried on in relation to this particular work. Now, I think any other approach to criticism is dogmatic. I don't care how good the ideas are or could be. That's one of the reasons why I don't have too much use for Freudians or Marxists or any other systematic criticism. I don't think it's relevant. It may or might not be relevant. I mean, if Meyer looks at the apples of Cézanne and gets all these ideas about the history of apples and human culture, the history of apples in paintings, the history of apples in regard to sex, all this to me, as I said before, is wholly legitimate from Meyer's response to the apples of Cézanne. But it doesn't at all follow that any of this would occur to me while I'm looking at a Cézanne, and I don't think that would be a disaster, that I didn't think of them in those ideas.

Tumin Is it also legitimate, as some political-minded cab driver once said, that all painting, except that done by Rockwell Kent and Siquieros, is a handmaiden and servile tool of capitalism?

Rosenberg Well, let's say, legitimate or not, it's rather typical. It's exceptionally narrow. He's only got two artists, after all, and not the best. But most people think about art that way. That is, they have a set of legitimized artists and the rest of art may be totally hopeless to them. In fact, that's exactly what goes on all the time. That cab driver is typical, in that he has a few icons which constitute the whole field of art for him. And that's what I was talking about before in relation to the criticism of the past fifteen years, in which a certain type of problem-solving has been the criterion for art.

Tumin I want to get back to the question of conceptualizing the judgmental and evaluational and critical process. Because it is possible to do it in science, to specify, say, a dozen criteria that somehow must be met by a work of science before you would say it's good, as against being a bad work of science. It's possible to do it with athletics.

Rosenberg You can do it with all sorts of things.

Tumin Can you not do it with artwork?

Rosenberg People do it all the time.

Tumin Do you think it's wrong to do it?

Rosenberg I think that the critic's experience of a particular work is the animating force which evokes various ideas, which, furthermore, are always evoked in terms of a given rhetoric. I don't leave out the question of style. That is to say, I can't have what I would consider a valid discussion, on my part, of a painting unless that discussion is carried on in a certain style, which happens to be the way I use words in thinking. In other words, the critic after all is a writer, and that is basic. Somebody who can't write can't be a critic. There is no such thing as having good ideas badly phrased in art criticism, any more than there is such a thing as having a very good idea badly written as a poem.

Tumin There is very badly written good science.

Rosenberg That can very well be. This is one of the important differences between art and science.

Tumin Or is it between criticism of science as against criticism of art? Do you think that's really different, too?

Rosenberg Yes, absolutely. There is no objective measure of a work of art.

Tumin There are no objective criteria?

Rosenberg There are no objective criteria.

Tumin The objective criteria in other fields are simply those which specialists agree upon. Are there no such objective criteria in the same sense in art?

Rosenberg No.

Tumin Why?

Rosenberg It's a phony analogy which people who are educated in the modern university keep trying to establish, that is, the analogy between art and science. They're always looking for the same kind of precision, the same kind of consensus.

Tumin I agree with you that precision is quite different in the

two fields, both in painting and science, and in the criticism
of painting and science, that consensus is present in science
and not present in art.

Rosenberg No, as a matter of fact, there's a very strong consensus in art, but it does not necessarily mean that it's acceptable. That is, art criticism, as Baudelaire said, is polemical.
You establish your idea about works of art, you don't accept
the consensus. Because your basic criterion is your experience of the work of art, and everybody's experience of the
work of art is different.

Tumin But they're not all wholly unique and fresh and innocent. They're always operating within a cultural context.

Rosenberg It may come about that some people agree about
some artists. And they may agree about them for a certain
length of time, too, in which case you would have what appears to be a consensus. If anybody carries this further, and
begins to inquire to what you and he and X agree upon,
when you think that Pollock is a good artist, you would find
that you are all talking about something else. Now you must
know that's true.

Tumin Is there no way in which to get consensus on a set of
criteria by which some works of art could be judged to be
superior to others, in the same fashion as we get consensus
on criteria by which to judge works of science?

Rosenberg There's no doubt that some works of art are in one
sense or another superior to other works of art. We're not
arguing that all works of art are equal. But the notion that a
consensus that would apply in the discipline, let's call it, of
physics or biology or something like that would necessarily
have its counterpart in art seems to me totally arbitrary. One
of the reasons why the sciences have become so important in
modern technological society, as against art, is precisely because the society is held together on a rational plane and not
held together, as it used to be, on a plane of a kind of univer-

sal recognition. That is to say, we don't assume that the intelligent person that we're talking to and with whom we might agree about various ideas has the same feelings that we have. We don't assume that he has the same background. We don't assume that he's had the same kind of unity or coherence in his life.

Tumin Why do you say that? If you and I go, let's say, if we talked for many years and we have sort of developed a set of unstated, commonly shared assumptions about some things, and if we go, let's say, to a movie or we go to a museum or we go to a concert, isn't it likely that we're going to have many of the same reactions, or at least we will know what the other one is likely to feel, given our knowledge of each other's reactions in the past?

Rosenberg Well, you're making a postulate which doesn't exist in the art world, that is, that we know each other for years, that we've been talking to each other, that we have various things in common to begin with that made us friends. We're now talking about a totally different matter. We're talking about a field of activity called art which has been invaded by many things. Let me give you some ideas of what invades art. Historically, Western art was invaded in the nineteenth century by Chinese art or by Japanese art, subsequently by African art, later on by pre-Columbian art, by the art of the streets and the backwoods, that is to say, by naive art, by ecclesiastical art, by all kinds of elements and styles. Now that does not happen in any science. You do not have a tremendous flood of phenomena and concepts that are unrelated to one another making their way into the center of physics and deciding what is valuable in physics. You have a continuous tradition which is one of the reasons why science has managed to hold its line of development more or less, and has been able, as they say, to progress. In art such a development does not exist. Think of the element of alienness that enters into works of art at any given moment. For example, right now something new has been dug up somewhere which nobody has ever seen before and is being put on display in the European museums. It's just been excavated and now is being put on display in a big museum and will undoubtedly influence artists and art itself.

Now, how can we enter into such a melange with the idea of a consensus? To me, this is totally absurd. Even if you get two people who know each other, who are sitting around with the same artists for half their lifetime, you get the most violent disagreement. I'll give you a concrete example. Barnett Newman had a retrospective a few years ago for which Tom Hess wrote the catalog, and he found that Barnett Newman was interested in Hassidism. He interpreted his work in terms of Hassidic number relations, and Annalee Newman, who is the widow of Barnett, was indignant at the way in which Tom translated Barney into a Hassid. Barney was interested in Hassidism. But he was also interested in baseball; he was interested in discotheques; he was interested in dozens of things. His triumph was to make a unity that transcended these interests, but that would also include them in some kind of a very individual way. The moment Hess reduced—and I'm underlining reduced—Barney's interest to Hassidism, he was completely wrong. Yet people have seized upon Hess's interpretation because they would like to find some specific content in Newman's paintings, and it's much more difficult to find this other content, that is, the content of being a modernist in New York who is interested occasionally in some Hassidic phrase and finds some interesting thought in a wonder-working rabbi. How can you have a consensus, when the object itself is an amalgam of so many cultural elements, psychological elements, elements of invention, elements of arbitrary decision? Is somebody supposed to see the art object in the same way that a pre-modern society saw such objects? To make a meaning out of New-man is, and again I go back to Baudelaire, a polemical act. I say his paintings mean this; somebody may agree with me, but nobody has agreed with me before I said it.

Tumin Well, but I see a level of possible consensus among you and lots of other people who might disagree about the elements in Barnett Newman and in other people, but who would commonly agree that an important quality in Newman, along with other first-rate painters or artists, is the extent to which, to paraphrase Baudelaire, there is the evocation of a rich imagination in contact with the experiences of his own life and with the objects in the external world, represented with great skill on the canvas.

Rosenberg But that's about the emptiest abstraction you could think of. A good artist is a good artist.

Tumin But so is it an empty abstraction to say that a scientific theory is elegant.

Rosenberg No, there's more to it. Many concrete, quite visible aspects of Newman's paintings have to be brought to light when you're talking about him, and it has nothing to do with his just being skillful. You see, when you use the word skill you fall into the typical humanistic trap, which is to associate modern art with the crafts of the Renaissance, and of all the art up to the modern time. That is, the concept of skill has to do with craft. By this time nobody cares about skill. You have to make up your own skills. Newman made up his own skill. His skill isn't the skill of any other painter, anymore than Pollock's skill was the skill of any other painter.

You make up your own art. This is the period of the one-man culture, and each artist attempts, in a kind of mega-lomaniacal way, as exemplified, say, by Mondrian, to capture the whole culture and stimulate unity which in the future will provide a consensus based on his invention. Read my piece about Mondrian where it's very clear that Mondrian had in mind the elimination of all other art in order to produce a society where everyone would grasp Mondrian emotionally without thinking about him at all. The ultimate purpose of modernist sophistication is to arrive at a state of absolute naiveté that would be equivalent to the immediacy of a tribesman in an African village. The ultimate aim of many outstanding twentieth century artists is to produce a kraal situation in which it wouldn't be necessary to have any art critics. You don't need art critics in an African village. Everybody knows exactly what the thing is by immediate apprehension. We talk about art because we do nothing else with it. We must arrive at our individual relations to it first, and then proceed to offer that experience to others. How much good it does, we don't know.

Tumin With what intention do you offer it to others? Leaving aside for the moment money, fame and all that stuff which may or may not be relevant, why do you write? Why do you write so forcefully about painting? Is any part of your motive an intention to try to get other people to see paintings as you see them?

Rosenberg Of course, of course.

Tumin Hoping they will come to share your criteria of judgment and perception?

Rosenberg No, not my criteria; my *opinion* about this particular work. I don't want them to become like me. I don't want to create a crowd of art critics. I don't want them to write about art. I want them to see what I saw in this work of art. That's all.

Tumin Rather than having a more general ambition of hoping to have a lot of people learn to see in general the way you see?

Rosenberg I don't know how I see in general. So if I had the ambition that you attribute to me, I'd be writing about aesthetics. And I have the least possible use for aesthetics. I see no interest in it whatsoever. I even read the *Journal of Aesthetics*. I find it practically impossible to find anything in it that's of interest.

Tumin So a book like Nelson Goodman's *The Languages of Art* is of no use to you?

Rosenberg Absolutely of no interest to me whatsoever.

Tumin Let me read one quotation and see if it's not interesting to you, because it raises some other interesting general points. Near the end of his book Goodman says, on the question of merit, "To say that a work of art is good or even to say how good it is does not after all provide much information. It does not tell us whether the work is evocative, robust, vibrant or exquisitely designed and still less what are its salient specific qualities of color, shape or sound. Moreover, works of art are not racehorses and picking a winner is not a primary goal."

Rosenberg So far, so good.

Tumin Goodman then goes on, "Rather than judgments of particular characteristics being a mere means toward an ultimate appraisal, judgments of aesthetic value are often means toward discovering such characteristics. If a connoisseur tells me that one of two Cycladic idols that seem to me almost indistinguishable is much finer than the other, this inspires me to look for and may help me find the significant differences between the two. Estimates of excellence are among the minor aids to insight. Judging the excellence of works of art or the goodness of people is not the best way of understanding them. And the criterion of aesthetic merit is no more the major aim of aesthetics than the criterion of virtue is the major aim of psychology." Would you agree with that?

Rosenberg Yes, I'd agree with that. They're all negative statements.

Tumin But you're both really discarding what other people would like to attribute to you or to aestheticians.

Rosenberg Aestheticians don't make judgments on works of art, they develop theories about aesthetics.

Tumin Let me turn to that domain called aesthetics because, in a rough way, art is in the domain of the aesthetic. Are there no special terms that distinguish the domain in which your enterprise as a critic is located from the terms which people use for other domains? Isn't there a specifiable set of concerns that you as a critic take on and that other people have found valuable, and your writing about them sufficiently informative and excellent to wish to hear more from you about those particular kinds of questions?

Rosenberg I don't know what those questions are. I think they've all disintegrated. If you look at the art in the past twenty years, it's extremely difficult to say that anything is left over from the old beauty and truth formulation. For one thing, art is definitely not concerned with beauty. What is it concerned with? It's almost impossible to say. The only definition I could think of in recent years was to say that it's concerned with anything that isn't in the category of something else. It has become a domain outside other domains.

Tumin But each domain is outside of every other domain.

Rosenberg But this one is outside of domains in general. In other words, if you make a psychological analysis and write it down and print it in a book or an article, it is recognizable as psychology. But if you make a psychological statement that has no reference to known concepts in psychology and is hardly identifiable even as psychology, you may hang it in an art gallery as a conceptual work of art. All I'm saying is that art is ultimately in the social-historical domain and, if society has decided to accept otherwise indefinable activities as works of art, it's pointless for you to say, "Society is wrong, art is really like *this*"—unless you set up the old academic "realm of the beautiful." When the realm of the beautiful collapsed, and the realm of the beautiful, of course, is related to other ideal realms, and art became a positivistic set of phenomena, you could not establish any set of criteria except the ones you establish on the basis of your own experience and which you enforce by the strength of your own rhetoric. That is to say, art has become totally polemical. I was defeated in the sixties by the overriding power of the public relations of what I consider to be terrible art. There was nothing I could do about it. I wrote one piece saying that criticism used to come before the work was accepted by society, but that now criticism comes when works are already beyond dispute. You can keep on repeating over and over again that X (I don't want to mention any names in this context) is not even an artist. He doesn't even use a medium. He's a guy who is an artist insofar as he's known to be an artist.

Tumin If two other people call him an artist, he's an artist?

Rosenberg No, it's like the phrase, he's famous for being famous. This artist is famous for being a famous artist. When you look at his work there's nothing there. But he's famous for being a famous artist. He will appear in various shows, inevitably. He belongs to the history of the decade and his "work" can bring all sorts of fancy prices from collectors and becomes a staple part of the museums. Now what am I going to do about that?

Tumin You would have something to say about why he's no longer an artist, wouldn't you?

Rosenberg I've said it and it's produced no effect whatsoever, except to bring denunciations. I know why he's not an artist and I know also why he's successful as a non-artist. That's more important because that's sociological.

Tumin In your article on Jasper Johns you said, "Reacting to painting as a social reality, Johns and other post-Abstract Expressionists looked back to Duchamp, as the disillusioned analyst of the relation between art today and other man-made things, and forward to Andy Warhol, as the artist

changed into a media celebrity and manufacturer of art substitutes." Now it's quite clear you have some clear notion as
to the limits and possibilities of art such that you're now
saying Warhol in these works is not an artist.

Rosenberg I said he was a manufacturer of art substitutes.

Tumin Now, are you not able, if someone says, why is this an
art substitute and not a piece of art, are you not able to say
why?

Rosenberg Yes, there's a previous article on Andy Warhol
which explains why he's a manufacturer of art substitutes.

Tumin In which you clearly state what an art substitute is as
against a piece of art?

Rosenberg Oh, yes, and how he became a media celebrity.

Tumin So you're not adverse to saying what are the criteria a
piece of art must meet in order to be called a work of art?

Rosenberg No, no. I don't approach the problem that way.

Tumin You aimed the problem that way by saying he's not an
artist any more.

Rosenberg In my article on Andy Warhol I explain exactly
what he does; why he's accepted as an artist; what he doesn't
do, and how he should be evaluated.

Tumin And therefore why you think he's not an artist.

Rosenberg No, that's not important. I agree with Goodman
that's not important.

Tumin "As the artist changes into media celebrity and manufacturer of art substitutes." You meant very pointedly to say
he's no longer an artist.

Rosenberg I was speaking of a trend in art, a change in the
figure of the artist. You want to pin me down to Warhol. A
species of gossip.

Tumin That means to say also you have certain touchstones or
criteria by which you're making that judgment. I'm not going
to press you to make them explicit. But why do you say,
"No, I don't have any general ideas?" Why do you say that?

Rosenberg There's no general idea involved in that, there's just the concrete idea that Andy Warhol represents a new kind of artist: "Media celebrity and manufacturer of art substitutes." I like that better than anything you're going to be able to drag out of me.

Tumin But by what criteria? You obviously have criteria, don't you?

Rosenberg Not necessarily. Maybe I just say it on an authoritarian basis.

Tumin No, you don't mean that. You mean that you do have firm ideas about what something has to be in order to be called a decent work of art. But when anyone presses you into a corner on that, you try to jump around the corner and not respond to that. Why? I can understand you don't want to be known for saying, "Here are only five criteria all works of art have to be to be called works of art."

Rosenberg You have an obsession with criteria.

Tumin You have an obsession with evading criteria. We have commonly opposed obsessions.

Rosenberg I don't believe in them. I have already explained to you that whatever concepts you use when you're discussing a work of art arise out of your experience with that work of art, and not because you have certain criteria. If you have certain criteria you have to apply them in all cases. And furthermore, I like some people who make art substitutes.

Tumin Fine, but you talk about experiencing a work of art. It's not a completely *tabula rasa* that you experience the work of art with? You experience it with a set of expectations, don't you?

Rosenberg No, I don't know what they are until I look at the work. Then I may discover that I have expectations. But they may be different in this case than in another. Take that thing over there. You see that photograph over there? That's a work of art, created by Saul Steinberg. It's a fake pho-

tograph. Now he's much better at creating fake art than
Andy Warhol. But his fake art is very legitimate.

Tumin Whereas Warhol's fake art is unintentionally fake?

Rosenberg It *is* intentionally fake. He even says so himself. I'm
not even insulting him. He says, don't even bother to look at
this stuff. He said to a woman who writes about art, "Let's
get the hell out of here and have a drink, you don't want to
look at this stuff." He knows what he's doing. He's fooling
around with his public, and it's perfectly legitimate to fool
around with the public insofar as it's that stupid. I want to
go back to what you said, you can't be that naive. One of
the things, one of the great ideas of Baudelaire was his idea of
the naive critic. If you want to read the conceptual development of this idea, read it in Baudelaire. He said the critic
should be naive.

What did he mean by naive? He didn't mean that he had
no brains, or that he was illiterate, or anything like that. By
naive he meant that he had a will to something, and that he
would pursue that desire regardless of what the situation
was. A naive person is somebody who wants something, has
a point of view. Now, whether or not that point of view can
be expressed as an ideology is another matter. I'm certainly
not arguing that the question of value is unimportant or that
it doesn't exist. I think it exists, and one of the most important things in our society is that people should have clear and
intelligent reactions to works of art. I don't believe that
they're going to arrive at these clear, intelligent evaluations
by developing a system of criteria. I remember when as a kid
I read Barnes' book on art, and he gave criteria for judging
works of art. Suppose you had ten criteria, memorized them,
and starting looking at a painting? You'd go nuts. It's not the
way one thinks—to count off traits.

If you had a set of criteria and you went around and said,

"All right, let's try A on this thing. Now we'll try B" . . . first of all, I can't even remember them. If I had *five* criteria I wouldn't remember them. I'd have to have them written down.

I once tried to do that in buying a house. I didn't know anything about houses and I had to decide whether or not to buy this house. So I said to an associate of mine, "You're interested in real estate. What does one look for when buying a house?" He wrote down eight criteria: Are the sills rotted? Is the water O.K.? And so on. I went out to East Hampton and I poked around to check the criteria. The pump wasn't working, so I couldn't tell whether the water was any good. The roof was leaking . . . that was bad. I went through the eight criteria. In regard to three of them I couldn't establish the facts. But the real problem was, I didn't know how to weigh the criteria against each other. If three things were lousy, that is, the roof leaked and two other things were no good, and two were good and two I couldn't ascertain, did this mean I should buy the house or not? My critic had failed to give me a scale. So I tore up the piece of paper and bought the house. As it happened, I did the right thing.

Tumin The analogy you're making, it seems to me, is both appropriate and inappropriate.

Rosenberg It's appropriate insofar as you have a practical problem. Criteria are useful in buying cars. But in art you don't have a practical problem.

Tumin Well, an art critic has a practical problem.

Rosenberg What's the practical problem?

Tumin What do I think about this painting?

Rosenberg That's not a practical problem. The practical problem is when a collector comes up to me and says, "Should I buy this for $10,000?" That's a practical problem. I never answer such questions. I say, "Go and see Clem Greenberg.

He gives advice to collectors. I just write about art. I don't
know anything about the market. I don't know how much
you should pay for anything."

Tumin Well, but for you a practical problem is that you have a
column to do. And you have to say something about something you've seen. You have to ask yourself, What shall I say
about it? Now, you're not going to talk about how the canvas was made of Belgian linen, which was extracted by a
process known to the ancient Assyrians. And you're also not
going to talk about the whiteness of the walls around the
frame, unless it gets in the way of your not being able to see
it. There are lots of things that are excluded from your view
when you take on the practical task of the critic, aren't there?

Rosenberg By practical task, you mean?

Tumin The things that you require of yourself, given your
enterprise.

Rosenberg Yes, sure.

Tumin Okay, that doesn't settle anything. But it leads to an
important question to ask you. Please go into the make-believe realm with me. If somehow you could have the power
to determine what should be hung in museums, would you
like that?

Rosenberg You mean, would I like the responsibility of
deciding?

Tumin The power to decide what should go into museums.

Rosenberg The thing that complicates that is the question of
what I think about museums and their functions.

Tumin Well, I don't want to get into that. I'll put it more generally. If you could shape the taste of a generation, would
you like to do that?

Rosenberg The taste? No, I don't believe in taste. That's an
obsolete concept.

Tumin Wrong word?

Rosenberg Yes. Not taste. *Values,* yes.

Tumin If you could shape the values of a generation with regard to works of art, would you like that?

Rosenberg Would I like it?

Tumin Yes, would you relish that prospect?

Rosenberg Do you mean, do I feel sufficiently confident in my own views to want to . . .

Tumin Yes, that's one aspect of it. Do you feel sufficiently confident in our own point of view to say that if only others were able somehow to share my point of view the world of art would be better off? I don't think it would be arrogant of you to say that, if that's what you felt like saying.

Rosenberg You're trying to lead me to . . .

Tumin I'm coming to art and politics. That's where I'm coming.

Rosenberg Your question is not one I can answer because if I did, as you say, shape the values of a generation, the question is, what would they do with that when they've had that experience. I have no way of knowing that. You know, I've had influence in certain places and for a certain length of time. I don't know what comes out of that. Very often, you know, people say to me, I was very much influenced by you, and then I see what they're doing. *Es vehrt mir nit gutt.* How do you know what other people do with your way of looking at things? Some of the worst art around today is definitely owing to my theories. No question about it. I can make a direct line from some of the works that I can least stand to a concept of action painting and various other ideas which I have let loose.

Tumin Well, as we all know, all great prophets get misused and abused.

Rosenberg I'm not sore. It's just that you can't tell what the logic of your ideas is in the minds of others. What would be nice, the thing that would be desirable and that to me would be a constituent aspect of a culture, would be that one's ideas should be related to a center of discussion, so that they should be elaborated in different directions at the moment that they appeared. In that way, they'd correct themselves in one's own mind, too. But one characteristic, as you know, of our culture is isolation. No matter how much publication or publicity you get, or no matter how much your ideas are talked about, you rarely have any genuine discussion of what they mean. So you don't get the kind of correction or elaboration of your ideas which could be useful to you. This is one of the characteristics of American culture.

Tumin That leads us to two connected topics—not connected with the critic, but connected with the artist. Sometimes it's said painters or writers shape the consciousness of a society. You're familiar with that kind of statement. Lots of painters and writers say, What the hell, we've never had the slightest influence on the consciousness of a society. Is that a question to which you can respond? Have there been times when paintings and other works of art have, in fact, had an important influence on the general consciousness of a society? Let's admit that in Christian art, when everything else was conjoint, and there was a homogeneous culture . . .

Rosenberg Well, then, you can't talk about influence. They're part of the same thing.

Tumin But have you seen occasions when painting has altered consciousness in important directions?

Rosenberg Important directions is the stumbling block in that question, because there's no doubt that, for example, in the realm of fashion, which in turn has a very strong effect on masses of people, painting has been very influential since the war. All you have to do is to look at fabric design and interior design.

Tumin All right, let's go beyond that and talk about political consciousness.

Rosenberg No, it's not possible that these changes should not in turn have an effect on what people think in general, that is to say, morally.

Tumin You think it has had an important effect?

Rosenberg Of course it has.

Tumin Give me a connecting link if you can. Give me a concrete series of connecting links.

Rosenberg You can't do that. If you try to create a set of causal links, if you try to create a causal chain, you're getting into the realm of the absurd. The only thing you can do is show a kind of synchronization of certain attitudes in art and literature and politics. Now of course we have the mass media, the effect of art on the mass media, and the effect of the media on art. This is a most important thing. You remember I talked about that in Stanford. Most contemporary discussions of art in relation to society are worthless because they don't take into effect the reciprocal pressures of art on the mass media and the media on art. The media on art, because it is the pressure of the masses on art. Let's say TV takes up painting. Immediately, an audience of hundreds of thousands. They don't know anything about art. The TV program is made up so they don't have to know anything about art. Of course a terrible distortion takes place inherently. The artist tends to collaborate in this because he's delighted to have such a hugh audience. People are looking at his paintings which are reproduced, of course in a totally falsified way, on the TV screen. So you get a constant interchange of falsifications, of stupid ideas, of clichés, all weighing on the art world. The situation today is fantastic. Every weekend I receive in the mail at least two announcements by galleries I've never heard of before. The number of operating art galleries is inconceivable to me. The Poindexter Gallery, which is twenty or twenty-five years old, folded up the other week. But the same day at least four new galleries sprang into view.

Tumin I can see the influence on galleries, and customers and publics. Do you see that influence from the media being exerted and responded to in any serious way by people whom you would consider serious artists?

Rosenberg You don't know how people are affected. I know some serious artists who are so morally decrepit that they would be affected by anything.

Tumin They would start painting in terms of what they think was now going to sell, given the new publicity?

Rosenberg No, but they might make works in styles that have been successful with the media.

Tumin Instead of going on to new problems?

Rosenberg "Problems" again. The wrong word. If they were a little hungry, they might think of a new idea. I know artists that have gotten new ideas because the old ones weren't selling anymore. But if you have a market that keeps expanding, you do more and more of the same thing. It goes without saying. What do you think artists are?

Tumin A touch of poverty is good for the semination of new ideas?

Rosenberg There's no question about that. How can you ask such a question? Affluence is heady, you know, and a very dubious condition to develop new ideas, or even to hold on to old ones.

Tumin But you wouldn't be willing to say . . . ?

Rosenberg Starvation is also bad.

Tumin It's impossible to state the best conditions under which you would get the freest flowing of ideas?

Rosenberg Yes, Tolstoy once said that government support of the arts is terrible, because an artist who is well off will never produce a work of art.

Tumin Do you agree?

Rosenberg No, because starvation is also bad. Tolstoy is the last guy in the world who should talk about a subject like that. If he had any sense of good manners, he would know that that is not a subject for him to discuss.

Tumin What else would you say about the impact of art on other institutions in society?

Rosenberg You mean, like on the Congress?

Tumin On political values.

Rosenberg We now have a politician in the Senate named Claiborne Pell who has made a big thing out of art. We have another one in the House.

Tumin On fundamental values? Where art really affects fundamental values?

Rosenberg It doesn't have a direct effect. If you're going to find it, you have to crawl through sewers. You can't find a direct effect of art on politics. Especially in the age of the media. What kind of effect can a painting have, compared to the constant pouring out of editorial matter, and phony stories in newspapers and on television?

Tumin Then why are the Bolsheviks of today so worried about their art?

Rosenberg You mean in Russia?

Tumin In Russia and Eastern Europe.

Rosenberg There's nothing more upsetting to a society than the loss of prestige of its accepted forms. The Russians are perfectly right about this. You'll find a discussion of that in one of my books—an analysis of why Kruschev was so upset when abstract artists showed up.

Tumin Why should he be upset if art is so inconsequential?

Rosenberg There seems to be a contradiction there. But in Russia—a tight society, as opposed, say, to democratic countries where art is in competition with the media, and the media are all saying different things, and there is a general melange, so that nothing is very authoritative—in Russia the notion that in some field freedom should reign, that is, that individuals should begin to make statements, visual statements which don't concur with what has been accepted as august and noble in art could be extremely upsetting. Valéry once said that one of the biggest cultural revolutions that ever took place was painting the nude. If people are used to seeing the human body in costume, and you suddenly take off the costume, it's a disaster. The strains go all through society, and not for sexual reasons either, but because the customary appearance of things has been disrupted.

Tumin So it's not the question of what particularly is said, but the fact that someone is speaking freely, rather than speaking in accordance with the accepted formula.

Rosenberg Exactly. The Communists always insisted that abstract art has no content, that it is purely subjective. Kruschev, I think, used the term masturbation. Well, he wouldn't get sore if people sat around masturbating in private. But what if hundreds of people came out and began masturbating in Red Square? The government would object—you're not supposed to do that. This is the kind of thing that would become an individual statement, which is intolerable.

Tumin Are you willing to say something about the social and political context that is most supportive of good art, all other things being equal? That is, what are the political and social conditions under which art as an enterprise can flourish the most?

Rosenberg You mean, are there some societies that are better for art than some other societies? That's a very serious question, because it's quite obvious that the social conditions that are best suited to art are those which produce a total social coherence. Primitive societies, medieval European society, the transitional society from medieval into a freer society. All these are good because values are well-established.

Tumin Why is that good?

Rosenberg Great art has been produced in those societies—

such as ancient Egyptian and Babylonian. These are societies that produced great art under conditions of slavery or near slavery. And in Africa and other pre-industrial societies, the arts flourish as an everyday activity. It's obvious now, in the late twentieth century, that this is completely valid art. We're not talking about some kind of clumsy whittling. This is great art that comes out of Africa and pre-Columbian American sources.

Tumin You really want to use the words "great art?"

Rosenberg I don't want to use the words great art, but there's no doubt that it's an art that deserves the highest respect. We don't know enough about it, and if we use the word "great" we're being foolish, because we don't know what the measure is.

Tumin So your use of the word "great" was a slip.

Rosenberg Yes, I would say I don't know how to measure a Benin sculpture against Michelangelo. I don't know what kind of a line to draw. But, I will say that all those concepts of art, the village . . . I mean, this is what you get from the anthropologists who keep telling you that, if you want to have great work you have to have a coherent society. We've heard it from T. S. Eliot; we've heard it from neo-Catholics; we've heard from all kinds of people that a disciplined, unanimous society will produce the best work. We've heard this also from avant garde artists, from constructivists. We've heard this, as I've said before, from Mondrian. You have to have, in other words, a total society. No private life, as Mondrian put it. Get rid of private life. Put everything in public squares, and you'll have a big square. You'll have a nice, well-wrought rectangle, right? Now, what's the matter with that idea? It's a very powerful idea. It keeps coming up in art all the time. It has a lot to do with that idea of impersonality, and reduction of the individual. That's the one thing. Get rid of the individual, and you'll have great art, spirituality, social coherence, communication, everything. Just get rid of that one little bedbug.

Tumin But no one said to Michelangelo, get rid of your bedbug.

Rosenberg That wasn't their problem. Their problem was to become more bedbuggy than ever. They were breaking *out* of something. Humanism was breaking out of those disciplines and into the belief in the individual. We're living in a period when the individual has become a suspect character. After all, who commits crimes? Dissatisfied individuals. Do away with individuals, and you won't have any criminals. Do away with individuals, and you won't have any social disruption. You don't have all kinds of things. In the propaganda of Communism, the individual is the hated element. Not only Communism, the whole industrial system hates the individual. The industrial system is not geared to providing you with what you want, it's geared to providing you, as a consumer, with what it makes. So you've got all these forces against the individual. He's the only thing that prevents the technological solution from having validity. But we've already contracted this disease.

Tumin Which disease?

Rosenberg The disease of individuality. We've had it, according to some people, for 700 years. According to others, it goes back as far as the Greeks; to still others, back to Abraham. There is the tradition that there is such a thing as being an individual. We can't be happy for some reason unless we've got something to do with it.

Tumin In that period great works of art have occurred?

Rosenberg You have to have that kind of art in order to satisfy that residual organism, the individual. There will be no art of any importance or interest without the decaying organism called the individual.

Tumin Are you saying, then, that the kind of society we have now, for all its pressures toward homogeneity, for all the dastardly pressures of the media, is nevertheless extremely rich in its possibilities for art precisely because of the great stress on individuality that also accompanies the contrary stress?

Rosenberg There is no stress on individuality.

Tumin But you are also saying that we have contracted the disease, which is a way of saying that many of us refuse to be only robots, or only automatons.

Rosenberg Look, some people can get very enthusiastic about self-immolation, and to get rid of their little bit of personality affords them a tremendous satisfaction. Conformism is the biggest force in our society today. You know that.

Tumin There has never been a society, however, in which there have been so many different sub-cultures to which you could conform, and in which, in effect, so much non-conformity, so much deviation, has been permitted.

Rosenberg By permitted, you mean what? You don't get locked up?

Tumin You don't get locked up, you don't get penalized, and increasingly every day greater and newer varieties of behavior are accepted as part and parcel of reasonable public behavior, however distasteful you may find them.

Rosenberg And your question is, is this good for art?

Tumin Well, I'm saying, isn't that a correct characterization of our society, and, if it is, is it or is it not good for art?

Rosenberg There's no doubt that the way things are is the only thing that we know of that's good for art. We cannot conceive, without entering into a destructive utopianism, of better situations for art than the one that exists.

Tumin You mean at any time?

Rosenberg No, now.

Tumin You mean, is that true of anybody in any society at any time?

Rosenberg No.

Tumin You're now making a judgment about all historical periods and saying this is really the richest?

Rosenberg Not the richest, it's the only thing we can do. This is a predicament. This isn't a situation that we have chosen. But there can't be a better one that we can think of. We tried that in the thirties. We tried to conceive of a better situation, and people became involved, as you know, with all these organizations and with social expectations. It was no damn good for art. The only thing we can think of that would be good for art is intensification and deepening of individual experience.

Tumin Which means, also, freedom. More and more freedom.

Rosenberg Yes, we can't think of a single thing that would benefit art today except to be more ourselves, more affirmative.

Tumin Are you being ironic, though, when you say that?

Rosenberg No.

Tumin You say we can't think anymore. It sounds like, how pitiful our imaginations are that we can't think of anything more than that.

Rosenberg That's the limit of my imagination anyway, and I've been watching this game for a long time, and I haven't seen a single idea that has come forward that wasn't worse than the idea that art depends on individuals. That is, all the modern art that I know of does that.

Tumin And who will have the freedom and the resources with which to try to express themselves?

Rosenberg That's right. We don't know how to promote freedom. It's a subjective matter. People have to seize freedom. We know all about freedom when it's not there. We know what could be done in Chile and Brazil. But we don't know what could be done here, because, in a way, there isn't much of a limitation on freedom here. The limitation is from within. There's no use saying that we're all corrupted by General Motors, or by television, because you don't have to be corrupted by General Motors or by television.

Tumin What, then, would you say about such things as the National Endowment for the Humanities, and the National Endowment for the Arts, with their various grant programs (leaving aside for the moment the question of whether some of their judgments have been good or bad)? In general, is the idea of providing greater resources for a larger number of people, whom various committees judge to be reasonably good and promising, is that good? Or do you find that a dangerous movement in our government?

Rosenberg I am studying those developments and I find them increasingly suspect.

Tumin Why?

Rosenberg Because of developments in both the Endowments relating to politics. I'm speaking of the powerful ideology of anti-elitism that's now being taken up in Washington and which is, culturally speaking, an equivalent of Stalinism. The attack on elitism is simply a disguised form of anti-intellectualism, and opens the door to every politician who wants to lay hands on money and jobs for his friends. Now, that's dangerous, because the art world today is financially very dependent on government money and on corporate money. And when you begin to study concretely the influence that is generated by those two forms of sponsorship, you have a lot to be alarmed about, because of their natural interests in regard to art.

Tumin What about the WPA art program?

Rosenberg The one thing that was good about the WPA was its lavishness; the fact that it had no criteria. This I know will startle you, and make you uneasy. Anybody that came along

and said he was an artist, they put him on. One artist got to
be a little better, someone else got worse; maybe the latter
wasn't an artist at all. It didn't matter—so long as there were
no criteria, the full weight of bureaucracy could not be applied to any individual.

Tumin Earlier we were talking about the possibilities of what
are the best situations for training young people in art, and
you were deploring the state of the universities, and you were
saying you don't know of a single good university art school
now, even though you used to believe that a young person
should be trained both in art and ideas, since they are very
important together, but that nobody's doing it right now.

Rosenberg Yes, and I started to say that someone else I know,
a professional art educator, shares the same view.

Tumin Why?

Rosenberg Because, he said, when he started his art department, they found *artists* whom they brought into the university and they produced a generation of MFAs. The next thing
was they got rid of the visiting artists, and they hired the
MFAs, so the second generation was taught by MFAs. The
first generation of MFAs had been taught by artists. But the
second generation of MFAs was taught by MFAs. So the
standards kept going down. That is, I think, a description of
what has ruined teaching in our art departments, the requirement of administrations for degree-holding faculty. By this
time nobody hires an artist any more, and they have established the kind of approach to art which comes out of a university, not out of artists' studios.

Tumin In that same regard, would you be willing to say, in
general, that critics serve art well, or serve it poorly, or we'd
be better off without most of them? What's your sense of the
impact of criticism on art?

Rosenberg Criticism today is also coming out of the universities to a very great degree. If you look at the art magazines,

you will see that they are filled with young people who have gotten MFAs and who are dying to get some recognition, and their approach is the same as the approach of the MFA artists.

Tumin Including that of the critics of the leading papers and the leading magazines?

Rosenberg Well, there are no leading papers and magazines. What are you talking about?

Tumin *The New York Times*.

Rosenberg *The New York Times* we don't have to discuss. *The New York Times* has a cultural program, and the people who write for *The New York Times* are about as apt for that program as can be imagined. It's all summed up in the title of the Sunday *Times* cultural section: "Arts and Leisure." You wouldn't want to bother people with serious ideas when they're enjoying that leisure, would you?

Tumin Should anyone pay any attention to what artists themselves say about art?

Rosenberg Oh, absolutely. But you have to know how to pay attention.

Tumin How? Give us some clues.

Rosenberg Well, that is to say, often they're not telling the truth, they're trying to delude you. Nevertheless they say things that are of utmost importance.

Tumin Can you know without eating dinner with them 200 times how to interpret them?

Rosenberg Yes, you can tell by looking at what they do and comparing it with what they say. Between the two, I'd anytime take a lying artist . . .

Tumin To a truth-telling critic?

Rosenberg To a truth-telling critic, sure.

Tumin At least the artist's lies are of interest in the total body of art?

Rosenberg Sure.

Tumin Are you of the same mind with regard to literary criticism?

Rosenberg Literary criticism is a totally different matter.

Tumin You think it's much more responsible and important?

Rosenberg It's an ancient activity and it comes out of people reading books and studying literature. Most reviewers, of course, have no talent, but so much of it goes on that some people were bound to do something worthwhile. There are plenty of fairly decent literary critics.

Tumin I take it you also don't count the museums of today, including the Museum of Modern Art, as any great assets in the production of interesting things in the world of art.

Rosenberg You mean in terms of their writing?

Tumin No, in terms of what they hang. In terms of the kind of relationship to the art world that they promote.

Rosenberg Their record has been very bad in the last twenty years. The great thing, as far as art in the museum is concerned, was the Museum of Modern Art in the thirties, when its function was very clear. That was to enlighten the savages in North America about what was going on in Europe. They did a wonderful job, and they had the best collection of modern art in the world. And without the Museum of Modern Art there would not have been any great developments in American painting and sculpture. That goes without saying.

Tumin Wait a minute. You mean a whole group of European painters who came over would not have been able to be shown, would not have hit a market?

Rosenberg No. They weren't known.

Tumin Would they have died unattended to, you think?

Rosenberg Whether they would have died unattended to or not, they would not have been part of the experience of American painters. That's the important thing. I mean, there were a few painters who knew Mondrian, but Mondrian when he died was an unknown person. In the thirties I went to the first exhibition in the U.S. of Paul Klee. The most expensive painting in the show was $600. Nobody knew Paul Klee. Most of the artists had never heard of Paul Klee. Even Picasso was hardly known in America. The Museum of Modern Art did a tremendous educational job. But it went off the track when the Americans began to produce advanced art. Alfred Barr didn't know what was going on. I suspect that he couldn't stand the Abstract Expressionists. The fact of the matter is, the Museum of Modern Art, like the Metropolitan, failed to buy Pollock or de Kooning, and had to pay huge sums for them later on.

Tumin Was it possible to say at that time, do you think, "Damn it, this man is an important painter. Buy him."

Rosenberg Some people said that.

Tumin Would it have been possible for you? Would that be the kind of judgment you would have been willing to make, and could have made at that time?

Rosenberg I never added, "Buy him."

Tumin Leave "buy" aside. This man is an important artist.

Rosenberg Yes.

Tumin You could tell thirty years ago that Jackson Pollock was an important artist?

Rosenberg Sure, that wasn't difficult. Of course, the point was also that we were all friends. It didn't take any great genius to say that this friend of mine is a great artist. As a matter of fact, I can document this. At the end of the war, I wrote a piece about art for the one-volume guide that came out of the American Guide Series, of which I had been the art editor in the thirties. In the article I mentioned a list of artists of the previous generation. The editor of the book told me the publisher wanted me to mention contemporaries. I replied that you couldn't mention contemporaries because to mention five artists, meant leaving out fifty. Mentioning ten meant leaving out a hundred. The editor insisted that the publisher wanted names. I said, "All right, I'm going to put in the names of my friends." He said, "Go right ahead. I don't care if you put in your grandmother." So I put in my friends. In that book, published in the forties, you will find that the great artists are Gorky, de Kooning, Pollock and so on.

Tumin One last set of questions, and then we'll fold up. It's commonly said, for better or for worse, that the great problem of many painters today is that no one knows what to paint about. You recognize that statement, of course.

Rosenberg Yes.

Tumin What's your response to that statement?

Rosenberg I agree with it. Barney Newman kept saying over and over again that the important thing for the artist today is *what* to paint. To pick one's subject, that's the important thing.

Tumin No, I don't mean that. I mean that they don't know what to paint. Not that that isn't the important question always for an artist. But people characterize this period as being one in which all previous things to paint about have been exhausted.

Rosenberg They said that in the forties and that's why Barney made that his slogan.

Tumin But do you think that's so, that all previous things have been exhausted and that painters don't know what to paint about? Not that it isn't important for them to care about what to paint about, but that they don't know what to paint about?

Rosenberg They never knew. An artist has to decide this question.

Tumin So this is not a special dilemma of the artist today. It's no more poignant, nor more pressing today than ever before.

Rosenberg Well, in the thirties the question was, "Is the artist supposed to paint the class struggle?" Then somebody said, "No, you're not supposed to paint the class struggle, you're supposed to paint the wheat fields of Idaho." Then some-body else said, "No, you're supposed to paint legends of America, like Benton." This has always been the question. When you decide that question, you decide all the other questions that go with it.

Tumin So the painter of today is in no worse situation with regard to that than ever before.

Rosenberg No. It has always been a great mystery of modern times as to what to paint. The modern world broke the academic certainty about what to paint. Choosing the subject became a kind of definition of the modern. The modern is that you paint reality, whatever that means. Every new movement has come up as a new form of realism. All movements, including the Bauhaus, always say, Realism. What is realism? What's to paint? What's important?

Tumin So, if I were going to sum up, I would say that, leaving aside those virtues of the periods of homogeneity of culture, and primitive cultures of which you've talked, that, in some sense, the situation of painting today is probably as good as it's ever been in that there's much more freedom and individualism than ever before, however much there is pressure toward conformity.

Rosenberg Now wait a minute. I didn't say that was a virtue. I said that's our predicament.

Tumin A predicament, but also a virtue because you think artists ought to be free to paint.

Rosenberg No, I don't think they *ought* to be free to paint. I think they have to be, not that they ought to be. They can't paint if they're not free.

Tumin Well, then they have to be free to paint, which is another way of saying they ought to be free. So they have to be free to paint and they are more free than they've ever been before.

Rosenberg I don't know if they're more free than ever before.

Let's say, more people have access to art. You raised the question that maybe it'd be better if a lot of them stopped doing it.

Tumin More have access to art. More have access to the resources required to engage in art. There are more museums and galleries than ever before. There is more of a public than ever before. They're more free to decide what to paint about.

Rosenberg Everything is hunky-dory, except . . .

Tumin Except what?

Rosenberg Except nobody has good ideas.

Index